A YOUNG MAN'S PASSAGE
JULIAN CLARY

EBURY
PRESS

1 3 5 7 9 10 8 6 4 2

This edition published 2006 by Ebury Press
First published 2005 by Ebury Press,
an imprint of Random House,
20 Vauxhall Bridge Road, London SW1V 2SA

Random House Australia (Pty) Limited
20 Alfred Street, Milsons Point, Sydney, New South Wales 2061, Australia

Random House New Zealand Limited
18 Poland Road, Glenfield, Auckland 10, New Zealand

Random House (Pty) Limited
Isle of Houghton, Corner of Boundary Road and Carse O'Gowrie,
Houghton 2198, South Africa

The Random House Group Limited Reg. No. 954009

www.randomhouse.co.uk

A CIP catalogue record for this book is available from the British Library

Jacket design by Two Associates
Interior by seagulls

Printed and bound in Great Britain by
Cox and Wyman Ltd, Reading, Berkshire

ISBN 9780091908720 (fromJan 2007)
ISBN 0 091908728

For Nicholas Reader

With thanks to:

Peter and Brenda Clary, Tess Greenwood, Doreen Howarth, Nicholas Reader, Linda Savage, Michael Hurll, Geoff Posner, Addison Cresswell, Nina Retallick, Merryl Futerman, Paul Merton, Kirsty Lloyd-Jones, Mandy Ward, Erin Boag, Paul O'Grady, Philip Herbert, Hector Ktorides, Andrew Goodfellow, Jane Janovic, Penelope Taylor, Barb Jungr, J. Friend, Sue Holsten, David McGillivray, Richard Nelson, Chris Stagg, Michael Ferri, Rupert Hine, Jeannette Obstoj, Janet Sate, Erika Poole, Mikos, Peter Mountain, Steve McNicholas.

Some names in the book have been changed.

MALLORCA

No one told me I had become an old queen. I came to the dreary realisation all by myself. I'd been hanging around the Club Barracuda, raising my eyebrows at desirable Spaniards, and was finally about to make my way home in the certain knowledge that I was of no interest and there were no athletic off-duty waiters drunk enough to emulate lust for me, when I came across my 22-year-old nephew. He was at once happy to see me and curious as to what I'm doing out at this hour at my age. It is after all 5.25 a.m. and I'm the oldest swinger in town. If only I could clear the air by having a nervous breakdown, then look back fondly at my youth, embrace middle-age spread and attempt something along the lines of living in the moment. I'm sure that's the healthy way forward.

Forty-five. It sounds grave. It sounds like a punchline. A doctor might say it to you at the end of a sobering prognosis. 'You see, you're 45...' Or a psychiatrist, while demystifying your current crisis, a publicist explaining your unseemly behaviour, a personal trainer excusing the aching muscles. Eventually I say it to myself in the mirror. Forty-five. It feels important. Good bones, careful diet and discreet Botox injections do what they can but facts are facts. I'd better start wearing dark colours and stop bleaching my hair. There need to be some other changes made in the pursuit of dignity, too. I've scratched a living for 20-odd years as a camp comic and renowned homosexual, bespoke Nancy boy and taker-of-cock-up-arse. That will all have to go. Soon. As did the rubber and the Lycra some years ago, replaced with corsetry and glamorous suits.

I'm pleased to note that I have evolved in some ways, even if I am still a single gay man living alone in a particular square mile of north London with his small mongrel dog. (The local services I require, incidentally, are minimal: a corner shop, an off-licence, a gay pub, a first-rate sushi bar and somewhere to walk the dog.) I'm happy now, primarily.

I knew instinctively, when I arrived here almost 25 years ago, that this was my destiny. It's as well to know. Ah, I thought then, I've come home. It's a different home now, and a different mongrel too, but this is where I belong in the great scheme of things. But why?

I feel honour-bound in the writing of this book to discover what the point of myself is. The universe is not as chaotic as it may first appear to be. Nature has a reason for everything. Why am I here? Did the world at that time really need an effeminate homosexual prone to making lewd and lascivious remarks? Does everything happen for a reason or did I just get lucky?

One theory, extracted from an essay I read during my formative years, goes along the lines that Nature produces a certain number of homosexuals in each generation. Their function is to stand aside from the rest of society (busy procreating, eating food covered in breadcrumbs and living the family thing) and comment upon it. We are the outside eye, the constructive critic, diffusing with our insightful observations the inevitably tense and difficult moods that result from domestic heterosexual drudgery. This has always appealed to me. I prefer to think that gay men, lesbians and transgender folk are part of the great scheme of things. Everything has its place. I am a Catholic, after all, and it's a comfort to me to know that God moves in mysterious ways. (He's not the only one.)

It may be that Nature's reasons change with time, and the current crop of freaks serves a different purpose. But I hope that I can discover the wisdom of my own creation in the course of this book. Surely, if we take a slow, selective troll through the chapters of my life, the least we can hope for is an understanding of the finished product? I'm rather hopeful. Prospective husbands need only read the paperback and proceed with caution. It will save so much time.

So here at 45 I will tarry a while, casting a bloodshot eye back at what may or may not be the first half of my natural life, but what can, come what may, unarguably be called 'My Youth'.

That's my general angle. I think I'll put the emphasis on the comedy. I am a comedian, after all, so we'll all be looking for a bit of uplifting sauce and slapstick, but expertly combined, correct me if I'm wrong, with what is loosely known as 'light and shade'.

You want the tears as well as the laughs, the lows, the traumas, the self-doubt, the drugs, the scandals. You want unexpurgated gay sex, and if you're a *Daily Mail* reader you'll want that followed by disease, death and loneliness. This may be just the book for you.

Once work gets a grip, depending on the work you do, it becomes the meaning of life for a while, as much an imperative as eating or sleeping. A career won't be denied; it chomps away at your allotted 24 hours and its hunger is satisfied only temporarily before the next urge, as sure as waves roll in from the sea. And even if your work is camp comedy, it's as all-consuming as a thesis. It has a life of its own.

In the throes of the early 1990s I might as well have been Sylvia Plath, so possessed was I. Buggery jokes, not bumble bees, perhaps, but I'd found my niche and took up the make-up brush as the poet does the pen, the teacher the chalk or the porno star the penis – i.e. with relish!

It doesn't last, of course. Things change: self-parody creeps in, laziness rears its sleepy head. Then there are well-meaning (or otherwise) TV producers who trust their own vision more than yours. Battle with them for a few years and your resistance may cave in, the path ahead obfuscated. By then you have tax bills and mortgages, expensive tastes and expectant friends to dish out for. What was once a joy becomes a job. You're not new and exciting, you're old and reliable, if you're lucky.

But why did I choose this particular line of work? It just happened, as things do. But here's how.

So prepare for a taste of a young man's passage.

It's not going to be easy for any of us.

LAMONT

One dull Sunday afternoon in December 1993 I lay on the carpet in front of the fire and thought about my life for a while. I couldn't indulge myself for too long as a car would be coming to collect me soon to take me to the British Comedy Awards. But the more I pondered my life, the harder it was to get up. My boyfriend had dumped me, my manager had lost interest, I was taking Valium during the day and sleeping pills at night. Even Fanny the Wonder Dog, while she hadn't exactly withdrawn her unconditional love, had taken to avoiding me: after 13 years of sleeping in my bed (under the duvet, head on the pillow), she now retired to a spare bedroom at night.

As far as I could work out, my life had gone pear-shaped two months previously when I moved house. Could it be that mere location coupled with bricks and mortar caused my emotional well-being to evaporate so suddenly? I lay on my back and looked up at the high ceiling. I tried to focus on the empty space, on the nothingness that hovered there. It was an unnecessarily large house. Detached, as I was, with a garage and a garden. This listed Victorian home was bleak, not impressive, as I had thought when I made the purchase. It was situated on a corner and the local Holloway youths congregated there, shouting unimaginative insults whenever they saw me, even heaving a brick through the kitchen window a few weeks earlier. It had been a mistake to buy it, but I was rich and it seemed a good idea at the time. I was trying to make sense of my newly acquired fame and wealth and saw 9 Middleton Grove, London N7 as an appropriate symbol of my status.

At the third attempt I managed to get off the floor and go upstairs for a shower. It was a black-tie event so I had better make an effort and pull myself together. These award evenings could be fun if you were in the right sort of mood. Of course, I hadn't been nominated for an award – I was presenting the award for the best comedy actress. Before I left the house I stroked a glum-looking Fanny and slipped a Valium in my pocket in case I had one of my panic attacks. I knew there was a lot of small talk ahead and I might get stuck talking to someone tiresome. In the cut-throat world of television, people sometimes enjoyed saying hurtful things. I had bumped into Chris Evans a few weeks before at the Groucho Club. 'How are you?' I said. 'Your career went off the rails a couple of years ago,' was his cheery reply.

When I got to the studio from where the bash was being broadcast live, I forced a smile and found my manager, Addison Cresswell, milling around the champagne reception. 'All right, mush? Our table's over 'ere.' He seemed happy and excited; maybe because two of his other clients, Jack Dee and Lee Evans, were nominated for awards. 'Should be a good night for the stable,' he said, talking out the corner of his mouth, as if he were a drug dealer discreetly offering a sale. His company, Off The Kerb, was hugely successful, and when he'd had a few drinks he would state his worth in no uncertain terms. Poking himself vigorously in the chest, he'd say, 'I'm a multi-fucking-millionaire, mate!' He was proud of the comedians he looked after, and viewed us a bit like racehorses. When he signed Jo Brand he said to me: 'It's good to have a female in the stable,' as if she might be serviced by Jeff Green and produce a mini comic genius.

I was presenting the penultimate award so I was free to watch the show for a while and think about what I was going to say. Before you read the nominations and opened the envelope to announce the winner, you had time for a bit of banter with the host, Jonathan Ross, and one quick joke. I hadn't thought of my joke yet, but there was plenty of time. I had some champagne and nibbled my Valium. I looked round the room. The set that year was an imaginative rural display of greenery, sprouting branches and scattered autumn leaves. A veritable Who's Who of British Comedy sat in the audience along with other television stars of the day. Near the front I spotted the Conservative Chancellor of the Exchequer, Norman Lamont. Fancy inviting him, I thought. How inappropriate.

ONE

Mother, I love you so.
Said the child, I love you more than I know.
She laid her head on her mother's arm,
And the love between them kept them warm.

'HUMAN AFFECTION' BY STEVIE SMITH

Whenever friends announce a pregnancy, I feel a sense of bereavement, and by the time they've finished the sentence they've begun to disappear, as if walking backwards into the mist.

I know why. I feel displaced. As a bachelor of a certain age, one wants one's friends forever available for evenings of white wine and general bonding. Boyfriends and girlfriends are unlikely to be welcomed into the fold. I don't want to know about their nesting or their breeding. I am the star of the show. All eyes and all attention must be upon me.

When you're the host to such gross narcissistic tendencies, it's not easy to pretend you're interested in a world before your time.

How on earth did they manage? I shake my head in sorrow, but perk up when I consider my parents and the generations before them, the chance meetings, the fateful couplings, the mysterious but unstoppable life force, genetic combinations and cellular activity that culminated in what I modestly refer to as 'me'.

I feel a connection, more imagined than real, with my great-grandfather, Michael McDonald, who came to London from Nenagh in Ireland in the 1880s, with his two brothers Dan and Tom. Escaping from hunger, poverty and famine, the whole family was bailing out. Three other brothers went to America and were never heard of again. 'I always like to think they went on to create the McDonald's burger chain,' says Tess, Michael's only surviving daughter, aged 92. Michael and his brothers, meanwhile, opened a grocer's store in Brentford High Street, west London. Dan minded the shop while Michael and Tom took the horse and cart around the posh streets of Notting Hill to sell their wares.

Around that time, in my wistful imagination like a heroine in a Thomas Hardy novel, Louisa Watts set forth from her home on a farm in Chipping Norton to work as a housemaid in Brentford. Louisa had a fine singing voice and had joined the Catholic Church some years before because they had the best choir in Oxfordshire. It might be that Louisa's mistress fancied an omelette for her tea one day and sent her maid to the grocer's, where Michael, as he handed over the symbols of fertility, caught Louisa's eye.

Their son, Hector, was my maternal grandfather. My paternal grandfather, John Clary, worked in a tobacco factory and met my grandmother, Elizabeth, in a pub. Perhaps she was drinking a snowball at the time, but there is no official record.

But let's talk about me.

'It was surprisingly one morning, and that's as far as I'm prepared to go,' said my mother when I asked about my conception. I already knew the deed was done at Clacton-on-Sea, and working backwards from May 1959, when I was born, I could see it was evidently during a late summer break at Auntie Flossie's bungalow. Now I knew the time of day!

I was 44, and I wanted to know. How was I...?

I had always assumed, it being the 1950s and all, that the miracle of life occurred after dark with the lights off, but no. Morning. Brazen as you please. Anyone could have walked in. Where were my sisters? Frances and Beverley would have been three and one at the time. Had Auntie Flossie taken them down to the beach to give my parents some time alone? How thrilling to think of my parents overcome by passion, intoxicated by the sea air, writhing and cavorting in the kitchen as the morning sun filtered through the net curtains.

I really wanted to know the details of that particular sexual act but as always my mother knew what my game was, and her 'that's as far as I'm prepared to go' had rather put me in my place.

The truth is my mother always knew within hours if she was pregnant. This being her third such experience, she was in no doubt. A vague nausea and a tenderness in the nipple region.

Somewhat chagrined at the prospect of bottling her own potential for a few more years as another life took over, but simultaneously overcome with those glorious, earthy feelings only hormones and heterosexual liaisons can produce, she soon got used to the idea of another child.

The blood pressure that had escalated during her previous pregnancies was now a serious problem. At eight months, a routine visit to her GP brought bad news. She would have to go to hospital at once. She refused. Frances and Beverley were so small. They needed her. If she had to go home, the doctor told her, then she must stay in bed and do nothing. It was vital for the well-being of the baby. She cried. Quite stressful, I should imagine. The next day there was a knock at the door. It was Auntie Flossie. Four foot nine and 62 years old, all the way from Clacton.

'I've come for your girls,' she said, and so she did. My mother's confinement, released from the responsibilities of motherhood, continued as prescribed. She stayed in bed, nursing the foetus within. She watched a lot of boxing matches on the television.

My mother had met my father six years earlier when they both worked for the Met Office in Dunstable, near Luton. (Fifty years later they're both still prone to glancing up at the sky and announcing to bemused visitors: 'Cumulonimbus coming in from the west, I see.') They were both 18 and away from home for the first time. My father had a motorbike. One thing led to another. You can quite understand it. 'Shotgun Boogie' and Frank Sinatra were all the rage. They didn't mean any harm, your honour.

Office life was some kind of big open-plan arrangement full of lots of young people who were good at geography. My mother made a name for herself by refusing to sit on a seat if it was still warm from the previous occupant. Apparently she would stand over the offending chair and fan it with a cotton handkerchief to encourage the cooling process. My father, with his film-star looks and easy-going manner, was quite a catch. No doubt they were all sniffing around each other like dogs on a council estate. Soon Peter and Brenda were an item.

During their engagement my father had joined the Metropolitan Police and was, it has to be said, a bobby on the beat. At the coronation of Queen Elizabeth the Second he was on duty, standing in the middle of Cambridge Circus directing traffic. My mother was with some friends who, along with thousands of others, were sleeping on the pavement in order to secure their spot to watch the great spectacle. Rumour has it she legged it over the barrier, ran to the roundabout where my father was doing his police constable duties, and kissed him to the applause of the assembled throng.

As you drive over the M4 flyover in Brentford, it curves disdainfully round the unpretentious spire of St John's Catholic Church. It was here in 1953 that Peter Clary married Brenda McDonald. They look remarkably happy together in photographs taken then. My mother seems positively coquettish and my father looks full of laughter. Clearly enthralled with each other, it is alleged they managed to keep themselves nice till their wedding night, which is something I suppose. Their sense of decorum had obviously evaporated by the time I was conceived. One might have hoped for a romantic weekend in Paris or even the grounds of a minor stately home, but it wasn't to be. I'm not bitter.

My father sold his motorbike to pay for their honeymoon in Guernsey. The entire hotel was full of honeymoon couples and there was a lot of giggling over breakfast.

Then they lived in Acton for a while, in a small flat on the top floor of a relative's converted house. Proper teas served on a proper table, napkins, fruit bowl on the sideboard, feeling very grown-up I dare say... By the time I was born they had moved into police flats: 1 Meadow Bank, Surbiton, Surrey. Brand new as well. Low rise, red brick, substantial lawns. Proper brick sheds for the rubbish bins and no smell of wee on the stairs.

The day before each of us was born, a nesting instinct possessed my mother and she went into spring-cleaning mode, emptying cupboards, cleaning windows and polishing floors. I was born at home. Brown paper under the sheets to save the mattress and brown paper up the walls, too, apparently, in case of who knows what. An enema had been performed to prevent Baby being born covered in unsightly faecal matter, and for that, at least, I'm grateful. Gas and air were administered to ease the pain of each contraction, so intoxicating my mother that she made unflattering remarks about Dr Pretzel. Given that he was delivering her baby there and then, the midwife thought it best to silence her. This she did by more or less sitting on my mother's face. A tough woman, the midwife, by all accounts. 'Very good, but didn't like children,' my mother recalled. 'Referring to your sisters, she said, "When are the two brats coming back, then?"'

Twenty-five years later, I went on a rebirthing course in Hampstead. A particular type of breathing is taught to you and a misty-eyed woman of a certain age gazes down at you. Soon an altered state was upon me. I struggled down the birth canal. I felt the warmth of an open fire, saw the tiles that surrounded it, stared up at the white knobbly ceiling, and heard my mother groaning as she expelled the afterbirth. I wanted attention. I cried.

I think it cost about £20.

I was named Julian after a Benedictine monk.

My mother had grown up in the village of Stoke Ferry, Norfolk. The McDonalds occupied the Manor House, and although they weren't lord and lady, the prestige that came with their residence didn't escape them. They had moved to the countryside when my grandfather took a job as accountant in a local sugar beet factory. During the war their substantial dining room was turned into a place of worship, and Father Julian Stoner gave mass there each Sunday. Local prisoners of war would come and fulfil their obligations alongside the villagers. I imagine swarthy Italians winking at veiled shop girls, sideways glances and shy blushes, but then I am a homosexual.

Father Julian was six foot six and the son of Lord and Lady Fermoy of Stoner Castle in Oxfordshire. He gave my mother her first holy communion and obviously made an impression. 'I decided to name you after him because he was the kindest man I knew,' my mother recalled.

When I was a few months old, my mother wheeled me to the shops. Prams in those days were big, metal affairs with massive spoked wheels, the size of a street cleaner's trolley. To transport her children about my mother wanted the top of the range. 'We saved up for ages when I was expecting Frances. We had no stair carpet but the pram was a priority. It cost £28 and your father got £6 a week. It was a London Baby Coach, the same as the Queen had. The most expensive. Grey colour. All coach-built. Too big, really.'

She parked me outside the butcher's, went in to buy some chops and went home. For several hours she quite forgot she'd even given birth to me. It was only the sight of the nappies fluttering on the line that reminded her. She raced back to the butcher's and I was still there, asleep in my pram. I could have been wheeled off by any old Loopy Lou, sold abroad into a life of slavery, made into sausages.

I've told my mother not to feel bad about it, though. I did the same thing with Fanny the Wonder Dog: tied her up outside the newsagent's and quite forgot she existed until lunchtime when I wondered why I had a cupboard full of Pedigree Chum. She was still there, looking bored and bewildered, three hours later.

M arried in the 1950s, when the 1960s arrived my parents had to get with it.

The ration books and valued chastity that were the reality of their youth were replaced with feminism, free love and the Beatles. My mother changed her hairstyle, a highlighted, tufted crop instead of the dark, trained top curl. My father grew side-burns. Money was tight on a police constable's wages so they earned extra cash in the evenings after we three were in bed by making lamp-shades and folding Christmas cards at five shillings per thousand.

So she was understandably tired out one afternoon when she mistakenly made our Sunday tea chocolate cake with Bisto instead of cocoa.

My great auntie Wyn – who was a regular Sunday visitor – was there and was given the first slice. My mother's chocolate cake was always cause for excitement. It was two chocolate sponges with delicious, sugary chocolate cream both in between and on top, decorated with swirls done with a fork, as creatively as my mother's limited time would allow. Auntie Wyn took a bite, paused, took a sip of tea and swallowed. She replaced the remainder of her cake on the plate and said nothing. The plate was part of a delicate, green and white bone-china tea service that was originally owned by my grandmother, and it was only used for Sunday tea. My sisters and I were served next and we all took big greedy bites. As one, Frances, Beverley and I spat our mouthfuls of cake out, Beverley missing her plate and indeed the table altogether. My mother was horrified by her children's vulgar display. 'Eat it!' We pulled faces and looked down at our plates with fear. 'I said eat it!' my mother insisted.

Luckily Auntie Wyn came to our rescue. 'Actually, Brenda, it does taste rather different…'

'Does it?' My mother indignantly took a bite. She spat hers out too. 'Bisto!' she said, identifying the culprit.

My father did shift work as a policeman and there were 'late turns', 'early turns' and 'night turns', when we had to creep around during the day and make no noise because 'Your father's asleep!' His job carried an element of danger, and when he got home my mother always asked if everything had been all right. She asked the obligatory question one night without turning to look at him. When he only mumbled in response she looked up and saw his face was bruised, battered and bleeding. In those days, banks had night safes where money or cheques could be deposited. Driving home after his late shift my father had seen someone being robbed of his cash as he tried to post it through the slot of the night safe. My father jumped out of his car and wrestled with the robber, who fought back violently. The robber got away but left his jacket behind. With that and my father's description, the man was soon apprehended and jailed. An article in the local paper praised my father's bravery. A few years later at school I exaggerated the story, telling my classmates that my father had been shot and wounded while single-handedly foiling an armed bank robbery. I obviously felt the need to be this dramatic quite regularly, because I remember other untruths I told quite clearly. When, as a nine-year-old, I was told by mocking classmates that I sounded like a girl, I solemnly informed them that, if they must know, I'd had a lung transplant a few years ago and had been the recipient of a girl's lungs. My feminine voice was the result of this life-saving medical procedure, and I'd rather they didn't make fun of me because I couldn't help it.

I was a happy, healthy child, but from the age of about six months I had a problem with my eyes. It was a form of eczema that made them red and itchy, and it came and went for years. As I slept, a yellow goo would be produced and I'd wake up in the morning with lids glued together by Nature's gunk. My mother had to bathe my eyes each morning to dissolve the gunk before I could open them and see. She used to take me to the skin hospital in Leicester Square for treatment. One day while we were there she was struck by one of her infrequent but incapacitating migraines. When these happened she had to lie down in a darkened room immediately. She phoned my father, who was on duty in Soho at the time.

My father worked in the traffic division for many years, driving around looking for violations, responding to calls and patrolling the motorways. He was first on the scene at many horrific car crashes, and was on duty when a British Airways 111 crashed in Staines, Middlesex. Once when I was late leaving for school and he was on early turn, he got me there in double-quick time, sirens blazing. On this occasion, his response to my mother was unsympathetic.

'You can't get home? Get the tube to Waterloo and the train to Surbiton.'

Once he understood the true urgency of her words he collected her in a police car and drove her to the nearest police station. There was no suitably dark room available, so she lay down in a roomy broom cupboard and told my father to shut the door and come back in two hours. As my mother told me this story recently I couldn't help but notice that my role, as a principal player in this anecdote, had been faded out entirely.

'What happened to me?' I asked, concerned.

'Well, the migraine was so bad I couldn't care less about you. I think you were left in the station canteen being looked after by whoever was about at the time.'

I remember waking up once in the middle of the night when a cat fight was going on outside my bedroom window, unable to open my eyes. The wailing falsetto sounded like the devil's death throes to me. I got blindly out of bed and crept as far as my parents' bedroom door before I started screaming. Within seconds my mother was there, clutching my head and saying everything was fine: it was only cats having an argument.

This mother/son scenario repeated itself when I was 34. In the midst of a black hole of depression and Valiumed to the eyeballs, I arrived at Swindon similarly traumatised by my drive down the M4. I stood on the doorstep and rang the bell, tears streaming down my face. 'All the cars were going backwards,' I said. 'I thought I was going to die.' My mother clutched my head and said everything would be fine.

It is incidents such as these, variations on themes subtly repeated like a quiet refrain in a piano concerto, that seem to imply there is, after all, some order to our lives, some recurring scheme or rhythm we may not even notice. We can't quite join the dots but we see them, like signposts along the way.

I was, for example, a sturdy baby. I enjoyed being sung to and I slept a lot. Today I listen to yodelling music and sleep a lot… As soon as I could walk I used to drape towels and scarves round my shoulders and attempt a toddler's version of swanning about… As I write I'm wearing a soft pink silk kimono that Jasper Conran made for me. I was once asleep in my pram outside the French windows when some rough girls came and threw dirt over me… I was recently trashed in an interview by Lucy Cavendish from the *Evening Standard*…

All similar experiences, don't you see?

When I try to remember my early childhood, it comes back to me in short, atmospheric film clips: a flowerbed full of marigolds with a path made from fire cinders, my father in his police uniform saying goodbye when he left for night duty, a green coat behind a frosted-glass front door, a high-ceilinged hall with a stained-glass window, the sound of stiletto heels on pavements and tiled floors, a kind, smiling, glamorous woman called Sylvia, my father in the kitchen, opening a container then saying, crossly, 'There's no ruddy coffee again!' I remember Norfolk fields covered in snow, and sitting on my grandfather's lap – he had a small lozenge-like growth on his jaw and when I or my sisters pressed it he made a funny prolonged quacking noise, as if we were pressing a front-door buzzer. I remember my grandmother's smiling, excited face when she greeted us at the front door of the Manor House, her placemats featuring scenes from classical ballets, the dark, shiny sideboard with two cupboards you opened by sliding a short wooden arrangement left or right, to the right if you wanted to get into the left side, and vice versa. I remember a television on tall, spindly, 1950s legs, built into a wooden case with 'doors' made of thin vertical slats of wood. When 'open' they disappeared into the sides of the box. You 'closed' the television by sliding them out with two thin gold-coloured metal finger-grips, designed to match the petite round 'feet' on each leg.

I remember lying in my bedroom studying the wallpaper at about the age of five. For some reason a design of climbing pink roses had been deemed suitable. Delicate buds sprouted from a thin green stem that twisted from left to right. Every foot or so the pattern repeated itself but the join was hard to discern and it was only a slightly quirky slip of a bud barely out of its green casing that gave the game away. The overall effect was of a wildly glamorous sequence of rose stems bursting forth on every available inch of wall space. In the small boxroom of the flat that was quite overpowering.

I had an Action Man (the first of many), while my sisters had Sindy dolls. They had boxes full of outfits with matching shoes and accessories, and my Action Man had a choice between camouflage all-in-ones or black slacks with matching polo neck. It was a ridiculous situation and I did the only thing I could. Very soon my Action Man was Surbiton's first cross-dressing experiment. (I blame the wallpaper.) Stretch fabrics looked particularly fetching on his well-toned torso and rippling limbs.

There was a girl who lived at the flats who wasn't quite right. She'd fallen out of the window as an infant and couldn't speak properly. Chains were put on all the windows. Judith's parents weren't going to let such a terrible accident happen again. But she had a fantastic dressing-up box, and whenever I went up to play we draped ourselves in oversized ballgowns and eased our feet into diamante slip-ons.

At the flats there was also a boy about twice my age I shall call Glen. I used to follow him round. He had a sweaty smell about him that excited me in a way I didn't understand. I spontaneously asked him for a fight once, not because we had fallen out but because I wanted him to touch me. He said no and then he stabbed a stag beetle with a stick and spread its creamy white innards across the pavement. I liked him even more after that. Years later, as I performed a sex act on a glass collector in the toilet cubicle of a Sheffield nightclub and experienced once again the

life-affirming wonder of the male ejaculation, I thought spontaneously of Glen and the stag beetle's innards.

The local sweet shop was called Frank's. It was run by three
brothers who happened to be midgets and stood on boxes to reach
the till. If you wanted something from a jar on the top shelf you
had to wait until someone tall enough to reach it came in. Frank
and his brothers later appeared in the film *The Private Life of
Sherlock Holmes*. Obviously the confectionery business was just a
stop-gap for them.

Three young children is quite a handful for any mother, so
washing, dressing, breakfast and bedtimes were all achieved on a
rota system. I'm not sure where I came in the feeding and dressing stakes but I was always last in the scummy lukewarm bath and
first to bed.

I attended several primary schools, starting aged four at Arundel
House in a smart red-and-yellow striped uniform. When I was
three my mother had sent a photograph of my sisters and me to
Father Julian, along with a letter in which she asked what school
he thought she should try for. How expensive was Downside, for
example? She still has his reply.

Talacre Abbey,
Prestatyn 2.2.63

Dear Brenda,

Thank you so much for the lovely photograph of the
children. Julian certainly does look brim full of character

and intelligence and I can understand you wanting to give him every chance. But Downside really is fantastically expensive. I believe it costs £1,000 to keep a boy there for four years, and this would be on top of about six years at preparatory school.

There are two daughter schools of Downside which might be worth your visiting, as they would both be relatively easy to get to from Surbiton. One is Worth, which used to be a preparatory school for Downside when I taught there, but which is now building up its own public school – it is in the most lovely setting and Downside sent the cream of its community to form the staff there. Three Bridges on the London–Brighton line is the nearest station, about four miles away. The other is Ealing Abbey, which was also founded and staffed by Downside and is, of course, <u>very much</u> cheaper, as it is a day school.

I do hope you are all managing to keep warm in this fantastic winter—

Bless you all always—

Yours affectionately

Fr Julian Stoner

Whatever the letter from my mother to Father Julian had said about my potential, I wasn't very bright. In fact, there was some suspicion that I was backward. (I gather 'backward' is a bit like being 'slow', as if we are all clocks on the wall.) Reading and writing were difficult for me: for several years I could only manage mirror-writing.

Arundel House was rather posh and costly and after a while the fees were too much, I think, and let's face it, I was hardly the star pupil. I was moved to St Joseph's in Kingston, which was a bit rougher.

I remember putting my hand up once and asking the teacher if I could go to the toilet. As several other children in the class had already been she got fed up, thought I was being cheeky and said no. It was a rather urgent number two so I asked again but was snapped at and told to be quiet.

I remember that stool with great clarity. Despite my best efforts to restrain it, it forced its way out to the semi daylight of my grey school shorts like a beaver emerging from its burrow. It sat in my shorts, steaming like an angry dragon, until the offensive odour alerted my classmates.

'Miss! Julian Clary's pooed himself!'

I was hauled out of the classroom, mortified but self-righteous – 'I told you I needed to go!' – and cleaned up.

My soiled pants were spirited away and I was told to put on another pair. They were huge and so near the end of their pant life – no elastic, several holes – they were just about ready to be used as a dishcloth.

For holidays we'd go to St Ives in Cornwall, or to visit my grandparents in Norfolk, or to the Isle of Wight where my father's sister, Aunty Doreen, and her husband, Uncle Bob, owned a guesthouse. It was in Sandown, and had a big sweeping staircase with a red carpet. There was a lounge, dining room, music room, lots of bedrooms and chalets to stay in and a big lawned garden. Doreen had a white albino Chihuahua called Pancho. Their son Michael, our only cousin, was six years older than me. Our favourite game as children was called Fight as Hard as a Lion – wrestling with lots of animal growling added. Michael, being the biggest and oldest, was always the most successful lion. An attack imminent, my sisters and I used to squeal with excitement as he ambled towards us, roaring like the king of the jungle.

My mother made us all laugh a lot from an early age. It wasn't always what she said but what she did. An old favourite was walking into a room with a pair of knickers on her head and saying something mundane like, 'Hot cross bun anyone?' She could diffuse a tense domestic mood with ease. One hot day she served up a beef stew. No one fancied it much and she silently scraped the considerable leftovers onto one plate. She then walked to the other end of the table where my father sat and without a word poured the entire meaty mess down the inside of his open-necked shirt. There was a stunned silence, then everyone laughed, apart from Beverley, who cried.

During lengthy car trips to holiday destinations my mother told elaborate and funny stories that she made up on the spot, keeping us enthralled for hours on end. The punchlines were improvised from our surroundings. One was about an old man who never washed. He had mice nesting in his beard and sparrows in his hair. 'And when we turn the next corner we'll see where he lived…'

We'd crane our necks to see the dirty man's home…

'A windmill!' said my mother with delight.

Another instructive tale was how the bungalow came to be invented. I won't offer you the full version or we'll be here for a hundred pages, but basically it concerned an impatient foreman at a building site. Once the walls of a house were complete he'd get a large number of workmen to lift the ready-made roof and, with the instruction 'Bung-a-high!', chuck it up in the air so it landed on top. One day, in his haste, he shouted too early and the house was only half built. Registering that it was not as high but not realising his mistake he shouted, 'Bung-a-low!' And that's the true story of how bungalows came to be.

For my father, departing on holiday was a military procedure: roofrack, trailer, tarpaulins all loaded onto the sturdy Zephyr. Anyone would think we were going trekking up the north face of the Eiger in slingbacks.

Before one holiday I remember Beverley and I spent the evening dressing up Sindy and Tiger in their going-away outfits (stripes for Sindy, a peach puff-sleeve smock affair for Tiger), and packing a varied selection for the rest of the trip. Tiger was my favourite toy. In fact, he was a leopard (judging from his spots) but I didn't know that then. Originally designed, I think, to sit on the back shelf of a car, he was soft and sleepy, his wild staring amber eyes replaced at some point with plain black buttons. I see him now on a shelf in my bedroom, looking kind and long-suffering despite being covered in a thin layer of dust.

Anyway, once we were all loaded into the car at the crack of dawn, my father cast a final eye over his troops. He glared at Tiger in his gorgeous silk frock.

'We're not going anywhere till Tiger takes that dress off,' he said with an air of determination.

From an early age I sensed that I wasn't quite the only son my father had in mind. I wasn't very boyish. Football and cars weren't my thing, try as he might to interest me in them. He tried to involve me in decorating once, telling me it would be a useful skill when I was grown up.

'Oh no,' I said. 'I'll get a man in.'

When I was seven we moved from the police flats in Surbiton to a police house in Teddington: 37 Blandford Road. It had a garden and everything.

When the time came for us to set off on our annual holiday, the Zephyr's roofrack and boot loaded up with luggage, it was pouring with rain. My mother began one of her long, improvised stories, which lasted until we reached our destination. It was about a disastrous family holiday when it rained all day every day and there was nothing for it but to go and buy a puppy. As it happened it never stopped raining for us either and so the story came true.

At a loss to entertain three children who were expecting fun in the sun, ice creams and sand castles, and unable to keep us cooped up in the damp cottage in St Ives all the time, my parents drove us all around Cornwall, stopping at various kennels to view the puppies. We saw all sorts and then had to decide. I was quite sure I wanted a beagle but they weren't ready to leave their mother and would have had to be sent to London by train in a box, so we decided on a long-haired miniature dachshund and called him Monty.

My grandmother wasn't impressed when she heard the news. 'Fancy getting a German dog!'

Our choice was not a wise one as things turned out. As the months passed it became apparent there was nothing miniature about Monty at all. He grew and grew until he was the size of a low hairy sofa. Bad tempered and destructive, he would bare his teeth and growl at anyone who so much as looked at him.

I had a farmyard animal set supplemented with lions, elephants and a hippo. I'd shove a plimsoll under the green rug in my bedroom and have an instant hillside. Tom the farmer rode round on his tractor tending to his sheep and cows, then moved further up the hill to where the more exotic creatures lived. One fateful day, Monty chewed off both his legs. His arms, which until then had reached out at 90 degrees, the better to clutch the steering wheel, were also nipped and twisted. They no longer boasted two manly cupped hands, forever in the gripping position – not that Tom let that stop him. He carried on as normal. As did his wife, I'm pleased to say. Jill, a bucket-holding, pinnied farmer's wife, lost both her legs up to the knee in the same incident. But she was there, leaning against the farmhouse door the very next morning.

Monty didn't just snap and nip and chew small plastic things, he attacked with intent. Excuses were always made for him until he bit my father. Then his days at Blandford Road were numbered. Off he went to live a life of luxury in the Manor House in Norfolk. As I recall the plan had been to have him put down but we children were so distraught at the thought of such premeditated murder that my grandparents stepped in and saved his bacon. The country life suited him and within weeks he was a placid, good-natured animal, doted on by his new keepers.

Despite this experience, my interest in animals grew. We got a black cat called Cindy from the RSPCA. She disappeared over the back of the garden into Bushey Park and didn't come home for weeks, and I lay awake at night imagining her creeping through the undergrowth, hungry and bedraggled but determined to find her way home. I was euphoric when she eventually turned up.

Then a neighbour's cat had kittens and we chose Robinson, a black-and-white number who did nothing her entire life but sleep in a cardboard box by the radiator. She died of kidney failure eventually, probably brought on from lack of use.

Rodents were the next phase. After a moderate amount of pleading and assurances that we would do all the looking after, all three of us were allowed to go to the pet shop and make a selection. Frances chose Jasmine, a guinea pig whose ginger and white fur grew into pretty floral swirls but who was otherwise devoid of personality, just blank, distrustful, staring eyes. A bit like people who live in Chatham.

My guinea pig Hildebrand, on the other hand, was as charming and delightful as a Jack Russell. She could recognise my footsteps as I minced down the garden path and would let out a cheery whistle like a London cabdriver passing a leggy blonde.

She had long flowing black and white hair which I used to comb endlessly with a baby's brush set and which billowed out behind her as she scampered behind me across the lawn. She was the Scarlett O'Hara of the cavy world, cocking her head coquettishly if she thought I had some celery or dandelion leaves hidden about my person.

Beverley, to be different, got a mouse. Pip was beige with pink eyes and, as it turned out, pregnant. When she gave birth to six hairless, slug-like young, we opened the top of her cage to get a better look and invited the neighbouring children in too. Mice take it badly if they're not left in peace at such a private time and Pip made her feelings clear overnight by eating her babies.

The next morning Beverley ran in from the shed screaming. It was a scene of terrible carnage: Pip sat in the middle of her cage, a look of Myra Hindley about her, her stomach swollen with her own consumed offspring, the sawdust around her and her manic mouse-face red and wet with their blood. Scattered around her like mini footballs were their heads. Clearly Pip wasn't the mothering type. This traumatic incident may well be the root cause of my dislike of all things beige.

There was more horror to come when the Labrador from the children's home at the end of our road leapt over the garden gate one sunny afternoon and attacked the guinea pig run. We came back from the park to find Jasmine dismembered on the lawn. I thought Hildebrand must have met a similar fate, but half an hour later she waddled out from under a rose bush and nibbled my toe.

Jasmine was replaced with Patch, a seriously tan boy guinea pig, so named because he had a small white dot between his ears. To say Patch was oversexed would be an understatement. His low machine-gun-like mating call could be heard streets away and he would slowly hop from one back leg to the other as if the weight and urgency of his guinea-pig semen was a source of some discomfort. Fortunately Hildebrand was a keen recipient. Unlike Pip, Hildebrand was a proud and fastidious mother. I would skip round the garden, she would follow me and her brood would follow her, conga-fashion.

When I was nine, my parents joined the property market and we moved to our first 'proper' home: 39 St Mark's Road in Teddington, a fairly typical semi-detached three-bedroom house built in the 1920s.

It was also directly opposite the Sacred Heart Primary School, which was very handy for me. I made friends with a boy called Barry Jones who lived up the road, the son of a big emotional Italian woman and a small, serious, preoccupied man.

He had guinea pigs too, and took on several of Hildebrand's litter. When his started breeding he just kept them all. They had a big walled garden and his brood lived in a disused greenhouse. I remember going round there several years later and the whole place was completely overrun with wild and untamed guinea pigs of every shape and size, dozens of them, many albinos, darting all round the place. I imagine some kind of pest control had to be called in eventually.

One of my mother's friends was Doreen Eldridge. She had three children too, and this coincidence made their friendship both inevitable and practical. I liked Doreen a great deal and it would brighten my day to hear her tap on the door and call:

'Yoo-hoo! Only me!'

I was a mere child, of course, and Doreen had come to see my mother, not me. I was acknowledged, patted and ignored as they settled down to morning coffee and biscuits. But this did not matter at all. In fact, it was all to the good, for Doreen's discourse was not about nappies or Jimmy Young, it was always up-to-the-minute scandal and revelation about people we knew, or repetitions of overheard conversations with sizzling punchlines. There was never a dull moment when Doreen popped in, and I would quietly and unobtrusively play with my farmyard animals or pretend to be reading a book while listening to the latest gossip. Thus by the age of eight I was a veritable *Who's Who* of Teddington Babylon, and as shocked as anyone by the particular goings-on of a woman, nay harlot, called Shauna (not her real name), whose activities enlivened many a morning's coffee break.

Doreen's main asset was imagination – a startling originality that swept her along faster than most could keep up with. She spoke very quickly, spilling the words out in no particular order, and the listener had the task of unravelling and ordering them if any meaningful communication was to be made.

Her appearance, however, was not disordered. She was tall and painfully thin, and from my position at floor level I would wonder at her long, sinewy legs, wound round each other like plaits of soft toffee. As she talked, Doreen would often sew. Nearly all her clothes she made herself; she would create summer dresses from curtains, aprons from summer dresses, tea towels from aprons and dusters from tea towels.

Doreen (also known as Do-Do) treated her children with the

same brisk vivacity that she treated everything else. She would break off in mid-sentence to call 'Nick!' (her youngest) from across the room, then, continuing her conversation, she would hold the struggling infant firmly by the shoulder while the forefinger of her other hand was busy clawing at his nose to remove some lumpy discharge.

As Doreen had a weak bladder, she was obliged to get up at frequent intervals throughout the night. Even this she turned to practical advantage. When she got up at 6 a.m. she would wash and brush her teeth before returning to bed for the final hour of rest. This would save time later on, and five minutes after the alarm clock went off she was up and dressed and shovelling breakfast into her children. Lunch would be over by noon and tea on the table at half past three in the afternoon.

If in the summer we went on a trip to the local open-air swimming pool, it was important to Doreen that we be the first to arrive. We would find ourselves sitting by the pool before it was warm enough to change into swimming costumes, and sleepy-eyed we would watch the attendant clean the scum from the water's surface.

I don't remember Doreen ever being depressed, but she was frequently ill and unable to carry on at the usual frantic pace. She was asthmatic and slept with an oxygen cylinder by her bed. Sometimes she would seem to run out of breath, and I remember her groping in her handbag for a small plastic contraption she called her 'puffer'. She would place one end of this in her mouth and inhale, and then her breathing would be easier. As well as asthma, Doreen seemed prone to all sorts of other afflictions. A superficial finger wound became septic and her finger was amputated. For Doreen this was a great talking point and she would waggle her stump in the air and shriek with laughter. Bronchitis and influenza also seemed to enter and depart her body as they pleased. The maladies kept her thin and frequently weak, but they served only to increase her desire for quickness and efficiency in every aspect of her day. On Saturday mornings she would often boast that she had done her entire week's housework, dusting, hoovering and all, by 8 a.m.

As her children grew up, Doreen was able to enter more fully into the swim of social activity in Teddington. Thus her conversation took on a different tone, centring in general on the Railway Tavern. Fortunately for me, the character called Shauna was also a regular there. I had grown quite attached to the infamous Shauna over the years and, like a wayward relation, I would have hated to lose touch.

For my mother, now free from child-bearing duties, time was more her own too. She chose college and career, but their friendship weathered the contrast.

In the summer I would still sunbathe near Doreen on her visits, bury my face in a towel and be presumed to be in the trance of adolescence. Sometimes, at the vital part of her anecdote, Doreen would lower her voice, something she had never done when I was six, and I was obliged to cease breathing and sprout antennae to capture the sordid climax of the tale.

We were raised as Catholics, washed and smartly dressed every Sunday for church, which we attended with our mother –

our father being more of an atheist. 'You live, you die, that's it,' he said, rather unimaginatively.

I loved church, the smells and the bells and the seriousness of it all. I had complete faith in the power of prayer and would close my eyes and press my mouth against the bitter dark varnished wood of the pew, reciting 'Our Father' and 'Hail Mary' over and over under my breath, dedicating one each to my parents, my sisters, cats and guinea pigs.

Christenings, first holy communions and confirmations were big family affairs. I had a pale blue rosary kept in a clear plastic case and a prayer book with a picture of a saintly-looking boy kneeling in prayer on the cover, who I thought looked a bit like me.

When I was ten I became an altar boy and, of course, it altered me.

I took my duties very seriously. The priest at the Sacred Heart Church was Canon Moore, a delicate, elderly man with kind, watery eyes. I loved lighting the big candles on the altar, reverently passing him the water and wine, and wafting around in my boy-size cassock and surplice.

There were a selection of these in the sacristy, and as you never quite knew how many boys were going to turn up, I made sure I got there early. There was nothing worse than being left with an ill-fitting cassock. Just an inch above floor length was what you wanted, although I would rather have it too long than too short. I didn't mind having to lift my 'dress' from the knee as I went about my holy business, rather like a well-to-do lady in an old-fashioned film. If the cassock was too short in the arm and stopped unceremoniously halfway down the calf, you felt a bit of a fool and tried to move about with slightly bent knees to disguise things.

To be given the task of ringing the hand-held gold bells during the transubstantiation was a thrilling responsibility. This is the climax of the mass, the moment the priest raises the Eucharist and says, 'The Body of Christ.' This isn't just ritual: the true Catholic knows that a real transformation has taken place, signified by the bells.

None of this drama was lost on me, and the special effect of the bells, if timed correctly and gently shaken with the merest ripple, could greatly increase the potency of the congregation's spiritual experience, sending shivers down their collective spine.

Nowadays the nearest I get to that sensation is the transformation scene in my annual production of *Cinderella*, when the Fairy Godmother turns rags into a ballgown and a pumpkin into a glittering coach. Light this moment properly through some gauze, add plenty of dry ice, some bad-tempered miniature ponies and a click-track of session singers ooh-ing and ah-ing ethereally, and you are indeed transported once again.

I went to confession regularly and once asked Canon Moore to pray for Hildebrand. She'd had an abnormally large litter and one was dying each day despite my mother's best efforts with an alarm clock and an eyedropper full of milk.

'And who is Hildebrand, my son?' he asked.

'A guinea pig,' I said.

I blushed furiously the next Sunday, mortified to hear the story repeated at the end of his sermon as an amusing anecdote. What of the confidentiality of the confessional? The holiness of the sacraments? Nevertheless I started weeding the priest's garden once a week for half a crown. It was mainly shrubs and very overgrown, but a rich source of dandelion leaves, which I proudly presented to Hildebrand and Patch. Their eyes glistened and their jaws swivelled.

My last few years of primary education at the Sacred Heart School were stress-free. I skipped over the road to school and rode my bicycle round Bushey Park. 'Never on the roads!' was one of my mother's rules, and I persisted in riding on the pavements until I was 16, oblivious to the angry old ladies forced to flatten themselves against privet hedges in order to let me past.

I continued to be fascinated by animals. I joined the RSPCA and various wildlife organisations, avidly read Joy Adamson's books about Elsa the 'Born Free' lion and wept buckets over the fate of her various cubs.

My mother and I continued to amuse each other, developing secret catchphrases, nudging each other during mass if we spotted someone wearing an unflattering hat. My father made a good straight man, and didn't seem to mind being the fall guy, although he'd get a bit cross if he fell asleep in front of the TV and my mother poked a knitting needle down his ear.

Years later I had a similar relationship with my pianist Russell Churney. He'd fall fast asleep in the tour bus and I'd use his open mouth as an ashtray.

I slowly caught up with my reading and writing, thanks mainly to an inspiring teacher called Mrs Lang. Petite and energetic, she

JULIAN CLARY

had red hair but I liked her even so. She was patient with me and seemed genuinely thrilled when I got something right. I wasn't exactly backward – I just did things back to front. The next year I was in Miss Lomax's class. She was thin and powdery and didn't take much notice of me so I fell behind a bit.

I was a bit in love with a girl called Catherine and gave her a Valentine's card.

Once a week I cycled to Hampton Wick to have piano lessons with Mrs Keable, who had a vase of dusty plastic chrysanthemums on display in her front window winter and summer. Each lesson cost a very reasonable half a crown, but she used to secretly give me sixpence back. Already in her eighties, she was a patient teacher and would demonstrate the correct way to play 'The Moonlight Sonata' despite the fact that her arthritic fingers made it impossible. I smiled politely.

Progress was slow, though. The mirror-writing problem resurfaced when I read music, and I somehow managed to play backwards. I finally mastered a piece called 'Swans on the Lake', from Book One. Simple and sedate, it became a family joke when a year later it was still the only thing I could play.

One week I turned up and the plastic flowers had gone. So had Mrs Keable, her bereaved daughter informed me. She had passed away during the week and there would be no more piano lessons.

As I hadn't displayed any shining talent as a pianist, no new tutor was sought, but we had an old upright at home, all candlestick holders and ivory keys, and I continued to thump out 'Swans on the Lake' whenever the fancy took me.

A few years later, when I had every intention of becoming a

famous pop star, I waited till everyone was out and wrote what I thought were fabulous songs on the now out-of-tune piano.

Then one day I came home from school and saw my father having one of his weekly bonfires. It wasn't until I wandered into the dining room and saw the empty space against the wall that I realised what he was burning. My piano.

'What are you doing? I play that!'

'No you don't,' he said.

As no one had heard me play, my story that I was writing the hits of the future wasn't very persuasive. At any rate, it was too late.

Always ready to cast myself as the wronged heroine, I salvaged a few keys from the pyre and flew up to my room in tears. I still have them somewhere, and about once a year I bring up the subject of the piano-burning. The fact that I didn't develop into the next Elton John we can put down to that needless incineration.

For my final year in primary school I was in Miss Ronson's class. A big-boned woman with a manly round nose and a booming voice, she lived locally in a bungalow opposite the shrew-like Miss Leeming. Neighbours watched to see if there was light on in both homes at the same time...

'He's come on leaps and bounds!' she informed my mother at the parents' evening.

Secondary school was looming and although Broom Road comprehensive school for boys was the obvious local choice, the select few could apply for a grant to St Benedict's, part of Ealing Abbey in west London, and suggested all those years ago by Julian Stoner.

My mother asked if this was worth considering for me.

'Oh Mrs Clary!' guffawed Miss Ronson. 'I said he was coming along, but I don't for a moment think he stands the remotest chance of getting in there. He won't even pass the eleven-plus!'

If only she'd been right.

TWO

"Will you walk a little faster?" Said the whiting to the snail
"There's a porpoise close behind us, and he's treading on my tail."

'THE LOBSTER QUADRILLE', *ALICE IN WONDERLAND*, LEWIS CARROLL

I passed the exam. This uncharacteristic flash of academic success I put down to my 'lucky pants', which my mother had bought for me a week before from Marks and Spencer. They were red tartan Y-fronts with a light blue trim and I wore them for any future exams or special occasions for the next ten years. My first boyfriend was to pick them up one day and read the label. 'Ages 9–11?'

If I hadn't gone to St Benedict's, it would all have been so different. It was the unholy monks who taught me the rudiments of glamour, alternative living and brutality. Until I walked through the gates of St Ben's on that fateful day in September 1970, I was a naive, uncomplicated, albeit slightly eccentric eleven-year-old, anxious to please, interested in guinea pigs, local gossip and church.

When I made my exit seven years later I was a languid, head-flicking teenager determined to avenge myself.

But we had better stick with the facts, and their consequences.

Everyone, especially me, was flabbergasted when the letter arrived saying I had passed the entrance exam and was accepted into St Benedict's. I think I probably did better in the interview than the exam. I was a perky, well-spoken boy and I had explained in some detail to the bemused panel of monks how to tell the sex of a baby guinea pig. My pedigree as an altar boy, not to mention my job as Canon Moore's gardener, also stood me in good stead. My mother was particularly pleased.

I felt a sense of achievement that was new to me, and I was very glad I didn't have to go to Broom Road as I'd encountered chaps from that school and they were rough and tough – characteristics in a boy I had not yet learned to appreciate.

St Benedict's was a public school, though, and the fees were more than my parents could afford, but we filled out forms and applied to Richmond Borough Council for a grant, which was duly given.

Barry Jones had also been deemed acceptable and during that summer holiday we played with our guinea pigs, cycled round Bushey Park and wondered what life would be like at our new school.

There was quite a lot of correspondence over those weeks, letters typed on quality notepaper, always headed with the school crest and Latin motto: *A Minimis Incipe*. One Saturday my mother took me to Peter Jones in Sloane Square to kit me out with what was required: not just a school uniform but a summer blazer, house tie, cap, cricket whites, cricket jumper, two rugby shirts, socks, shorts, boots, satchel, fountain pens – on it went. A lot of this was a waste of money, of course. I played rugby twice a week but it was a matter of personal pride to me that I never once touched the ball. I didn't understand the rules, for one thing. Shirt, shorts and socks were pristine from one week to the next, laundry not required. With one exception. Shivering on the side-lines, the ball landed in my arms as I hugged myself against the cold. Jolted out of my quiet contemplations by people screaming my name, I ran towards the goal and put it down at the spot I'd noticed over the months was of great importance. I turned expectantly, expecting congratulations, but none were forthcoming. Apparently I'd run to the wrong end, scoring for the opposition.

Some summer reading was also recommended, hair length specified and a copy of the school rules supplied so I could learn them and adhere. It was all a bit daunting.

As was getting there. I'd been used to simply crossing the road to get to the Sacred Heart, but now I had to get to Ealing by 8.50 a.m. and not be late. That was one of the rules. From Teddington this involved walking to the station, catching a train to Richmond, getting on the 65 bus to Ealing Broadway, then the E2 to Eaton Rise. For my new life I'd have to leave home at 7.20 a.m. My mother would lay the table the night before, partially segmenting my half grapefruit with a sharp knife and turning it upside down in a cereal bowl so it wouldn't dry out. In the winter she would make me porridge, standing at the stove in her dressing gown.

At the time this was deemed worth it because St Benedict's was considered to be such a special school and I was lucky to be going there. I did this for seven years, was rarely ill or late, and it never occurred to me to play truant.

Unlike my sister Beverley, who left for school every morning for a whole term but then went around to her friend's house and hid in their loft all day. She was only rumbled when the parents' evening rolled round and her form teacher said, 'Beverley who? I've never heard of her.'

Her rebellious nature manifested itself in another curious way; when told to go and have a bath she would lock the bathroom door and sit on the windowsill smoking, swishing the water round occasionally in case anyone was listening. She'd then wet her hair in the sink and come downstairs supposedly bathed. Unfortunately she had no slippers on and my mother noticed the tell-tale dirt between her toes.

So, one September morning in 1970, I arrived at the big, red Victorian mansion in Eaton Rise, London W5, that was St Benedict's middle school. Here I would stay for two years until graduating to the upper school, a rather forbidding mix of old and new buildings just down the road, teeming with big boys with deep voices.

The middle school was a kinder, gentler place, lots of lino and polished banisters leading to the very top of the house where lino gave way to carpet, where the headmaster's office was. The classrooms, three for each year, were on the lower two floors, and to the side of the playground was a 1960s prefab building where school assemblies and PE classes were held.

Each year was streamed, which meant clever boys were assigned to 3(a), average boys to 3(1) and the least bright to 3(2). I was in 3(2). After the initial shock of being named and shamed as the bottom of the pile, I decided we were the boys who had the most fun: at least, if you're counting laughs per minute.

Not all of us were stupid; some were just naughty, asking inane questions just to annoy the teacher, humming quietly to make others laugh or even, if you sat next to the right boy during French (when the lights were dimmed and the blinds drawn to facilitate the instructive slide show), given to undoing their flies and guiding your hand inside. I'm sure that kind of fun didn't go on in 3(a), where they were all far too busy being bright and brilliant.

All boys were known by their second names only, which took a bit of getting used to. Especially if they had names like Noonan, Lavarini, Girenas or Pecko, which sadly some of them did. At that age I couldn't get my mouth round Pecko even if I tried.

At the end of the first term, Smith, Spragg and Nutt were promoted to 3(1). This was a bit like entering a new social stratum and peer pressure demanded friendship be replaced with disdain.

I quickly made new friends with my own kind. One boy invited me to sleep over at his house and plied me with cider. We then embarked on a curious game of strip poker that meant I had to remove an item of clothing whatever the cards said. When I continued to lose despite having nothing left to shed, he said, 'Ah, that means I get to do whatever I want to you.'

And so he did. I didn't really know what was going on, but it would have been churlish to stop him. A few weeks later I was invited to go one Saturday to the Science Museum by another boy.

As we travelled home on the tube he whispered in my ear, 'I've heard about you. I can't wait to get you home...'

So I was a kind of boy-scout version of a gangster's moll, passed around like a bowl of cheesy balls.

Our headmaster, Father G, was kind and paternal. Late forties, tall with a ruddy complexion and big yellow teeth. His eyes twinkled with wit and warmth. He taught us Latin and geography twice a week, and I looked forward to his lessons. He had a dry sense of humour and would send up his own authority by making mock-angry-headmaster announcements. If he asked a question my hand always shot up, even if I didn't know the answer, because we always had a bit of banter between us whatever the outcome.

The ordeal of the long bus journey home was eased somewhat when I discovered the benefits of sitting downstairs. The top deck was always the preserve of schoolboys and smokers. When the bus got nearer Kingston, the workers from the Hawker Siddeley factory got on and came upstairs, smelling of oil and carrying tartan zippy bags containing their now empty Tupperware lunch boxes.

One day it was full upstairs and that's when I discovered the joys of sitting downstairs betwixt and between the women, who of course talk more intimately to each other than the men, who are too busy coughing and rolling their own.

Once I heard a woman say to the stranger beside her: 'I've got three children you know, and a husband on a machine...'

I told the story at the dinner table that night and so enjoyed the laugh I received that thereafter I used to travel downstairs deliberately, the better deck for eavesdropping on elderly ladies going to or from the shops.

Other tantalising snippets I recall overhearing were:

'Don't mind me, I've got skin cancer.'

'The morning isn't the same without a sausage.'

'Shut up, Julie, you're nothing but a fucking foul-mouthed cow.'

'Stop dribbling, Doreen!'

And my all-time favourite:

'But there ARE no motorbikes in Harlesden...'

Being a St Benedict's boy, I would obviously stand if the seating was limited. It was a school rule: 'All boys shall offer their seat to people on the bus.' How times have changed.

About half our lessons were taught by monks; the remainder were taught by real people. My favourite lesson was English language and my best teacher was Mr Moore. He was dramatic and a bit fey, but a brilliant and inspirational teacher. Once a week we did Exciting Writing, where we could make up our own stories, usually on a topic we'd discussed beforehand. Once, as soon as he entered the classroom, a volatile boy called Heinz flew at him, shouting and screaming incomprehensibly for a couple of minutes. This boy was always in trouble and had been beaten by Father G several times in his carpeted office. We all froze. When Heinz stopped as suddenly as he'd begun, Mr Moore calmly told us to open our exercise books and write down our reaction to the staged drama we had just witnessed.

When our second year started, we were treated as the 'big boys' of the middle school. In a year's time we would enter the upper school and we needed to be toughened up. Father G's smile was flashed with less frequency and a harsher tone was used all round.

A selected few boys of our year were named as prefects, but none of us plebs from what was now Lower 4(2). Surprisingly, I was awarded the role of 'apple boy', a lesser honour but an honour nonetheless. It brought with it a tiny amount of status and meant I spent morning break distributing Cox's apples for a penny a time through a kind of stable door opposite the toilets.

Sport was a big part of the curriculum. We had PE lessons twice a week, rugby or cricket twice a week depending on the season, and last thing on Wednesday afternoon was swimming – compulsory unless you had a note from a parent to excuse you. A coach would arrive and take us to the public baths in Ealing. Each night before bedtime I used to pack the necessary 'kit' in my school 'shoe bag'.

One Wednesday I forgot my swimming things. I was as sorry as anyone. Particularly so as the Strip Poker Boy often required me to share a changing cubicle with him. He once said to me as we got changed, 'Hear that noise? That's them next door having a wank.'

And there was really no other explanation.

When the time came for everyone to go off in the coach for swimming, I and three other boys, similarly trunk-less and note-less, remained in the classroom, knowing we were in trouble.

'We'll get the whack,' said Mercieca, unconcerned, a friend and fellow rebel of Heinz's and no stranger to corporal punishment. No one had ever laid a finger on me, punishment-wise, and I couldn't have been more scared if you'd told me I was about to mount the electric chair. A dinner lady at the Sacred Heart had once slapped me on the back of the legs for talking in the queue and I was in a state of complete outrage for weeks, even though it didn't hurt much.

We heard Father G approaching and the door opened. He looked furious and his face was beetroot-red.

'What are you doing here?' he asked us coldly.

We whimpered our various excuses.

'Get upstairs to my office,' he spat.

When we arrived in the carpeted office, all bookshelves and easy chairs with a stately desk by the window, we stood and waited in silence for a minute until he followed us in.

He marched to his desk, opened a drawer and, with something of a flourish, pulled out a leather strap. It was about a foot long, half an inch thick, studded with brass round the perimeter. It wasn't adapted – it was clearly manufactured with the express purpose of inflicting pain. As each year master had a different variation on this weapon, must we suppose that, at some point in the academic year, various disciples of Christ sat around a catalogue and hummed and hahed about the various merits of the cane or the strap?

'Three whacks each. You first, Mercieca,' said Father G.

Mercieca stepped forward with the nonchalance of a veteran, leant across the seat of a worn armchair and placed each hand on the wings attached to the back. Father G approached, lifted the flap caused by the two vents at the back of Mercieca's jacket and swiftly, in one movement, lifted the front panel of his cassock and tossed it over his right shoulder. With the strap in his right hand, his face distorted, eyes bulging and lips thrust forward, primate-like, he grunted as each swipe of the strap hit its target.

There was no pause between the three strikes, it was a brief, frenzied attack, then he stood back, inhaling noisily.

The other two boys followed and I was saved until last. None of the others had made any noise, or reacted much at all. I did. I cried out in pain and was told to shut up. When we got back to the classroom and gingerly sat down, Mercieca said, 'Blimey! He hit you much harder than us!'

It wasn't just the stinging pain or the humiliation of having my backside flogged for a mere matter of forgetfulness, it was the terrifying transformation of Father G from paternal, holy priest who fed me the Body of Christ at mass to furious strap-wielding monster. It was a lesson in life that I would never forget.

The next day in geography he tried to resume the jolly banter that had always been a hallmark of our relationship. I was having none of it. If he asked me a question I gave a monosyllabic answer and gazed wistfully out of the window: also, presumably, a beatable offence, but he got the message.

I never willingly spoke to him again.

Beatings were an everyday occurrence, though, and I'm sure that part of me felt I had somehow graduated. I was 'one of the boys', or so I liked to think. Usually boys were beaten in the carpeted office over the armchair, but if your crime was a particularly heinous one then a 'public execution' was in order.

Later Robert Heinz had one of these, although I can't remember what for. He was called onto the stage during morning assembly (after prayers), his misdemeanour announced and then he was told to bend over. We all held our breath as he was given six very hefty stripes with all the energy Father G could muster. It was terribly shocking to witness, a bit like seeing news footage of someone being beheaded in Rwanda.

Afterwards in the cloakroom he dropped his trousers and showed us the thick, blood-red welts that criss-crossed his buttocks, one or two on the back of his thighs where the headmaster had missed, or maybe Heinz had been involuntarily propelled forward with the velocity of the previous hit. Heinz wasn't tearful about it like I had been – he was furious, calling Father G all the names under the sun.

A week later he got his revenge.

We were all in on it. Heinz had sneaked into the office during lunchbreak and stolen the strap. Everyone had a close look at it, this evil weapon that had caused so much pain to so many of us. I held it upright and it flopped from side to side like one of those extra-extra large penises you occasionally encounter (or I do), which take forever to become fully tumescent.

The next morning at assembly there was a tangible atmosphere of excitement. Father G stormed in, face like a bag of spanners. No prayers, no announcements, he got straight to the point.

'Some boy in this school has stolen the strap. Unless it is returned to me by three o'clock this afternoon, or unless someone tells me the boy responsible, I shall beat the entire school.' Then he left.

We were all aghast. A mass public execution had never been known!

A few cowardly boys (notably all from the 'a' stream) pleaded with Heinz to do the decent thing and save us all, but not many. We were brave and resolute.

So at five minutes past three that afternoon, the entire middle school of St Benedict's was told to line up in the playground. Almost two hundred boys waited in silence until Father G marched out brandishing a cricket bat.

'Who's first?' he barked.

And then he beat us all. One whack each. Just a token really, a symbolic mini sting which only succeeded in uniting us all in adversity. I made sure I was towards the back of the queue so he'd rather run out of puff by the time he had his second bash at me.

My religious fervour waned a bit after that, although when Hildebrand died following a nasty bout of cystitis she was given a full Catholic requiem mass. I placed her in a shoebox full of cotton wool, buried her tearfully among the rose bushes and marked the spot with a home-made crucifix. Afterwards I stood there having a good cry and my father told me not to be such a sissy. (A bit late for that advice.) I kept a lock of her hair in a matchbox and carried it around in my blazer pocket until well into the sixth form.

With Hildebrand gone, I felt the need for my own pet and rather fancied a kitten this time. My parents said no to this as we had two cats already.

'Robinson can be your cat from now on,' my mother offered, but I wasn't having that.

There was a pet shop next to Richmond station that I

frequently popped into on my way home from school. One day I saw they had some kittens in the window. I stood there watching them for half an hour until the shop was about to close, then rushed in and bought a little black and white male I called Pao, after the main character in a book I was reading at the time about a Chinese boy. He cost 52½ pence. I tucked him inside my blazer and caught the train home, thrilled but full of trepidation as to what my parents' reaction would be.

As I turned the corner into St Mark's Road, I saw my father standing in the driveway waiting for me, as I was late home. He didn't spot the kitten until I was a yard or so away.

'You can take that straight back!' he said, really rather cross at my defiant purchase.

'They're closed now,' I said.

'First thing tomorrow, then. We are not having another cat! You've been told that already.'

That night Pao slept in my bed, under the bedclothes, down by my feet, purring loudly. The next morning his return to the pet shop was deferred to Saturday, as I couldn't possibly be late for school. Over the next few days Pao charmed everyone, as kittens do, but my father stuck to his guns.

'He's going back to the shop. I will not be defied.'

Saturday morning arrived. Just before I left the house my mother took me aside.

'If for any reason they won't take him back then I suppose you'll just have to bring him home again,' she said with a knowing look.

I took Pao all the way to Richmond and back to the pet shop.

They would take him, they said, but there would be no refund of my 52½ pence. That was all the excuse I needed and Pao and I hopped back on the train to Teddington. My father looked secretly pleased; he'd stood his ground but the kitten could now stay.

Pao grew into a lovely cat who knew I was his master; he slept down at the bottom of my bed and would sit on the garden wall waiting for me to come home from school. In the mornings he would follow me down the road when I left, running ahead and blocking my path for a final stroke until I told him to go back home.

There was only one drawback. Being a male cat, as he grew older he took to marking his territory by spraying his pungent, acrid urine. Unfortunately one chosen spot was on the kitchen counter, up against the display of kitchen utensils. We were greeted most mornings with a soup tureen full of cat's piss.

I had happy times outside school. Barry Jones's elder brother, Gary, had been a coxswain for Kingston Rowing Club but had grown too big for the job, so Barry and I went along one Saturday for a try-out.

The job of a coxswain is rather exciting and important, especially when you're only twelve. Apart from the coach, who is cycling along the towpath shouting handy hints through a megaphone, the cox is in complete control, not only of the steering, controlling the rudder with two toggles either side of the seat, but the speed and pace. During a race you also need to bully the oarsmen into giving their all with every stroke, even when they are completely exhausted. For a prepubescent boy this is quite a power trip.

To help in these endeavours I too had a megaphone, a mini tin one, fixed to my head with plastic straps.

Most of the year was spent training. The oarsmen ran and weight-lifted three times a week, then we would go out on the river in the boat at weekends, maybe the odd evening too if there was an important race looming. The regattas happened each Saturday in the summer months: Molesey, Wallingford, Marlow, Reading and so on, culminating, if you were good enough, in the splendour and glamour of Henley Royal Regatta.

In the winter you would train in the boat on Saturday afternoons and Sunday mornings. There were a few marathon events, such as the Tideway Head in March, where crews from all over the country raced in a mad free-for-all from Chiswick Bridge to Putney, a gruelling endurance test for oarsmen and coxswains alike, especially as we then had to row back to our headquarters in Kingston afterwards. On one occasion I was so frozen through after this event I had to be lifted out of the boat and carried into the kitchen where I was propped on a chair and my feet placed in the oven to defrost.

The clubhouse itself was (indeed, is still) situated in Canbury Gardens, just by Kingston Bridge, a short bicycle ride (on the pavement) from Teddington. The boats were all stored on the ground level in three big bays. At one end, giant clanking metal shutters could be winched open, then the boats carried out across the shingle to the river.

Upstairs were changing rooms, a kitchen (because oarsmen

are always hungry), a bar (because oarsmen drink a lot of beer), a gymnasium and the clubroom itself, with its wooden floor and lots of black plastic leather-effect sofas and chairs. On the walls were wooden panels listing previous captains and presidents and winning crews, some of whom could be seen in the old sepia photographs sporting big baggy shorts and handlebar moustaches.

During my first year at KRC I didn't take it very seriously. Barry and I would turn up on Saturday and hang around to see if any crews needed a cox. If not, we'd just lark about the clubhouse, maybe clean a boat if asked.

The club's eccentric caretaker was a pipe-smoking Scottish man of about 60, called Jock. He was short and bald with a big moustache, like the men in the sepia photos, and gnarled seafaring hands. He seemed to more or less live on board his own flat-bottomed skiff boat, and it was his job to open up the clubhouse at weekends, serve behind the bar and generally boss everyone around. He was very moody and would shout and holler at anyone who crossed him. He seemed to be pretty much in charge of us boys, giving us chores to do, such as peeling potatoes or waxing a boat before a race.

He was also a bit of a dirty old man, and if he got you on your own in the kitchen he would come up close, his hands furiously scratching about in his pockets, and say things like: 'I expect you boys like a bit of horseplay, do you, when you're alone together, aye? Play with each other, eh?'

Then dissolve into a strange lusty giggle, all the while tugging away at his cock inside his trousers.

We obviously all knew about his peculiar ways and would avoid getting stuck on our own with him in the kitchen, but one or two of the boys went on dubious 'overnights' with him, sleeping in his leaky boat under a canvas contraption somewhere downriver. Nothing was ever said, but it's hard to believe there wasn't scratching and giggling involved.

Not me though.

'Leave yourself alone!' I said to him once, tired of the dirty talk and furtive wanking. 'Or I shall tell my parents!'

Jock aside, the rowing-club crowd were jovial, sociable rugby types who loved rowing and sport in general but didn't take it that seriously. They could drink for England in the bar once training was done, and in fact some of the set didn't row at all, simply turned up every week to down lager and make merry. Most people had a nickname: Vampire, Groundhog, Lurch, Shirley, Skidmark and Birdshit, to name a few.

I was christened Fuck-Pig. This was laddish vulgarity: their label for me, a pretty blond girlish boy. In fact, they were kind and protective towards me. Eight drinking, swearing oarsmen were better role models than one strap-wielding monk.

Some of them had girlfriends who would come along to regattas to cheer on their burly boyfriends, or to the clubhouse after training where they'd sip white wine and mother us boys.

Word soon got round that I had a nubile older sister. Frances was now 16, a tall, glamorous blonde who had just started the dance and drama course at Arts Educational and wished, if you please, to be known henceforth as Frankie.

I took along a holiday snap of Frankie in a bikini and passed it round the bar one day. The reaction was most encouraging, so I offered to introduce her to anyone who would buy me a Mars Bar. First off the mark was Lurch, and I delivered her to him the next weekend.

The next year – 1972 – Fuck-Pig struck it lucky. I was given my own 'eight' for the season, and as it turned out they were a brilliant crew. I'd learned the rudiments of coxing the previous year, but under the tutelage of our coach, Don Somner (Groundhog), I discovered which part of the river to aim for to find the fastest-flowing stream of water, how to push the opposing crew over without getting disqualified for clashing blades, and how to get the best performance from my men, a lesson that has been invaluable to me ever since.

That summer we won every week, moving through the ranks from novice to elite. We were invincible. After each win we would go out and celebrate, often ending up at Kingston's Berni Inn, where my boys ordered steak and lager and I was given a shandy or two. I was their mascot, indulged and looked after.

I remember one celebratory evening at the clubhouse when I had too much to drink and was sick in the toilets and then taken home, still in a bit of a state. My mother slept on my bedroom floor that night, concerned I might choke on my own vomit. The next morning, hung over and in disgrace, I was sent back to KRC to clean up the mess I'd made and then grounded for two weeks.

But I was a useful cox: in a close contest, aggressive steering and pertinent instructions can win the race. The boats themselves were delicate and expensive, and even the oars were costly to repair, and as the 'driver' a cox had considerable responsibility. I only disgraced myself once, but in quite spectacular fashion. One year I was cox to a hopeful four at Henley Royal Regatta. The evening before our first race we went out on the river to train and try out the course. That done, we headed for the landing stage and, aware that other crews and coxswains were watching, I attempted a swish and speedy landing, but mistimed it. I could see Don Somner's frantic signals to slow down but ignored them. I'd show the opposition what a daring, chic master of the Thames they were dealing with.

There were a few last-second shouts from coach and crew but it was too late: the bow hit the bank with a sickening crunch. I'd not only caused irreparable damage to one of KRC's finest boats, but ruined our chances at the most prestigious regatta in the rowing calendar. We had to borrow an inferior vessel for our race and lost dismally. It was all my fault.

I was in deep disgrace. There was no jolly fun with the boys for Fuck-Pig at Henley that year, and my blonde locks were left untousled.

But to be fair, they didn't bear a grudge, and my boat-smashing faux pas was soon just a club bar story that I rather enjoyed hearing repeated.

A bit like the bowl-of-soup incident.

KRC's arch rivals were Molesey Rowing Club, and once a year the two clubs would compete for a day and then have a grand, if tense, dinner, which would take place at the clubhouse of the alternate hosts. Legend has it that I wasn't happy with the soup at Molesey's club one year, so I carried my bowl to the top table where their leader, Captain Croucher, sat resplendent in black jacket and club tie, and poured it over his head. Apparently it was piping hot and didn't result in the hearty back-slapping from my fellow Kingstonians that I'd expected.

Although the rowing world was one of dedication, tough and exhausting, it had a unique social structure. No one lost sight of the fact that it was primarily a recreation for all involved. The homoeroticism of such an environment passed me by at the time, but who is to say that my subconscious wasn't taking notes? Maybe fate was preparing me for the life that lay ahead. I certainly got a rush from being in charge. Eight men in peak physical condition jumping to my every command: to get that kind of thrill nowadays I'd have to go to some underground club in New York I suspect.

'You were very assertive for a twelve-year-old,' recalled Richard Nelson, my 'stroke' – the oarsman at the front of the boat who sat directly opposite me and generally set the pace.

He was 25 in 1972 and looked after me like I was a younger brother. It was his sweaty face in the forefront of my vision during a race, his agony I witnessed closest, his sweat I smelt and his sofa I would sleep on when we all staggered out of the Berni Inn and they were all too pissed to deliver me home to St Mark's Road.

At the opposite end of the boat from Richard, in the bow position, was Grant Watkins, or Grantley, as he was known. Originally from Australia and only 18, he was the youngest member of the crew. Like most Aussies he was forever cheerful and adventurous, given to uttering meaningless phrases like 'wacko-the-diddle-o'. For him a penny was a 'brass ra-zoo'. Always being silly and jumping around or falling down to make people laugh, he was never without his camera. He had his own darkroom and would develop the pictures himself, sometimes superimposing someone's head onto another body. One December he made a short comedy film starring me and him and showed it at the Christmas party. Indeed, he went on to become a talented TV and film editor.

He drove a battered old Mini and he once took me out to the countryside and then let me take over the driving. I hadn't quite mastered the difference between brake and accelerator and we crashed into a farm gate. We were both cut and bruised and the Mini more battered than before, but we decided not to tell anyone about the incident. (It was my father, an expert and advanced driver, who taught each of us three children to drive when we were old enough. We all passed our tests on our seventeenth birthday. He was a strict and unforgiving teacher, and as an irritable teenager my emergency stops became a means of self-expression, the brakes sometimes being applied in anticipation of the command. Even now if he's in the car with me he says, 'Mirror, signal, brake!' or 'Where's the fire?' if I exceed the speed limit.)

Twenty-odd years after I crashed his Mini, Grantley was working in New York as a film editor in a large open-plan office. He stood up from his workstation and fell to the ground. Thinking it was one of his pranks, people watched and waited to see how long he'd lie there. In fact, he was dead.

Having mastered the art of reading, I devoured books. I started with children's classics, such as *Swallows and Amazons* by

Arthur Ransome, disdainfully skimmed a few Enid Blyton offerings, but by the time I was twelve I was chomping my way through Thomas Hardy, George Orwell, D.H. Lawrence and George Eliot.

My mother took us to the theatre and the ballet as often as she could afford it. We saw *The Marriage of Figaro*, *There Goes the Bride* (starring Peggy Mount, Bernard Cribbins and Bill Pertwee at Wimbledon Theatre), *Giselle* (with Anthony Dowell and Marguerite Porter) at the Royal Opera House, and Rock Hudson and Juliet Prowse in *I Do! I Do!* at the Phoenix Theatre. A highlight was Rudolph Nureyev in *Romeo and Juliet*, *The Sleeping Beauty* and *Don Quixote* at the London Coliseum. We once sat on the front row and when he did a pirouette his sweat splattered across our faces. 'We must never wash again!' my mother whispered.

She also took me to the proms at the Royal Albert Hall to hear Tchaikovsky's *1812 Overture*, but omitted to tell me about the cannons going off towards the end. This being the 1970s, when the IRA's bombing campaign was in full throttle, I hid under my seat until it was explained to me that this was all part of the show.

On Saturday evenings we had 'tea on our laps': sandwiches, sometimes muffins, sometimes fresh prawns. We watched the *Generation Game* and *Bilko*. On other days we ate at the dining-room table. We were cautioned never to turn our forks over.

'You might have tea with the Queen one day.'

In fact, my mother had a bit of a thing about the Queen, maybe because they are of similar age. She'd often say out of the blue, 'I wonder what the Queen is doing now?'

She also taught us how to eat our food so that the final mouthful had a morsel of each component. Three peas, maybe, the last bit of broccoli and the last of the shepherd's pie. This was considered proper.

When we'd finished, if we wanted to do something or go somewhere we'd ask, 'Can I get down now please?'

If it was a special occasion, such as a birthday, we might go to the Happy Garden Chinese restaurant in Hampton Hill and make each other laugh with our attempts at chopsticks.

We played cards, too, if there was a family gathering, for a penny a game and three pence for the winner. Kaluki was the favoured game, or Chase the Lady if we were feeling daring.

It wasn't so much the game that mattered as the banter that went with it.

'Gawd Blimey,' my grandfather would declare when he looked at the hand dealt him.

'"Gawd Blimey," said the duchess as she waved her wooden leg.'

'You ought to be poleaxed.'

'Flick it!'

'Strewth!'

'Lawks-a-mercy!'

'Brown bread by the river's brim.'

A frequent visitor was Auntie Wyn, spinster sister to my grandfather, and my godmother Auntie Tess.

Auntie Wyn lived in Brentford, at 32 Adelaide Terrace, the very house my grandfather had grown up in. In those days it had been a gravel road with a sister terrace facing it, but that had long been demolished to make way for the A4, and then as a final insult the M4 flyover was built above it, so the terrace stood now, defiant but dusty, vibrating with the double helping of thundering traffic.

Brentford was not far from Ealing where I went to school, so it became the tradition that each Wednesday I would hop off the bus on my way home and stop for tea. My mother by this time had qualified as a probation officer and was working at the Brentford office. On Wednesdays she worked late, then picked me up from Adelaide Terrace at about 7.30 p.m.

In her seventies by then, Wyn had been engaged several times in her youth but never married. The most serious betrothal had faltered when he refused to convert to Catholicism, a prerequisite of a 'mixed' marriage in those days. As the prospect of a married life receded, Wyn simply never left home. Nor did her brother Gordon. He lived with her at number 32, but was of scant value as a companion. They had fallen out many years ago – it was rumoured over a game of cards – and now lived separate lives under the one roof, refusing even to meet at mealtimes.

Thus it was Auntie Wyn and I had our tea together (always a ham salad featuring a boiled egg) at five o'clock each Wednesday in the kitchen. The wallpaper I remember was of blue tits sitting on the branches of a tree. We would then clear the plates away and set the table again for one. As it got near to six o'clock she would start glancing up frequently at the clock above the doorway, and at one minute to six she would stand up determinedly and leave the room. Wyn and Gordon passed each other in the passageway without a word in this way every day for the remainder of their lives. I'd stay put in the kitchen for a little while and say hello to Uncle Gordon before joining Auntie Wyn in the lounge to watch *Crossroads*, although she could never quite grasp the plot.

'What on earth is going on?' she would ask me, totally flummoxed if there was any variation on real time, such as, God forbid, a flashback sequence. A while later we'd hear the front door slam, which meant Uncle Gordon had gone to the pub, and I could return to the kitchen to do my homework, although I spent most of my time studying the blue tits and listening to the clock tick.

The acrimony between them continued beyond the grave. Wyn had been plagued with a weak heart for many years and when I was 16 she collapsed and died while on her way to see the doctor. As next of kin, we needed Gordon's permission to erect a gravestone, and this he refused to give. We had to bide our time for several years until he expired too. The final irony was that he was then buried in the same grave as her.

Auntie Wyn was a frequent visitor to St Mark's Road. She loved coming along to the regattas, where the family would have a picnic on the riverbank and cheer me on. Then we'd go home and play Kaluki. She had cataracts, though, and couldn't really see the cards, let alone the boat races. When she finally had them operated on she could see even less for a few weeks and had to wear thick dark glasses while she recovered. We took her to see the rhododendron and azalea display at Isabella Plantation in Richmond Park and her head swivelled in amazement at the pink and purple flowers.

As we grew older and no longer suffered from carsickness (I once vomited in my father's jacket pocket on the way to

Norfolk), our summer holidays became more adventurous. We borrowed a tent and after a trial weekend in a forest near Guildford, where my father and Frances mastered the art of erecting the aluminium tent frame and hammering in the tent pegs, we loaded up the trusty Zephyr and set off for the Costa Brava, heading for a resort called El Delfín Verde.

We caught the cross-channel ferry to Dieppe and travelled through France, eyes peeled for the GB sign on passing cars. 'There's one!' we'd cry, and all wave happily, reassured that we weren't the only intrepid adventurers in what seemed like a far-off foreign land. Beverley was horrified by the French hole-in-the-ground toilets and refused to use them, graciously agreeing to 'go' behind a haystack in the countryside instead while we all waited in the car. As she primly emerged, scurrying back towards us, two days' worth of effluence finally ejected, a plume of steam was seen curling skywards from behind the haystack, rather giving the game away.

The fortnight's vacation was done on a strict budget ('About 50 quid,' my father recalls) so there were no overnight stops in hotels. After a long day of driving and waving at fellow Brits, we'd find the nearest campsite and erect the tent and the beds, and lay out the sleeping bags. The stove, utensils and food would be next and then my mother would attempt something imaginative with a tin of frankfurters.

We awoke one morning to the steady hum of a torrential downpour, a common feature of our holidays, wherever we were. We hadn't bargained for this on our training weekend, and while my father and sisters slid around in the mud in their flip-flops, folding and rolling up the sodden tent as best they could, my mother and I took refuge in the car, occasionally winding down the window to tell them to hurry up.

Our conspiracy to amuse ourselves by annoying my father was not very kind, but it was fairly relentless. Generally he'd go along with it, shaking his head in mock disbelief at these two Queens of Sheba who declined to do any of the hard labour involved in a camping trip for five in foreign climes.

Boiling eggs for our tea that night she handed him a seriously fractured one.

'I'm afraid yours cracked, Peter. And your toast burnt, too. Most unfortunate.'

'Thank you!' he'd say, laughing gamely. 'Dear oh dear...'

But we arrived at our Spanish resort in the end, found a delightful spot under some pine trees and began the holiday proper. We baked in the sun, swam in the sea and chortled at our northern English neighbours who cooked chips on a camping stove every night while we had sophisticated rice dishes. I was bought a snorkel and thought I was the next Jacques Cousteau. I made friends with a boy of my age (twelve) who was horribly lobster-red from the Spanish rays but that didn't stop him encouraging me to touch him where the sun don't shine when we investigated the local caves.

We were sad when the time came for us to leave, but we shook the sand out from our sleeping bags, and once my father and sisters had loaded everything up, our new friends, including the lobster boy, gathered round to wave us off.

There was an awful gurgling noise when the engine was turned on. We'd been parked on a slope and oil had seeped into the clutch, or something technical like that. My father got out and fiddled under the bonnet, sweating and wiping his hands and then his forehead with an oily rag. The leaving party began to mutter, lost interest and wandered away.

We eventually crawled out of the campsite way behind schedule and started our journey, unable, it seemed, to progress beyond second gear. Halfway across the Pyrenees a thunderstorm added to our troubles and we pulled into the nearest campsite. Once again my mother and I watched from the comfort of the car as the others struggled in the wind and the rain to erect the tent, assisted by several community-minded fellow campers.

By the time they had finished, lightning, a great fear of my mother's, was ripping across the sky. (If a lightning storm occurred while we were at home she removed all her jewellery, rushed round turning off lights and unplugging anything electrical, and made us huddle in the middle of the room well away from the windows until the danger had passed.)

'Get in the car, quickly!' she shrieked, thinking we'd be safest in there with the rubber wheels. She wouldn't let anyone get out, and we sat huddled in the steamed-up car all night, peered at with curiosity by the drenched helpers from nearby tents.

In the morning the rain abated, the unused tent was sheepishly dismantled and packed away and off we went. That day the car broke down completely in a small dusty Spanish town. The local garage had to send to Barcelona for a suitable gearbox and we hung around in a lay-by for a couple of days, out of food and out of patience. I added to my father's woes by sticking my foot through the dashboard and snapping the Zephyr logo in two.

'You great steaming idiot!' he said.

We got home eventually, of course, and I looked forward to returning to school and writing the obligatory essay: 'What I did during my summer holiday' – deeming it wise to omit the business in the cave with the sunburnt boy.

THREE

For sweetest things turn sourest by their deeds;
Lilies that fester smell far worse than weeds.

SONNET 94, WILLIAM SHAKESPEARE

Despite the beatings I had endured in the middle school at St
Benedict's, it was a relatively cosy environment.

You could get lost in the upper school, consisting as it did of
a great modern concrete-and-glass assembly hall attached to the
less ostentatious block of airy classrooms, which in turn was
connected to the original 'house', dark, ornate staircases and levels
you never ventured onto unless summoned to where the monks,
masters and prefects had their offices and suites.

There were corridors and staircases all over the shop and
strange, unexpected burrows where monks would appear or disappear from like something out of *Alice in Wonderland*. There was a
grand oak-panelled reading room and library, with mice carved
into the chair legs. You could go there to study, and silence was

ensured by the presence of a monk or master on a raised pulpit-like desk, who threw a threatening glance at anyone who so much as cleared their throat.

There were various smells pervading the various parts of the school, a rich menu of sweat, urine, cigarettes, chalk dust or floor polish, depending on where you found yourself.

And looming over us all was the abbey itself, quite cheery with its sandstone colouring and surrounding trees. Huge and unfussy with the obligatory spires and stained-glass windows, it is both modern and gothic, functional and mysterious.

Each class had a form master who would remain with you until you reached the sixth form, and each year had a division master, a less intimate, more fearful figure to whom you would be sent if you did anything wrong, and who had the authority to beat you and the weapon to do it with.

The form master for upper 4(2) was Mr Klepacz, a youngish man who wore flares and had frizzy hair like Marc Bolan and a moustache. He was quite down-to-earth and rather shocked me once when I asked if I could be excused to go to the toilet by saying, 'Go on then, go for a piss.'

Division master for the upper fourth year was Father Kasimir: short and stout, in his late fifties or early sixties. He didn't seem to wash much or change his cassock, the same stains and sprinkling of dandruff from his silver head of hair apparent on his shoulders and beyond week in and week out. He walked with a strange, purposeful strut, as if he just knew he was about to discover some wrongdoing round the next corner. He always seemed to be cross, possibly because his dog collar was worn far too tight round his thick token of a neck. I was scared of him, which I'm sure was the general idea.

As it turned out I had good reason to be.

Although now in different classes, Barry Jones and I were still friends, travelling home together on the bus, and meeting up at Kingston Rowing Club where he was now a cox too, even if not blessed with such a glamorous, successful crew.

On the first day of the new term in the upper school, in the autumn of 1972, we met up at break time and he introduced me to a new boy called Nicholas Reader. Nick, who was dark haired with full lips and perfect white teeth, had been sat next to him over in upper 4(1) and Barry had been given the responsibility of looking after him and showing him the ropes, as it were.

Nick lived near the school in Ealing with his father, whom he called 'Bill Boy'. He was far more worldly wise than us, cooked his own meals, read *Melody Maker* and *Record Mirror*, watched television until gone midnight and showed a daring disrespect for the school rules. He was also very smart academically, ahead of the game in Latin and ancient Greek (which only a few of the brightest boys studied anyway), and funny, able to mimic classmates and monks, draw hilarious caricatures and slip in and out of an array of comic personas. Within days he'd given each monk and master a nickname. He also pointed out that 'Father Fox' – a smiling, somewhat fey monk – glided about silently as if his cassock concealed a set of wheels.

I was delighted to discover it was possible to make fun of those in authority. It had never occurred to me before. Every time Father

Fox glided by on lunch hour patrol duties, we would nod at each other knowingly and laugh. For a whole term we took to following him around like private detectives. I would follow him down one corridor while Nick loitered at the noticeboard, then he would take over. In our schoolboy eyes the man was simply touring all the school toilets in the hope of finding who knows what. We couldn't do anything with this knowledge but we were certain we had his number.

We were secretly laughing at everyone's expense, not just the teachers. Parents, the goody-goody prefects, the bullies, the rugby types, the dimwits et al. We were ruthless. Everyone was caricatured and given a code name. We were in different classes, so we would save up incidents or anything we deemed a faux pas to tell each other in the break.

An unfortunate-looking boy called Gallagher, who spoke as if he had a permanently blocked nose, was told off in my class once for wearing a bracelet.

'But, sir,' he cried, 'them's me love beads!'

We howled over that one for weeks and it became our catchphrase of the moment.

Pretty soon Barry Jones became the victim of our disdain. I don't think he did anything in particular to deserve it, he just wasn't quite on our wavelength. Nick and I so delighted in each other's company that Barry got squeezed out. We were now exclusive to each other, turning on our weaker friend with all the cruelty of hungry pack dogs in the wild.

Once Barry didn't come to school for a couple of days, but we didn't care.

To the untrained eye we were model schoolboys, well spoken and well behaved. We observed the school rules, handed in our homework on time and kept ourselves nice. Until we ejected Barry, our private amusements were known to no one. Then one day Father Kasimir exposed me with such a torrent of invective that I wrote it down.

Private Diary, 14 May 1973

Today during RE class Father Kasimir turned to me and in a worked-up, loud voice said: 'Oh yes! Butter wouldn't melt in your mouth, would it? But underneath you are a filthy bully. Oh yes – I know! I suspected you all along. Oh, I'm disappointed in you, you great bully! You are like a rock with beautiful flowers over it but underneath is maggots and earwigs, filthy stinking earwigs!'

Twice more in the class he said similar things. Then as I opened the door for him when he left, he said, 'Come with me!' and in the corridor said in a calm voice: 'You know what I was talking about in there, don't you?'

'Yes, father.'

'Well, try and be nice to poor Jones. He's been very ill you know, seeing special doctors and having nightmares. You didn't know that, did you?'

'No, father.'

I did feel a pang of guilt for my old chum, but nightmares and 'special' doctors all seemed a tad overdramatic and unfortunately the whole episode lent itself rather well to our particular brand of parody. My friendship with Barry had run its course and no doctor, special or otherwise, could do much about it.

Nick and I were now free to be best friends and neither of us had much time for anyone else. The fact that we were always together, whispering and giggling, didn't go unnoticed. We became more overtly camp with each passing day. We started to be known throughout the school as 'Daffodil and Daisy', or 'Pinky and Perky', and cries of 'Poof!' or 'Queer!' were shouted by just about everyone whenever we were 'in public'. Walking down a corridor from one classroom to another became a hazardous exercise, and as the years passed the persecution only increased, becoming more vehement, vocal and ultimately violent with each term.

Then my mother gave me *The Prime of Miss Jean Brodie* by Muriel Spark to read, and the philosophy of the book's heroine became our Bible. We saw ourselves as 'la crème de la crème', and when Miss Brodie told her girls to hold their heads 'up, up like Sybil Thorndike', we took her at her word. Miss Brodie championed individuality and eschewed conformity, and so would we. We drew parallels between the Brodie set and ourselves, between the Marcia Blaine School for Girls and the dull, stifling modus operandi of St Benedict's.

I struggled through maths and physics, yawned through history and geography, but I couldn't wait for English. My very own Jean Brodie came in the shape of Frances Hanley. She was young and beautiful with flowing red hair and her classes were a joy to me. She let me exercise my imagination and was full of encouragement for the results, returning my essays to me peppered with big red ticks in the margins.

She wasn't at all stuffy, like the dusty old monks who taught most classes. And although our class was always quite noisy and a bit of a handful, she inspired us all, and was having none of my nonsense when I rather pompously wrote at the bottom of one essay: 'The lack of imaginative sentences is probably due to the lack of silence I require for successful work.'

She replied, 'No, if you really want to concentrate you will do so. Besides, don't try to stifle a little noise – it's life, exuberance, real.'

Most of the stories I wrote as a schoolboy feature strange, often mad, diva-like women, for example: 'Mary Ross was outrageous. In everything she did she wanted to amaze; every head must turn in wonder at her, everyone must notice her. It is only when people point that she is happy.'

On my end-of-term report she wrote: 'The sky is his limit!'

Love blossomed in the staff room for Miss Hanley and soon she married Philip Lawrence. When she left to have children I was devastated, and although I continued to do well in English, it wasn't the same without her. Frances Lawrence used to bring a record player into class and tell us to write whatever the *Enigma Variations* suggested to us. Her replacement told us to write a story about ice hockey – not something within the scope of my experience. I ask you.

My attempt survives.

'OK, lads, put yer gear on.' I went to my locker and got out my pads. I sat down on the bench beside Buddy Holder.

'Looks like a hard one!' he said, sucking his teeth

then letting them go suddenly, making himself look very serious.

'Oh, really?' I said, pretending I didn't know what he meant. He gave me an amazed, almost cross look and pulled his mask on.

Nick had an extensive record collection which I borrowed and absorbed. At that time David Bowie was in full throttle as Ziggy Stardust, and we started with him, soon branching out to the delights of Lou Reed, Dana Gillespie and Iggy Pop. Glam rock amused us too, and all of this served to give our already effeminate natures some credibility, at least to ourselves.

Our greatest love was reserved for a number of soul divas. Aretha Franklin primarily, but Patti LaBelle, Linda Lewis and Thelma Houston were favourites too. Anyone loud and black got our approval.

Our classmates were all into Led Zeppelin and Deep Purple, music so far at the other end of the spectrum it only strengthened our resolve to have nothing to do with them.

We were very excited when we heard that LaBelle were doing a concert in London, riding high on the success of their single 'Lady Marmalade', which contained the line, 'Voulez-vous coucher avec moi?' The audience were instructed to wear something silver, so after my father dropped us off outside Drury Lane Theatre we rushed to the loo and stuck silver 'merit' stars all over our faces and thought we looked fabulous. The show was a theatrical extravaganza, beginning with Patti LaBelle's descent from the

ceiling in a silver space-age costume, festooned in feathers, shriek-
ing as only she could, and continuing with Nona Hendryx giving
her all in 'The Revolution Will Not Be Televised'. We were totally
smitten: the dressing up, the emotion, the glamour of it all
absorbed by our impressionable brains and incorporated into our
day-to-day lives. We now knew there was a life outside school
where childish name-calling and cane-wielding monks had no role.

My head was similarly turned by visiting my sister Frankie in
the chorus girls' dressing room at Richmond Theatre after a
performance of *La Vie Parisienne*, given by the Kingston Amateur
Operatic Society: the make-up, the costumes, the excitement were
all things I wanted to be a part of my life, too. Frankie soon
became a professional dancer and I was fascinated by her new
career and the contents of her wardrobe and make-up box.

During her first job in panto, at Eastbourne, she started
having a passionate affair with a guitarist in the band, and in her
dressing-table drawer one day I found a stash of his intimate love
letters. I rushed into school the next day to tell Nick of his specific
request to 'sit on my face'. This, of course, became our catchphrase
of the week.

The sex life of Frankie and Kevin we lived and breathed, recre-
ating the private moments I had read about in the most explicit
and disgusting cartoons. These we drew during the less engaging
classes, folded and hid in the palm of our hands and swapped
discreetly in the corridor between classes. Luckily our furtive
communications were never spotted and confiscated or we'd have
been in serious trouble, doubtless receiving the beating of Father
G's dreams.

Apart from Frankie and Kevin, the cartoons featured Bill Boy and Big Bren (my mother) and a gallery of invented characters (Millie Slut, Gay Lusac, Rose Steptoe and Sambo, to name a few), saying and doing the most obscene things we could come up with. Schoolboy sexism and racism were commonplace. One I drew that Nick remembers featured a girl saying, 'Oh, Sambo, I just love the way you pass chewing gum from your mouth to mine when you kiss me.'

To which Sambo replied, 'That ain't chewing gum, honey chile, I just has de heavy cold.'

In the cartoon fantasy world we created, Millie Slut and Gay Lusac were glamorous superstars, often depicted in full colour clutching awards for 'the worst LP of the year', falling into the orchestra pit during disastrous world tours or simply proclaiming their own fabulousness while dissing their rivals, sometimes pleasuring themselves with cucumbers at the same time.

Meanwhile we did lots of extracurricular reading: Muriel Spark, Iris Murdoch, and Jane Austen, the gossipy nature of her novels being right up our street. When Father Edmund asked who had read any D.H. Lawrence novels and I replied, 'Yes, all of them,' he was horrified.

'*All* of them? What, even... *Lady Chatterley's Lover*?' He was more horrified than impressed.

Off we went to more concerts: Lou Reed, Roxy Music and in particular Dana Gillespie. She had just been signed to Bowie's Mainman label and was doing a series of gigs to promote her album *Weren't Born A Man*. ('Ooh what a drag I ain't got a tail to wag.') The cover featured Dana in stockings and suspenders, wearing a red basque and a feather boa. She was the original Mary Magdalene in *Jesus Christ Superstar!* and a former British waterskiing champion. She was fabulously buxom, reeked of jasmine oil and wore lots of Indian jewellery. We wrote to her and she replied, sending us each signed photos and stickers.

We went to lots of her gigs at places like Brunel University and the 100 Club in Oxford St. She sang her own fabulously raunchy songs with titles like 'Get My Rocks Off' and concluded each gig with a selection of old bordello songs such as 'Organ Grinder', or a voodoo song from New Orleans 'I Walk on Gilded Splinters'.

She was also reasonably accessible. We got to chat to her afterwards, inhale her jasmine perfume, be photographed with her and get her autograph. Amazingly Nick once stayed the night at her 'bunker' in South Kensington, when he missed the last tube home. I was terribly jealous when I heard he'd snuggled up with Sneezy her Yorkshire terrier in the spare room, sleeping next to a guitar given to Dana by none other than David Bowie.

After one gig I nipped onto the stage and nicked the glass she'd been drinking from to add to the 'shrine' I'd created in my bedroom.

'I always thought you were gay,' she said recently. 'You had the mannerisms.'

Indeed I did, but it wasn't something I was ready to confront just yet. Dana was our icon. We had pictures of her in various states of undress on our bedroom walls. She was our icon, and in some senses our beard.

From admiration to aspiration is but a small step, and by the age of 14 Nick and I decided we were pop stars in the making. He was to be known as Nick Charles and I was Groupie Gypp. Until my father burnt it I wrote songs on the piano, but we both saved up for acoustic guitars and wrote dozens of songs each with just a handful of chords. I mastered A, E and G, but Nick rather surprised us both by playing the rather tricky B7. I even took guitar lessons with a clinically depressed woman called Wendy Beak who lived near Teddington Lock. Because of her condition she would only teach sad songs. Once 'Smoke Gets In Your Eyes' was learnt she wrote out the lyrics to 'Somewhere Over The Rainbow', except in her version it read:

Somewhere over the rainbow,
Skies are grey...

We were prolific songwriters, knocking out a couple of what we were sure were hit singles most nights, with titles such as 'Hot Hands, Cold Heart', 'Boogie Down The Inside of Your Leg' or the sacrilegious 'Love On The Altar'.

We would each record our compositions separately on cassette, being as innovative as we could with our limited guitar skills, pitch pipes and maracas. We would then spend a Saturday afternoon having a 'photo session', which involved hogging the Woolworth's photo booth in Richmond, wearing sunglasses and draping ourselves in colourful scarves. When Nick got a Polaroid camera for Christmas we were able to indulge our fantasy without suffering an angry queue of punters waiting to get their passport photos, impatient with the two girly schoolboys taking forever behind the grey curtain.

We would then design our 'album' cassette covers, agonising over the felt-tip graphics and title (*Eclipse* and *Sweet Touch* were two of mine, the latter featuring a bastardised snap of me moodily stroking Pao the cat). When we were both ready we would 'release' our new albums, which just meant that I handed mine to Nick and he handed his to me. But we did this with some reverence and then nervously awaited each other's 'review', which was invariably favourable.

From time to time we'd put on concerts. We didn't feature many of our own songs during these, preferring to sing along to the fuller sound of our favourite records. I'd wait till I knew everyone was going to be out for the evening, then I'd invite Nick over.

Keeping our choice of songs secret from each other, we'd push back the furniture in the lounge, create a lighting effect of some kind by redirecting the angle-poise lamp towards the ceiling, then decide who was going to go first. If it was me I'd leave Nick sitting in the lounge while I went upstairs to get ready, donning a little make-up, some costume jewellery and a pre-chosen item from Frankie's wardrobe, most famously a purple feather waistcoat my sister had made herself for a party.

When I was transformed into Groupie Gypp, I'd call to Nick from the hallway, he'd start the first track and I'd make my dramatic entrance through the lounge door. I'd sing along to Aretha or Patti for half an hour, Nick would clap and whistle, then it would be Nick Charles's turn to be the star. It was always necessary to keep half an ear cocked in case we heard the parents' car on the driveway, in which case the performance had to be very suddenly aborted due to circumstances beyond our control.

Unfortunately my exertions one evening left the underarm feathers matted and sweaty and Frankie was understandably furious when party night arrived.

'You've ruined it, wearing it to one of your bloody concerts!' she accused me. I could hardly tell her I'd been giving a concert, not going to one.

We were totally convinced of our impending superstardom. Puffing on menthol cigarettes after our lounge gigs, we'd talk about 'when' not 'if' we were famous pop legends, even discussing our early retirements at the height of our careers.

'I think I'll go out on top and become a recluse.'

'It's important to break America first...'

Our careers as million-selling recording artistes imminent, we were more dismissive than ever of our peers, and our attitude didn't endear us to them either.

One song we wrote, 'Don't Take The Juice', was about life for us at St Benedict's.

Don't take the juice, boys,
There's no excuse, boys.
I'm sorry if I seem to be cracked, boys,
Sorry but there's no money back, boys.

We were called 'queers' and 'homos' every hour of the school day. We were pushed and shoved and hit over the head with books. The fact that the school staff turned a blind eye gave the real bullies in our midst the green light to continue.

'You bring it on yourself, you know…' a master said to me once.

The danger began each morning as soon as I got on the bus. Even sitting downstairs another boy from St Benedict's might get on and take a seat behind me. Someone once set fire to the nylon lining of my coat, resulting in a very passable Joan of Arc impersonation. A brick flew past me, inches from my head, as I walked down Eaton Rise.

As we got older it was a thrill for younger boys to join in, having a go themselves at the odd couple, who in normal circumstances would be off-limits because of their age and size. We weren't just the Nancy boys for our year, but for the whole school. We were famous, albeit in a dangerous form.

When Quentin Crisp's *The Naked Civil Servant* came out, both as a book and a television play, Nick hennaed his hair and I bought a rinse-in sachet called 'Winsome Wheat', from Boots. Instead of calling us 'Pinky and Perky' or 'Daffodil and Daisy', we were both now addressed by the all-purpose 'Quentin'. His persecution and passive acceptance of his lot struck a chord with us. When he said, 'Life is a dash from cradle to grave across open country under heavy fire,' we knew what he meant.

A new set of catchphrases was born, our favourite being: 'Look at me! I am an effeminate homosexual for all the world to see!'

We did our best to emulate Crisp's famous calmness when cornered by macho thugs, but didn't always succeed. A nasty little runt, several years younger than us, had been following us around for days, calling us names and refusing to go away. Nick pulled a thin branch from a tree in the playground and gave him a frenzied whipping, not stopping even when he begged for mercy. Nick seemed as shocked as the runt. Afterwards we amused ourselves wondering how the porky little pig would explain the marks on his thighs to Mummy at bath-time.

The boys who had led me astray in the middle school were now my accusers. Strip Poker Boy less so, to be fair, and he pinched my bottom if no one was looking and breathed heavily behind me in the lunch queue, but there were no more sleepovers and there was no more poker. In fact, he was expelled from the upper school for refusing to take a beating that was, in his opinion and that of his parents, unjustified. He became a window cleaner, whistling at me one day as I alighted from the bus at Ealing Broadway.

I had no friends at all apart from Nick. If he was off school for any reason, I spoke to no one. I went to the reading room or the library during the lunch hour to pass the time and lie low.

Our lives were difficult but we enjoyed the celebrity status. We knew there was a more interesting world outside of St Benedict's. Buoyed up by Muriel Spark and Quentin Crisp, we were just biding our time. We wore odd socks and too much Denim aftershave, mildly provocative acts but not something anyone could cane us for, we hoped.

'Julian is always either languid or superior' read my school report. Well, yes, I was.

When we were in the upper fifth, our division master was Father Edmund. An extraordinarily tall, thin monk, like something out of an El Greco painting, with black shiny hair and big wet lips, he was universally known as 'Pole'.

One of the many school rules was that you weren't allowed to enter any classroom other than your own. One lunchtime, Nick was waiting at the door of upper 5(2) for me to put some books away in my desk and carelessly placed half a foot over the forbidden threshold. Suddenly Pole loomed behind him. 'What do you think you're doing in there?' he demanded. Of course, Nick explained that he was merely waiting for me and, of course, Pole was having none of it. Here was an opportunity to beat the gayness out of one of us at least. I heard and almost felt the four cracks of the cane Nick was dealt, even though Pole's office was two flights up.

When we reached the sixth form, our plans to take the music business by storm suddenly didn't seem so far away. We had never sung our songs to anyone but each other, and we were very secretive about our catalogue of tapes. Nick could actually belt out a number with considerable gusto but I think we both knew my voice was, shall we say, unusual. But it was mind over matter. If I wanted it badly enough, it would happen. And if we were to be the next Hall and Oates then some progress had to be made before we left school.

We decided to combine our creative talents. I renamed myself Marvin Shark and together we called ourselves the Mind and Body Floor Show. Next we wanted backing singers, so we placed an advert in the *Melody Maker* that read: 'Two funky black chicks wanted for blue-eyed soul band. Send demo tape and photo.'

I can't remember how many replies we received but we ended up with Carmelita and Pauline. They were a scream, gorgeous girls with fantastic soulful voices and they screamed with laughter at our funny voices and mannerisms. But bringing outsiders into our private world was a risky business. The girls sat around Nick's lounge patiently listening to our plans, but we were decidedly shifty when it came to rehearsing. Of course, they wanted to know what numbers exactly did we have in mind? Where were we going to perform them? I said I could arrange a gig at the long-neglected Rowing Club, but it never materialised. Amused but disillusioned, the girls had better things to do than commute to Ealing each weekend and humour two peculiar boys who were unable to deliver the goods they seemed so sure about. Carmelita and Pauline faded away, and with them the Mind and Body Floor Show.

But with the fortitude of youth and our undiminished faith in our own destiny, Nick and I simply changed tack: theatre – that was the thing!

The school play that year was to be *Romeo and Juliet*, and my old English teacher Mr Moore was in charge. Nick took on the role of Tybalt, Prince of Cats, and I, undaunted by the fight scene integral to the part, was to be Count Paris. It's not usual to get a laugh on the line 'Oh, I am slain!' but I managed to.

After the dress rehearsal Mr Moore's wife and second-in-command, an exotic Spanish lady called Conchita, took me aside and said, 'Too much with the rouge, Julian! Too much rouge!'

Next up, as a stepping-stone to Hollywood, we joined the Strawberry Hill Players, a cosy unhurried organisation near Teddington, but rather like us they were all talk and no action. After a few evenings of tea and biscuits in the church hall, and just the occasional glance at the script of Wilde's *Lord Arthur Savile's*

Crime, we decamped to Putney and the no-nonsense Group 64, a reputable amateur dramatic society run by the resident director Maurice. We were both cast in *A Man For All Seasons*. As Sir Richard Rich I had no less than three costume changes, while Signor Chapuis (Nick) was glamour personified in his black embroidered tunic and cloak.

Performing at last, dressing up and wearing make-up and being applauded for it, we felt we were on our way.

Note: I recently received a badly spelt letter from the St Benedict's Development Office. They need to build a new sports pavilion and are after some money. 'I hope that you will reflect on the privileged start in life the school helped to give you and that you will feel, like me, that St Benedict's with its strong Benedictine ethos merits your generosity.' They shouldn't hold their breath.

FOUR

Had we but World enough, and Time,
This coyness Lady were no crime...
But at my back I alwaies hear
Times winged Charriot hurrying near.

'To His Coy Mistress', Andrew Marvell

Nick was to be a feature of my life for evermore, but we were never lovers.

Nor did we discuss our desires. At the age of 18 I had never been out to a disco or a nightclub. I spent my Saturday nights at home with my mother and kept myself nice.

I once overheard two boys on the bus talking about their frustrations. 'I'm going mad,' said one. 'Haven't got me leg over in two weeks.' I realised I wasn't exactly living life to the full, but with only one friend and no invitations, what could I do? I was also strangely prudish, reacting with tight-lipped disdain if anyone, male or female, showed an interest in me.

Frankie was dancing in Paris at La Nouvelle Eve and invited me to go and stay for a week. Again I inhaled the glamour of the dressing room, sequins, eyelashes, feathers and all. But I was horrified when the barman at the club asked her if he could take me out. When I declined, Frankie took me aside.

'If you are gay, I just want you to know that everyone in the family will still love you.' It was a perfect opportunity for me to come out, but I denied what was clearly obvious to everyone else. Maybe I thought the whole world would be hostile like St Benedict's. Despite appearances, I think I hoped to turn out like David Bowie, confounding expectations and not being disappointingly obvious. It's fair to say I was confused.

Neither could I discuss my theatrical ambitions with my parents. Nick auditioned and was accepted at the Guildhall School of Music and Drama, while my future was a bit of a blank. I was unable to say I wanted to act. I was unable to say I was gay. On the brink of adulthood I feared that my ambitions would all be failures and my proclivities my downfall. As adolescents do, I kept all my thoughts secret, terrified of ridicule.

'Have you thought about joining the army?' my father suggested, hopefully.

When I politely dismissed this and vaguely mentioned some sort of work in the theatre, my mother enthused about a life in administration or working backstage. She could imagine me running a little arts centre somewhere...

An academic exploration of drama seemed acceptable to all parties.

At the eleventh hour I applied to a number of universities and went for three or four interviews. At Kent University I got chatting to a girl called Noreen from Cambridgeshire. She had jet-black hair and big, sad eyes like someone from an Iris Murdoch novel and wore a fawn mac. At the end of the afternoon we swapped addresses and the next day she wrote to me.

Dear Julian,

Though it seems rather presumptuous to write to you like this after such a brief encounter today, I find, not entirely to my surprise, that I have to. I know very little about you, and you even less about me, that is probably part of the attraction. When I found myself interested in you I realised that you were different. Understandably you could be wondering what on earth I'm talking about and then again it might strike you as logical. I don't think the difference between you and everyone else can be defined but nevertheless I think it exists.

Whilst I don't think I know you in anything but the polite, tolerant way in which people treat each other under such rigid and timetabled conditions, you can't help detecting certain things which trigger off the appropriate emotions or reactions, and you certainly triggered off something. I've had the feeling like the one you get before going to the dentist ever since. I rather deliberately took my pen out, waved it under your nose and hoped you'd ask to borrow it. (Confession.) You did – thanks. I'll end this almost pathetic and somewhat desperate, admittedly deliberate plea to know you better in the hope that I didn't bore you and that you will consider it. Please reply.

Noreen

I was impressed with the classy blue notepaper and the neat handwriting. No one had written to me in such a serious, adult way before. We began a rather intense teenage relationship, mainly through letter writing with the occasional wander round art galleries. I made sure we never went anywhere she might expect a kiss. Eventually she wrote to me: 'I feel like an unwanted bun that's hardened and stuck to the cakestand.'

Once when I visited her in Cottenham we went on a picnic in a field and she grabbed her chance, pushing me back on the blanket and caressing me through what I seem to remember were black velvet trousers, but that was the extent of our intimacy, despite the encouraging news that she had condoms with her. We retreated to our letter writing, all of which I kept and numbered, peppering our missives with poetic quotes: 'Soon may I hear and see you too!' (*King Lear* adapted). But Noreen was still confused. Letter number 16:

If you didn't want me, except as just an acquaintance, you wouldn't clutch my hands, you wouldn't let me touch you and you wouldn't look at me as you sometimes do. But on the other hand I dare not kiss you because of fear that it's not what you want.

I don't know what you'll say.

Please be truthful if you can.

'Please trip me gently, I don't like to fall.' That's a Bowie lyric altered somewhat to convey a pessimistic attitude which one hopes is not necessary.

Happily her fantasy of us both going to the same university and consummating our love evaporated and the letters, gripping though they were, stopped eventually. I missed her letters, though, and the feeling of being important to someone.

When the requisite A-level results were mine I was accepted on the drama and English course at Goldsmiths College, University of London. I had never imagined being a student. I'd seen them on the news from time to time, protesting and sitting down in the middle of roads, but they didn't seem very stylish. My mother made me promise never to take drugs. This had been her mantra to each of her children when they flew the nest, and my word was solemnly given.

In early October 1977 my father drove me to the hall of residence that was to be my home for the next two years. Blackheath House, 20 Blackheath Rise, London SE13.

As he drove away, leaving his peculiar son outside the big peeling unkempt house, he tells me he thought: Whatever is to become of him? I was a strange mix of naivety and world-weariness, consumed with secret ambitions. I was tall and thin, with long, carefully groomed hair and colour-coordinated clothes. I spoke softly and slowly. I was always passive and never confrontational. Part monk, part pop star.

As it turned out, I had arrived a day early. As my parents had now moved to Swindon in Wiltshire, there was nowhere to go. Blackheath House was yet another red Victorian mansion, with accommodation for twelve male students. The resident tutor was a bit cross with me for arriving ahead of schedule, but let me in and told me to select a room. I would have to share. I climbed to the top of the house, which I thought would be quieter, and chose a large room with a slanted ceiling. The carpet was dark green and rough to the touch. Two single beds, two desks, two noticeboards, two wardrobes, all quite cheap and cheerful. I went for the bed nearest the window, unpacked and put my Dana Gillespie pictures up on my noticeboard and arranged the fruit my mother had sent with me in a round Pyrex bowl.

Downstairs the common room was sparse and grubby, what furniture there was spilling stuffing from Stanley-knife wounds, and if you sat on it for any length of time you'd come away with mysterious bites. Down a step from the common room was the kitchen, mostly given over to white Formica lockers where students could lock away their meagre supplies. A back door opened onto a small overgrown garden, where, it transpired, Rose the cleaner would chuck any unwashed pots, pans, plates or cutlery left in the sink.

The other eleven students arrived the next day, and Nick, a cheery punk-rocker type studying geography, was my room-mate. What he made of me I've no idea, but he smiled a lot and shook his head, chuckling with amusement at his strange new roommate. I observed that much, and thought: It could be so much worse. That night we all went to the pub round the corner. Nervous and socially inept as I was among such blokey types, I nevertheless immediately sensed that this was not going to be the ordeal that school had been. They drank lots of beer while I sipped a Coca-Cola. They were fun, and seemed to be amused by me. On the way back to the Rise, they ran through the grounds of the nurses' home shouting and whooping, while I kept primly to the pavement. They were flushed and excited by their own daring when we met up on the doorstep. That night Nick was sick in my fruit bowl. He was terribly apologetic the next morning, and rinsed the vomit from my apples under the bathroom tap.

The next morning we all set off together on the bus from Blackheath to New Cross. As we left the house I picked up my first letter from my mother, which I read on the journey:

Dear Julian,

I do hope you are all right. Shall I bring a blanket up for you when we come? I don't know how you are managing without saucepans. I expect you've been busy settling in and getting to know people and places. I hope you like it, eventually if not immediately. It's very quiet here without you. The day after you left, I forgot you were not around and shouted something of interest out to you!

We've found a badminton club at Wootton Bassett. They play Mondays and Wednesdays and we intend to go along on Monday for the first time. I missed bridge last night because I had a bad migraine but Daddy went.

On Monday I'm going to a Detention Centre at Usk, which is in Wales. New ground for me.

Have you got your grant yet? I hope so. If you don't receive it soon, let me know and I'll have to give you a loan for your lodgings.

There's not a lot of news since I saw you. I can't write more because I've still got a bit of a headache left over from yesterday. Hope you'll understand.

All my love,

Mummy.

Got your coat yet?

PS Received your letter today. Interesting. Perhaps you should always carry the A–Z wherever you go?

It was funny to think of my parents at home without me, leisure activities taking care of the hours that for years had been dedicated to their children. A week later she wrote again.

I was interested in the snippet of news regarding your cell-mate being sick in your fruit bowl. Not so much because he was, but your rather nonchalant attitude. I suppose it's all part of being away from home and having to cope with all eventualities. Time was when you would have died at the very thought.

I'll have to stop writing soon as Kevin Keegan is on in a match. Love to you. Don't spend too much on Christmas presents. You are not getting much spent on you!

Love from Mummy.

PS Have you managed to find the church yet?

I sat next to a girl called Linda at the 'welcome' gathering in the theatre that morning. She had spiky hair, glorious cheekbones and wore a green glittery tie over a man's white shirt. She told me she was the lead singer in a band called Linda and her Genitals. She had worked with the Royal Court Youth Theatre and was cool, confident and intelligent. Afterwards we wandered through the hall for the Freshers' Fair, and signed up for the Drama Society and the anti-Corrie Bill pro-abortion march. I hovered at the Gaysoc table but didn't like the shirt the boy manning it was wearing, so moved on.

At lunchtime, wearing our 'A Woman's Right to Choose' badges, we went to the bar. Linda shrieked with punky laughter when I ordered a Coca-Cola. She ordered lager for me instead. It was on special offer.

In the first few classes, where we often had to pair up and do 'getting to know you' exercises, we gravitated towards each other whenever possible.

Between the English and drama departments, we were offered a stimulating mix of academic and practical work. Greek tragedies, war poets, Edward Bond, acting and improvisation classes soon filled our timetables. I raced from lecture to seminar to studio with a happy heart unknown to me at school. The silly superiority that Nick and I had paraded evaporated now. It had only, after all, been a defence mechanism in the face of aggression. Now in a new world – by choice not force – I was shocked into near normality.

Instead of one friend I had lots. I was no longer on the outside looking in with disdain.

There was even a dance class. I wrote excitedly to my parents: 'I'm feeling loose already and can twist my legs into all sorts of positions. Today we listened to a recording of *The Cherry Orchard* in Russian and were told to tune in to the different emotions.'

Being immersed in higher education had obviously had some effect on my letter writing, as this reply from my mother indicated:

> Thank you very much for explaining or translating for us expressions you now use in everyday conversation, which clearly would be over our heads. We would never have got the meaning of your sentence, which contained the word 'vociferous', without your help! Nevertheless I have some doubts as to your alternative word (noisy) being quite accurate enough for us to be sure we can substitute vociferous. For instance, can one really describe the traffic as being vociferous, or can one say your father is a vociferous sleeper? Perhaps you shouldn't yet throw away your Thesaurus! Still, you are clearly destined to get a good degree. And kind with it, since you know we don't understand long words so put alternatives down.
>
> Pao is missing you, and is a disturbed cat, acting as if psychotic. (Ask someone what this means.)

Apart from the course work, the third-year productions were always looking for actors, and auditions were held at lunchtimes.

Within a few weeks I had my first part. 'I've got myself into a play called *A Scent Of Flowers* and I play the undertaker and the priest. Both parts are very funny although I don't think much of the play as a whole,' I wrote.

After that I was in a different play every few weeks, from Shakespeare to Poliakov. Nine productions, no less, in my first year. I even played a lumberjack in one show. 'At the moment we're having trouble making my voice gruff enough for the part.'

As if I didn't have enough on my plate, I also developed an infatuation for a boy I saw in the refectory one day. He was quite short and slight and wore a battered leather jacket, and I would seethe with jealousy as he canoodled brazenly with his girlfriend. He slouched a lot and had tousled hair and moody lips. An art student. I think his name was Michael, although I never spoke to him. In my diary I referred to him as 'the Boy From New York City' – not because he was, but because he seemed streetwise and daring. It was also the title of a hit single at the time by Darts. Also, I needed a code for my diary in case my secret documentation of each and every sighting was discovered.

I was quite happy in my private agony, swooning from afar. He sometimes caught me staring at him and would look back, more bemused than smouldering. Spotting 'TBFNYC' became a kind of hobby for me; I worked out the prime times for a sighting and would position myself in the refectory where I had a clear view of all possible approaches, heart fluttering in anticipation. I didn't tell anyone of my feelings.

My curiosity about sex was gathering pace. Soon just looking and longing would not be enough. My virginity was becoming a burden. I was not aware that anyone fancied me in the slightest, but it seems they did. One day after college a boy on my course called Chris invited me to the Rosemary Branch for a drink. He was a lanky, hippyish type with a northern accent and a straggly beard. He had kind eyes and rolled his own cigarettes. He lived in a hall of residence right next door to Goldsmiths, and as we had an early lecture the next day he invited me to stay over with him. Oblivious to his intentions I said yes. It would save on the bus fare. He had the luxury of a single room, so I tried to sleep on the floor in a draught. After a bit of late-night chat, he said, 'Why don't you get in with me?'

When I hopped in he said, 'Good lad,' and kissed me. The beard scratched me as his passion mounted and the pink, wet tongue waggled around in my mouth like a newborn panda. His penis jabbed away at my thigh until he came. It was a bit like having sex with an Irish wolfhound. Or so I imagine. I felt quite grown-up the next day, but far from sure that I had been fully deflowered. Nevertheless it was a step in the right direction. Chris gave me secret smiles and knowing invitations to the pub for the next week or so but I didn't want to repeat the experience. I sometimes went to the college bar with Linda or my other new friends, but often I went home to write my essays. I took to writing comic monologues for my own amusement, and a couple of plays. These often featured tough, working-class girls, the type I'd observe at the bus stop at New Cross.

'Marcia, Marcia, look at the arse on 'er!'

You would hear that cry every day in the playground

when Marcia and I were kids. Mostly from me. Well, it was true, anyway. She's got a lot to thank me for, she has. I've been the making of that girl. She'd never have gone on a diet if it wasn't for me. I toughened her up. You see scraggy rooster where once was succulent chicken. That's bad news if you're a hungry wolf but a blessing if you're Marcia. She's a masterpiece. When someone stole her plimsolls in the third year I told her not to mess about. Burn the bleedin' school down, I told her, you can borrow my matches. So she did. Marcia got reform school, the rest of us got a month's holiday while they repaired the damage. She came out of that reform school a sight to see. Hard as nails and with a tattoo saying 'I Love Leslie' on her inside thigh. No one calls her fatty any more and she's got me to thank.

I got an evening job at the Old Vic Theatre in Waterloo as an usher, selling programmes and ice creams. During the performance I would do 'foyer duty', which meant ushering in late-comers and sitting on the stairs reading a book. Miguel, a half Portuguese Royal Ballet student who worked behind the bar downstairs, would sometimes call up to ask if I wanted a drink. I asked for a Coke but he said no, have a gin and tonic. After work we walked to the station together and one time he said, 'Would you like to come and stay with me for the weekend?'

Wising up at last to the subtext of the casual remark, and realising for the first time that he was gay and, what's more, had his eye on me, I said, 'Yes, that would be lovely.' I thought he meant sometime soon at our mutual convenience, but at Waterloo he bought two tickets to Dalston. He smiled and gave me an imperious look, which I'd seen before from Rudolph Nureyev when he took his endless curtain calls.

Miguel was quite a catch. A lean, handsome, curly-haired boy. At 24 he had taken to ballet rather late in his youth, but as he chatted to me on the tube that night he revealed a self-confidence that thrilled me. He told me about his life and his ambitions to dance, his belated epiphany. Then he locked eyes with me and told me I was beautiful. No one had ever paid me a compliment like this before. A week before in the refectory, a fellow drama student called Wendy Hallam had turned to me and said, 'You're such an Adonis!' – but her tone of voice implied a hint of sarcasm. Miguel's words were from the heart and I almost wanted to cry. Much to his amusement, I'd had no idea our casual chats over the previous weeks had been part of the courting process, and I was somewhat taken aback to find myself whisked off to north London in this fashion, but by the time we got off the train at Dalston Junction I was in love.

The flat, above a betting shop, was small and untidy. In the kitchen piles of dirty plates filled the sink, and we watched as a fat mouse scurried about the floor, selecting only the freshest morsels from the many on offer. Miguel's flatmate, an amiable smiling woman, wafted in wearing a faded kimono, looked me up and down and said, 'Here he is then...' Clearly up to speed with Miguel's romantic intentions.

In the bedroom were orange curtains and piles of sweaty dance clothes. Miguel quickly made the bed before we got into it.

He could sense how nervous I was and we lay there for ages talking before he kissed me. This time it was most satisfactory. He
climbed on top of me and parted my legs determinedly using some
balletic manoeuvre with his knees. Baby Lotion was his lubricant
of choice – a smell to be forever associated with him. I was tense,
unresponsive and barely breathing. My inexperience revealed, he
coached me and reassured me throughout the proceedings, but
any virginal protests were denied, his determined personality
apparent even between the sheets.

'You'll get used to it,' he said afterwards, in a business-like
way. He was rather thrilled to be my 'first'. Miguel was misty-eyed
the next morning, stroking my face and kissing me awake. Passing
a stool the next day was a painful experience, a bit like (I imagined)
giving birth, but this too made me feel grown-up, at last.

That night I wrote a monologue for a character called Lucille
Spinks (aged 62). It seems somehow relevant.

I met a man on the tube once, name of Albert. He took
me back to his flat and we had sexual relations. It wasn't
a love affair, it was a sex affair. Albert was black as the ace
of spades, and his body all muscle and no fat. All was
hunky dory and a little occasional straightforward sex
might have done wonders for me. But Albert, sad to say,
was very partial to your anal intercourse. I'd be laying
there slipping into the land of never-never and before I
knew it was Christmas he'd stuck a finger up me bum and
was reaching in his disco bag for some lubrication. And
that was just for foreplay. Come the main course I was sick

in a bucket. Talk about square pegs and round holes. No thank you. Sex and bottoms have very little in common as far as I'm concerned, and I couldn't abide the practice. I felt like a poodle flattened by a Doberman pinscher.

'Leave it out!' I said to Albert, but it was no good. He was set in his ways and he nearly got set in mine. I thought of England, I thought of Berlin, but it was no good. With respect, lying there with your face buried in a pillow is no way to spend your time, however short. You can't get a grip on your turds the next day, neither. So it was a case of happiness or haemorrhoids. It was on your bike for Albert, and I settled down to a family pack of Murray mints and a toothache.

I, on the other hand, showed more perseverance. The affair was conducted almost entirely in Dalston, after shifts at the Old Vic. I shared a room after all, and Miguel had a double bed. I felt like a fully fledged homosexual at last, a card-carrying member. Nick from school, now a trainee actor at the Guildhall, had signed up too, and we discussed our menfolk on the phone like moaning housewives.

First attempts at love are a bit like first attempts at wood-work. I was full of enthusiasm, immersed in the task, but the result was neither sturdy nor functional. After three months we were firewood. I was busy rehearsing a principal role in *Twelfth Night* for another college production most evenings. Miguel got fed up with the prolonged separation and told me over the phone, as I stood in the lino-covered hallway at the bottom of the stairs in Blackheath House, to decide: him or the play. I thought for a moment. There was a meaty part to be had on both sides of this equation, but what should I do? Orange curtains or velvet tabs?

Well, let's just say that my Andrew Aguecheek was a triumph, still fondly talked of by those who were lucky enough to catch it. I wonder if it has been thus ever since? Love scorned in favour of career? Many's the husband there at the beginning of the tour and absent by the end... and I am no stranger to the mid-TV-series personal problem. These days, I cling to the wreckage for dear life. But at 19, dipping my toes into the world of gay love for the first time, I was remarkably unconcerned.

Linda and I made friends with a girl called Renata, soon renamed 'Neen'. She seemed posh and cerebral at first, but in fact she was a scream. A keen gossiper like Linda and me, she had a Germanic talent for cutting to the chase and a clucking, seductive laugh. The three of us basked in each other's company. 'Who else was interesting in our year?' I asked Linda recently. 'Well, *we* were the interesting people, really,' she said. Linda, Neen and I were the core, at the very throb of any social or theatrical event.

We were terribly exclusive, guarding our 'area' in the refectory with all the enthusiasm of Nicholas van Hoogstraten. Others were welcome to visit, such as Janine, a pretty, ringleted girl, all long skirts and lace shawls. (She turned up in tears once because a Jamaican woman had stopped her as she walked through Deptford Market with her Asian boyfriend and told her, 'Pork and beef don't mix...') Stephanie, luxurious of hair and buxom as a Rubens nude, contributed a kind of rustic Diana Dors glamour. There were a couple of Steves, one who wore military jackets all the time and would clearly have been happier at Sandhurst. When Linda asked him for a cigarette one day he made the unfortunate response, 'I'm sorry, I'm down to my last seven.' Steve McNicholas was funny and delightful, but thought better of uni life and left to form a band called Pookiesnackenburger. Later he co-created *Stomp!*, the innovative stage show where young men in vests make a lot of noise with dustbins. Chantal was a cashmere sweater and pearls kind of gal, destined to fall victim to one of my early attempts at audience humiliation.

We soon took over the Drama Society. No one else got a look-in. We hijacked the annual budget for the culmination of our ambitions at that time: a fully staged production of Coward's *Private Lives*, to run for a full week in the main theatre. Directed by Neen and starring Linda and myself in the roles of Amanda and Elyot. Family and friends came to watch.

Dear M and D,

It's been one surprise after another. After your *grande* arrival on Wednesday, when I was taking my make-up off yesterday I had a message that Noreen was downstairs. I told her about the show when I rang her at Christmas and she remembered the dates. Such a surprise as I haven't seen her for ages. Hasn't changed, mind you, still wistful and old-fashioned, but it was nice to see her. We had nearly a full house last night so it should be packed out tonight. The record player broke, so we had to improvise our way out of that. My nerves vanished after the first act and I really enjoyed myself. I recorded it too. I wonder who will turn up to surprise me tonight?

Went out to dinner with Linda's shoplifting cousin after the show last night. (She's in court this morning.) It was very embarrassing but highly amusing. She complained about the wine and the price of everything then demanded breast of chicken and nothing else in her curry! But she did pay the bill – with some very suspicious-looking luncheon vouchers.

No more news really. It was lovely to see you all.

Be home soon as you know,

Love Julian

Emboldened by this success we decided college life needed a bit of light relief, so we staged a series of lunchtime cabaret shows called *Camping on a Shoestring*. Again the stars would be Linda and me, and Neen would produce. What others thought of our shameless ambitions and relentless self-promotion I don't know, but there was no stopping us. We booked the coffee bar for a week, renamed it 'Nina's Nooky' and set about putting some sketches together. There was an advert in the *Stage* selling '100 music hall gags', '100 drag queen gags' and, intriguingly, '100 ad libs and heckler stoppers' for £2 per assortment, so we sent off for them. Most of them weren't very funny, but we got one or two gems such as: 'My father was a boxer... and my mother was a cocker spaniel.' And: 'Who did your hair for you? Was it the council?'

Then in a dusty old shop in the backstreets of Soho, we found a pile about four feet high of Victorian musical monologues and humorous songs. They were dated and sentimental, occasionally even offensive: 'Wot's De Good Ob Grousin'? (An Old Nigger's Philosophy)' being just one example, but we found a few that were definitely worth a spin: 'I May Not Be Clever But I'm Clean!' sounded like a winner, as did 'I Wonder If My Mother Ever Knew?' and 'The Man With The Swollen Head'.

The show started with Linda and me dressed as two cleaning ladies called Glad and May. The agony of their domestic drudgery was made bearable because they at last had a captive audience.

'Hello, I'm Glad and I'm glad to be here.'
'And I'm May and I may be glad to be here!'

We were loud and anarchic and had a number of catchphrases: 'I'm human, you're human, everybody is human', and 'It's uncanny and unnatural'.

'We used to work in a factory. Monkeys could have done the work we was doing – hairy monkeys covered in hair – then one day in walked Lionel Fart. He took one look at me – one look was all it took – and he said, "You, May, have got something that not every woman has got." And Glad had a little bit herself, tucked away within. Anyway, he whipped it out, there and then – he whipped his tape recorder out, and it was next stop Hollywood.'

At a given moment we'd whip off our headscarves and Oxfam coats (mine was primrose yellow, Glad's was hot pink) and underneath we were Amanda and Elyot once more, but a Vaudeville version. As ridiculously posh as Glad and May were common, we over-enunciated horribly: 'I've nehever lohoved hany hwun helse for han hinstant!'

Although we can't sing we then launched into 'Someday I'll Find You' and some of the musical monologues found in Soho.

Stephanie was allowed a show-stopping impersonation of 'Carmen', the Spanish tea lady from the refectory. (She would give us cut-price biscuits if the supervisor Olive wasn't looking.) To the tune of 'Don't Cry For Me Argentina' she sang: 'Don't cry for me, pretty lady, the truth is, it isn't worth it, they say it cost fifteen and a half, I charge you twelve and a half, you don't tell no one, you don't tell Olive!'

Glad and May returned after Steph's spot for the highlight of the show, the Handbag Competition. Linda would say, 'Do you know, May, I feel like a rummage...' which was our cue to dive into the audience and secure a bag each before they could be lifted to safety. 'There's a prize for who's got the most interesting handbag...' we told the audience before a callous and unrestrained autopsy of the contents.

It was a lot of studenty nonsense really, but these lunchtime shows were a hit so it was a natural progression for us to move on to *An Evening With Glad and May*, in which we were somewhat grander. 'Both of us have gifts bestowed upon us by powers beyond the realms of your limited imaginations. Glad's mother was a spiritualist, her father was a comedian – she's a happy medium.'

Somewhat influenced by Dame Edna Everage and Bette Midler, we called ourselves 'Housewives Extraordinaire', and got our friend Simon 'Hunky' Hughes to interview us as 'Michael Parkinbox'.

As May, I had a troublesome son called Janice.

'I was just tidying his room the other day, Glad, and I wasn't prying – but I'd just rolled back the carpet when I found... this! A suspender belt. It's uncanny.'

    'And unnatural,' added Glad.

'It came as a shock when I'd just forced the lock

Of the wardrobe and out fell the gear.

There was lipstick and rouge and a dress that was huge,

And earrings, one for each ear.

He must look a sight, I thought, dressed up at night,

So that's where he goes after tea.

While I finish the grub and Ken's gone to the pub,

He's upstairs looking prettier than me!'

We seemed to have a penchant for comic rhymes. Glad's husband, Vick, had recently expired after a nasty cough and cold. ('Towards the end he was known as "Vick the nasal spray".') Being vegetarian she buried him somewhere leafy and green: the cabbage patch. She spared no expense and on his gravestone was the following inscription:

> *Vick was vegetarian,*
> *I thought him such a hoot.*

He used to nibble nuts
And he liked a bit of fruit.

We didn't rehearse a great deal, and when we did we just made each other laugh. I'm quite sure much of the act was funny only to ourselves. We enjoyed being reckless and making it up as we went along. It was an antidote to all the 'proper' plays we were involved with, and with each other there, we had no fear of being lost for words. Mostly, everyone waited for the handbag competition, a hit-and-miss but rather daring bit of improvisation. I hooked out Chantal's handbag on one occasion and read the entries for her diary that week. Unfortunately I shared with everyone the news that she had visited the doctor on the Wednesday with itchy nipples. Chantal never spoke to me again. Do hope the problem has cleared up by now.

Linda and Neen were both a year older than me, and wiser in every sense. I had just left my sheltered, suburban life in Teddington. Linda had a council flat in Deptford and Neen shared a house in Clapham where everyone had half a shelf in the fridge and adhered to a cleaning rota stuck on the back of a door. Both had boyfriends, past and present. Slowly I absorbed their feminist ideals, left-wing politics and sense of style. My carefully ironed shirts and colour-coordinated tank tops, 'loon' trousers and slip-on shoes would not do. My hair was worn in a carefully blow-dried sweep with a fetching side-parting. I don't remember a specific makeover but if Linda shrieked and Neen hooted when I arrived at college I knew I'd made a mistake. Slowly I transformed, finding collarless granddad shirts in thrift shops, braces, baggy trousers and boots. I had two favourite T-shirts, one with a big picture of Hilda Ogden, the other featuring Bet Lynch.

'Let's bleach your hair,' said Linda one day and I let her. She produced a packet of Born Blonde and set to work, not allowing me to see the results until she'd finished. Every few minutes she'd poke around under the cap and say 'Nothing's happening'. The last time she looked her eyes widened and she rushed me into the bathroom to shampoo the bleach out.

'Oh Jules! Jules!' she said with horror when I'd towelled myself dry. Only then was I given access to the mirror. The result was a garish mix of sunset orange streaked with primrose yellow. We both collapsed in mortified hysterics.

'Get me a bottle of gin!' I said when I could speak, and Linda rushed out to the off-licence. (I'd got a taste for cheap gin that term.) It didn't seem so bad when I was drunk, but it was. You do occasionally see teenage boys at bus stops with frightful hair that is clearly the result of a similar home-bleaching experiment. I went around for months like that. Linda laughed every time she saw me. I broke the news of my look to my parents by letter:

Now we come to the little matter of my hair. I enclose the photograph to let you become accustomed to the change before I descend on Wiltshire *au* flesh. I think the village shop and the priest should be given prior notice but we'll let the rest discover for themselves. Oh, what a mistake it is. I collapsed in a heap on the bathroom floor when I saw it and venturing out has become a major ordeal. The refectory came to quite a standstill this morning.

I couldn't see my friends – I just heard them screaming!
However, it won't last for ever and when I'm old and grey
I may be glad I did such an outrageous thing.

We went on pro-abortion marches, discussed whether or not all men were potential rapists and loathed Margaret Thatcher. Once I went with Linda to a meeting of the SWP, although I was rather bored by the comrades. One night at a party I was handed a joint. Forgetting my promise to my mother, I took it. After a few puffs I fainted, and when I came round was sure I'd had a terrible accident.

'Get me some trousers!' was all I said, repeatedly.

For my second year as a resident at Blackheath Rise I shared a bedroom with Steve, who wasn't half as much fun as Nick had been. Although he never vomited in my fruit bowl, he snored. Not just heavy breathing and the occasional snort but a proper foghorn, window-rattling snore.

'Steve! You're snoring!' I used to say every few minutes. He was most apologetic and took to bringing his boots over to my bedside before retiring so I could throw them at him when it all got too much. Since I aimed for his head with some success, he devised a new method: gaffer-taping a boot to the end of a broom handle so I could prod him out of his slumbers a little less violently.

One day in the grubby kitchen in the Rise I took a swig of orange juice that was off and it made me sick. Although I recovered quickly enough, the nausea came back a few weeks later, then went, then came back, and so on for the next year. The doctor told me it was nerves, and I got little sympathy from Steve.

'Having your once-a-month again are you?' he'd ask when he entered the bedroom to find me groaning on my bed under the moleskin fur coat I got for a snip at Greenwich Market. (I thought I looked glamorous and chic, but as photos prove, I was mistaken.) I used to read his diary when he went out and came across this somewhat unsympathetic description: 'Greta Garbo has the shits again.'

A month later I was revising for the second-year exams at my parents' house when I was sick once more. I must be nervous about the exams, I thought. My parents were away but came back to find me curled up in agony on the stairs, so thought it best to call an ambulance.

At St Margaret's Hospital in Swindon a doctor lubricated his rubber-gloved finger and inserted it up my bottom. When a sharp press to the right caused a breathtaking increase in pain, he confidently identified a case of acute appendicitis and told the nurses to prepare me for surgery.

Five minutes later, six rubber-gloved medical students appeared, all wanting to digitally invade me in the interests of their future diagnostic abilities. After the third stab of finger-induced agony I put a stop to it, explaining that under normal circumstances they could jab away all night, but now was not a good time.

Out of action for a few weeks I missed the exams and was told the boring news that I'd have to sit them at the end of the third year. I got a nice 'get well' card from the Rise, signed by all.

The last I heard of my old roommate Steve, he'd become a prison officer, which seems about right.

Someone who was most concerned about my confinement in hospital was the front of house manager at the Old Vic, Patrick James. With his stubby neck, fleshy lips and immaculate suits, he was the Paul Burrell of his time. He'd had twin 19-year-old sons, one of whom had fallen to his death from a helicopter, but whatever his contribution to family life had been back in Ireland, he was now a salacious queen and no mistake. His big moment came each evening before the doors opened when he took the stage for the fire drill. 'Mr Jet is in the… stalls bar!' he would announce with a trembling voice, and the ushers, situated by the doors on each level of the theatre, would hurriedly usher out the imaginary audience. 'This way out please! No need to panic…'

When I came back to work looking pale and interesting, his flirtations went up a gear. Starting with extra shifts and progressing to gifts of silk ties and expensive aftershave, he whisked me off to Joe Allen's restaurant to wine and dine me. I became very partial to Brandy Alexanders and he once bought me nine on the trot, sure that this, at last, would lower my resistance. He pounced on me in the back of a taxi that night, but to no avail. I was having none of it.

He wrote to me:

I'm not sure I can go on much longer with the fantasy – maybe, if not probably, of my own creation – of the relationship that does exist between us. I had hoped for something more. The crux of one of my favourite plays – de

Montherlant's 'La rie dont le prince est un enfant' – is St Paul's dictum: 'Woe to thee O Land whose king is a child.' It has haunted me all my life and now seems more potent than ever. I feel deeply unhappy, ashamed at my lack of control and totally unsure of where it leads me.

It didn't lead him into my trousers, that was for sure. Once I got Nick from school a job at the Old Vic too, Patrick quickly transferred his affections to my equally disinterested friend. We had to play along with him as we loved our job: the Prospect Theatre Company were in residence and Derek Jacobi's *Hamlet* was a sensation, not to mention Barbara Jefford as Gertrude, whose fabulous sweeping turns we imitated in the aisles each night.

After selling the programmes before the show, the procedure was to take the money and unsold programmes up to Patrick's office, where he'd log the sales and the cash onto a sales form. Nick and I, suspicious as to how he paid for all the expensive gifts and the Brandy Alexanders, took to creeping into the office unobserved to analyse his bookkeeping. All was quickly revealed. If we'd sold 50 programmes, the form said 20. Patrick James was on the fiddle.

We weren't sure what to do with this information until Nick had a brainwave. He wrote a short story about a theatre manager called James Patrick, guilty of a not dissimilar scam at his fictional playhouse, and gave it to Derek Jacobi to read. Very soon afterwards Patrick was relieved of his post and returned to Ireland.

Third-year students had to make their own living arrangements, so I moved into a dull terraced house in Brownhill Road. I was the only lodger to John, a somewhat creepy confirmed bachelor in his fifties, fond of cardigans and prolonged eye contact. I'd been there a few days before I noticed the ornamental whips adorning the walls. Curious. John never seemed to go out and I would lie in bed and listen to him creeping about the house long after bedtime. In the morning the whips had been rearranged... I thought I should think about moving. When he brushed past me in the kitchen one day and exhaled lustfully in my ear, I went to my room and packed my stuff. For the next few months I lived with Auntie Tess and Uncle Ken in Syon Lane, Osterley, and over Christmas I worked at the British Gas headquarters at Marble Arch. Elaine and Micky, the two women I worked with, were rather preoccupied creating their wardrobe for the coming season, and little photocopying was achieved. My job mainly consisted of meeting anyone bold enough to approach the photocopying department and tell them that we were very busy indeed, snowed under, in fact. Couldn't possibly photocopy a single thing till next Friday. Best to send the job out if it was at all urgent. Spread out on the other side of the door were patterns and fabrics for summer dresses and jaunty blouses.

I was sitting in a Greenwich café one day, moaning to my friends about how hard it was to find a room somewhere near college that I could afford, when the waitress said she had a room available in her flat. Within days I had moved in to 54B Hardy Road in Blackheath. It was a big, sunny upper maisonette in a posh road. Lynda, the waitress, lived there with her black cat, Samson. I had a large bedroom with a double bed and a church pew. The rent was £12 a week, inclusive. I wrote to my sister Frances.

Living here keeps me in very good spirits. Lynda had the fumigators in so the fleas have gone. Something had to be done: I had 30 bites on one leg. Lynda had none, so they obviously liked me. Being popular has its drawbacks, you see. I got beaten up on Monday night. Linda and I had been out to the theatre and we were just standing at the bus stop in New Cross. There were two boys standing behind us, but we didn't think anything of it. Suddenly I felt an arm round my neck and then they put the fist in. I was so shocked I didn't know what to do. I thought they were going to kill me. Perhaps they would have done more damage than they did but Linda bravely jumped on one of them and pulled him off. Then I fell on the pavement and expected them to put the boot in but they ran away instead. They didn't try to take our bags or anything – that's what amazes me. They just wanted to beat me up. But apart from a cut lip and a bouquet of bruises, I'm unscathed. Straight afterwards we saw a police van outside the chip shop.

Me: I've just been assaulted.

Police officer: What did they look like?

Me: Ugly.

I'm going to start decorating my room tomorrow, I

think. Although I may put it off until after Christmas because I'm too lazy and too poor at the moment. I think that's all the news. Except you must see the film *Yanks*. I cried six times.

See you soon (if not before),

love Julian.

A Nigerian woman whose name I can't recall lived in the room opposite me. She had a stunning smile but she was very shy and hardly ever came out of her room. She never used the kitchen, preferring to cook on an electric ring in her bedroom. She would scurry to the kitchen in her blue dressing gown late at night to wash pots and plates before dashing back. She never went out, but she appeared in the hall one Saturday afternoon – which was in itself unheard of – wearing a silk two-piece with a matching hat.

'I'm going to get married,' she said in a very flat voice. Lynda and I said congratulations, and off she went. An hour later she came back to her room and carried on as before.

When she moved out, Cathy, a glamorous nurse from Greenwich Hospital, moved in. She altered her uniforms to show off her legs and figure, and wore pale blue eyeshadow. 'All right, doll?' she used to say. We would sit at the kitchen table discussing her marriage prospects. 'I'm after a doctor or a lawyer,' she said.

Back at Goldsmiths we decided to form a theatre company and go to the Edinburgh Festival. Under the guidance of David Gale, Company Work Theatre was a no-frills theatrical cooperative. Shows were performed in 'the round', everyone was equal and there were no stars. We were to perform *As You Like It* in the afternoons and *Twelfth Night* in the evenings, but there was a morning slot available too at the Walpole Hall if anyone had any suggestions. I rather boldly put one of my plays forward for discussion. *The Axe and Victims* was a black comedy about a rapist. (Attacks were happening on a daily basis. As Grandma Lucy said, 'He broke in halfway through *Charlie's Angels* and I'll never know what happened in the end!') It was rather bad taste, but surprisingly it was accepted.

Rehearsals were fraught. I wrote to my parents.

Yesterday I was not a happy man. I went as co-director to a rehearsal of my play. When I left, I was no longer co-director. Firstly, people kept asking me impossible questions about why their character is the way it is, what sort of background they came from and other matters of logic (which has never been my strong point). Then a troublesome actor called Giddon lived up to his reputation, throwing a tantrum because he didn't understand why his character had to say the line: 'I like Vera Lynn. I admire her teeth.' I wish they'd just learn the lines and DO it, leaving the Stanislavski technique where they found it. Anyway, once again I wished I'd never written the thing. Max, my co-director, said I made him nervous and our ideas were too different. By mutual agreement I've now handed over to him and I shall keep well away. What the end result will be we'll have to wait and see.

You'd have laughed at me the other day. We were

rehearsing *As You Like It* outside. In one scene, a lord and others are eating a banquet. Orlando enters, grabs me by the neck from behind and says, 'Forbear and eat no more!' As he said this we staggered backwards and fell into a fishpond. Right in, suit and all, up to the neck. We had to go and have a bath and borrow some clothes. Onlookers said it was the funniest thing they had ever seen.

My mother wrote back: 'Don't get temperamental about your play. After all, everyone connected with it is intent on doing it well and making the production successful. Don't get too possessive about it. Just imagine how Shakespeare must feel as he looks down on some of the efforts put on under his name!'

The 'no frills' policy was very clear when we arrived in Edinburgh to find our accommodation was a scout hut. Eighteen foam mattresses were laid out side by side and meals were cooked by each of us in turn in the adjoining kitchen. When my time came I cooked goulash with rice, but mistakenly used pudding rice. It looked as bad as it tasted.

One night we had a barbecue outside the scout hut. 'I didn't enjoy that much,' I wrote to my parents. 'The conversation digressed and became rather serious with talk of "What I personally think is…" and "All I've got to say is…" concerning the function and future of the company. They are a funny lot – probably because they're mostly actors. They rarely DO say what they "personally think", although barriers are beginning to be broken, living so closely together.'

With three different shows a day to perform, we were rather busy. It wasn't a laugh a minute, more like one a week. Putting the word 'work' in the title of the company had rather set the tone for the experience. And while I was as left-wing and group aware as the next thespian, I didn't see why glamour and glitter should be perceived as the devil's work. I wanted to wear make-up and theatrical costumes and add the odd flourish to my performance. Sleeping in scout huts and queuing up for vegetarian chilli rather took the fun out of things. Whatever my future was, I wasn't prepared to 'muck in' to that extent again. Power to the people and all that, I secretly thought, but if it wasn't too much trouble I'd like the star dressing room, hot and cold running water and some complimentary top-of-the-range skincare products thrown in.

Of course, sleeping 18 young people in a scout hut for three weeks is asking for scandal. There was plenty of late-night whispering, giggling and midnight walks. I tried to keep myself nice but I was awoken one night by a hand invading my sleeping bag. Pretending to be asleep, I tried to guess from the touch and size who it belonged to; too small to be Sir Toby Belch, I thought. The hand reached down and began to caress me. I turned, almost involuntarily, and we began to kiss. Then I realised: the hand clutching my manhood belonged to a girl.

FIVE

'The supreme object of life is to live...
It is true life only to realise one's own perfection,
to make one's every dream a reality. Even this is possible.'

OSCAR WILDE

Heterosexual sex was a revelation to me. So snug, warm and wet – I was full of admiration for Nature's cleverness. I mastered the basic manoeuvres of intercourse in the missionary position, but the taking of the vagina from behind, known rather sordidly as 'doggie position', soon became a firm favourite. I also learned how important it is in the straight world to sustain sexual activity and not peak before your partner is ready. This I achieved by reciting mathematical tables (not out loud, though). Another useful trick was to sign my name, imagining the penis is a pen. Whether this works with anyone else's name other than my own I couldn't say, but the unpredictable twists and turns of writing 'Julian Peter McDonald Clary' with such a novel instrument certainly had the desired effect. The female orgasm (unless she was acting) was a Dyson to the male carpet sweeper, a whooping cough to our throat clearing. What with nipples and breasts, secretions, G-spots and sundry other erogenous zones to discover and excite, it's a wonder I ever bothered with men again. The female body is peppered with erogenous zones. To me, as a beginner, it was a bit like learning to fly a helicopter; I didn't know where to begin.

Of course, we didn't attempt any preliminary lessons in the scout hut. We waited until we got back to London and the privacy of my room at Hardy Road. The world of boy/girl romance was suddenly revealed to me. That was it, we were lovers. We lay in bed half the day eating boiled eggs and listening to 'Cool For Cats' by Squeeze. If she was woken early by the concert violinist who lived next door, she opened the sash window in my bedroom and shrieked, 'Stop that bleedin' racket!' On Valentine's Day she gave me a card in which she'd written:

> *I can't resist your silky style*
> *The diamonds in your head*
> *And though you are a super star*
> *You bring me tea in bed.*

I shall call her Michelle. We had been flirting with each other for weeks before it all began. I had announced one day that I was contemplating a love affair to see me through the winter. Who did she suggest? 'Me,' she answered firmly. She had big brown eyes, and although she didn't exactly stare at me she would, I noticed, rest her eyes upon me. During rehearsals we had sometimes held eye contact for a little too long. Now we were embarking on something major. At that age you don't analyse things much, but it was hardly practical: I was gay and she had a boyfriend. But she was an alpha female, not to be denied, and I was besotted. For her birthday I gave her some big brass earrings. On one was engraved: 'Will you marry me?' On the other was: 'Why ever not?' I think we both knew we were doomed in the romantic longevity stakes, but we were helpless. We couldn't do without each other.

The arrangement was she slept with me during the week and her boyfriend at weekends. Clothes and toiletries accumulated at my place for weekday convenience, and for four days a week I was her man. Her ritual weekend defection to the 'other' boyfriend became the source of some unhappiness. Consequently I was always a bit tortured on Friday, but all smiles by Tuesday. Eventually I grew accustomed to the arrangement. Secretly I rather admired Michelle's refusal to adhere to social convention, although when a third suitor entered the fray I think we all felt a trifle mucky. We struggled gamely on for a few months, but it wasn't fun any more.

I remember taking a suitcase full of her clothes over to her flat towards the end and emptying them on her front doorstep. There were tears and tantrums. We never quite let go of each other, and even these days, 24 years later, although we see each other from time to time, we do not socialise with each other's husbands or discuss our personal lives. When I look into Michelle's eyes, my heart still races and I imagine a life other than the one I have lived. I have never reprieved my heterosexual life, or dabbled again in that procreative world. I have thought of it – sometimes longed for it – but it has not come to pass. Those sacred, carnal pastures belong to Michelle alone. Once you become a renowned homosexual you subconsciously, if not culturally, feel obliged to keep within those boundaries. And if your sexuality is your career, or at least a defining aspect of it, you do not ask any questions.

I do not cast any doubt on my homosexuality (Lord knows, we've all got better things to do with our time) but in analysing my life for your reading pleasure, my relationship with Michelle must be given its due. It was a happy, if emotionally stirring, interlude in this my gay life thus far.

At the time I didn't dwell on things for too long. I wrote some dreary poems, but soon after our affair petered out I returned to the gay world with an enthusiasm that surprised even me. I got a job as a bar man at Heaven nightclub behind Charing Cross station. Taking a handsome boy home after work wasn't so much a perk, more a part of your job description. My job there came to an end on 'toga night'. As is not uncommon on such themed nights, all the bar staff wore minimal loincloths to help the atmosphere along. A crusty old punter draped in a beer-stained sheet leered at me all evening then asked me, 'Is it yes or no?' Once I understood that the question requiring an answer was whether I was his for the night, I answered in no uncertain terms and he complained to the management. The next night the manager, David Inches, 'let me go'.

My days at Goldsmiths were nearly over, too. I wrote to my parents: 'No one talks about anything but exams and work and what they're going to do afterwards. Whatever will become of me? I change from being worried and depressed about it, seeing myself ending up as a disillusioned teacher or office worker, to being very excited, thinking that now is the time I've been waiting for, and now it all happens.'

After university the plan was to get acting work. We signed on the dole, sent hopeful letters to the National Theatre and the RSC, and got a few dismissive replies. In those days you couldn't get far without an Equity union card. Linda and I got our provisional card by doing Glad and May gigs wherever anyone would take us. Old people's homes provided us with a few of the required contracts, although the old dears weren't terribly taken with us. They watched our nonsense for a few minutes then started playing cards.

On my 21st birthday Linda and I did a Glad and May gig in a pub somewhere in Shepherd's Bush. As it was a special occasion we got a taxi back to Hardy Road from Blackheath Station. I paid for the fare with our wages – a £50 note, and, without noticing, got change for a fiver. Linda wasn't pleased.

After pestering the local paper we got some publicity. 'Cheek and chat are where it's at,' announced the entertainment page of the *Lewisham Gazette*. 'Gaudy, fast-talking housewives Glad and May have found just what they wanted in a nervous pub customer's handbag.' Our big break, or so we thought, was a centre spread in the *Sun* on 17 July 1980. 'Come to the Cabaret!' wrote Roslyn Grose. 'All over Britain song-and-dance is coming up on the menu nearly as often as fish and chips. Glad and May are a pair of housewife superstars who would make Dame Edna Everage gnash her dentures with envy. They're so young and pretty they make other women feel nervous – especially when they nudge each other and ask: "Feel like a rummage?"' Someone recognised me in the newsagents and I was thrilled.

To make the most of this national coverage we put an advert in the *South-East London Chronicle* saying, rather naively, 'Glad and May, Housewives Extraordinaire, will entertain you at your office party'. I only got one call, from an Indian man, who asked what the show entailed.

'Well,' I said, 'we come out dressed as two char ladies talking about our lives.'

'And then?' he asked.

'Well, then we turn into Amanda and Elyot from *Private Lives.*'

'And then?' he said, breathlessly.

'Then we sing a song and do a handbag competition.'

'And then? S-s-sex cabaret?' he whispered hopefully.

I hung up.

I remember a few of our gigs. The Queen's Head, a tiny pub in Steine Street, Brighton. We were introduced by Simon Fanshawe, who said afterwards, 'There are two things going to happen to Julian. Firstly, he's going to become a huge star. Secondly, he's going to be seeing a *lot* more of me!' One out of two isn't bad.

We were also booked for a Saturday night at the famous, if notoriously rough, south London drag pub the Vauxhall Tavern – home for 15 years to Lily Savage. Booked to do half an hour, we only had 20 minutes of material, so I asked my old schoolfriend Nick, now a graduate of the Guildhall School of Music and Drama, to warm up the crowd with a few show tunes. We were all in a state of terror beforehand. Nick sought comfort in a bottle of sherry before he went on. After a couple of numbers the crowd were turning ugly. Nick's microphone was unceremoniously unplugged and Lee Paris, the resident compère, introduced us.

'We've got something a bit unusual for you now, ladies and gentlemen – a double act, one of whom is a real live woman!' The audience growled their disapproval. We raced through the act getting no laughs at all, and in no time were into the hand-bag competition. There weren't many on offer but we grabbed what we could. Linda opened hers first and pulled out a letter. 'Oh, look!' she said, 'her husband's in Pentonville Prison!' We both knew it wasn't wise, but it was too late to do anything but read on – a harrowing, personal letter from an incarcerated husband to his darling wife. Desperately trying to squeeze some comedy out of the letter, we sounded suspiciously like two inex-perienced students making fun of a sad, private communication.

''Ere, Glad, I wouldn't mind being banged up, how about you?'

'Oh no, May! I was sent down once and it left a terrible taste in my mouth!'

That's when the ice cubes started to be thrown. A slow hand-clap started at the back of the pub and swiftly gained momentum. The burly woman who owned the bag stood at the front punch-ing her fist into the palm of her other hand. We hurriedly retreated to the dressing room where we stayed long after closing time in case we were lynched.

Meanwhile, we scoured the back pages of the *Stage* where acting jobs were advertised. There were lots of profit-share companies doing group-devised plays that would tour the outer reaches of Wales, or worthy theatre-in-education productions funded by the GLC. Sometimes we'd get an audition. Linda got lucky first, a contract for a year's work with the Chipping Norton Repertory Company, strangely enough the very place my great-grandmother came from. I went to quite a few auditions but rarely got a re-call. Not only was I extremely uncomfortable and nervous when expected to impress a panel, but my languid mannerisms and breathy voice, let's face it, excluded me from most roles. I didn't really go in for versatility. But eventually my persistence paid off. My first job was with the Covent Garden Community Theatre. Legend has it that just as I started my audition speech a shaft of sunlight broke through the window and gave me an ethereal glow. The panel of jolly left-wing types thought I was some kind of Second Coming and gave me the job on the spot.

The show was called *I Was A Teenage Sausage Dog*, written and directed by Andy Cunningham. I was to play Auntie Vera. It wasn't glamour drag: I wore a rainbow-coloured Afro wig, a woollen minidress and Dr Martens boots. Aimed at children, it was an anti-vivisection romp about Vera's dog Fluffy Wuffles (played by a collie puppy called Georgia Georgio) being pursued by evil scientists who wanted to perform unspeakable experiments on him.

We rehearsed in the Holy Trinity church hall, opposite Holborn tube station. The acting style was loud and cartoon-like and we performed in community centres, adventure playgrounds and the occasional London pub, travelling round in a battered red van. As soon as we were all on board and en route to our first gig of the day, a joint would be rolled and passed around. To begin with I was worried about my promise to my mother, and about fainting again, so I just mimed my inhalations. Soon enough, however, I got the idea and the weeks passed in an amiable, stoned haze. But this was just the start. We also took our show off to various summer hippy fairs, such as the Elephant Fayre in Suffolk. Drugs of every sort were all the rage there, of course, and along with everyone else I took magic mushrooms and LSD, which made the corn in the fields turn a heavenly yellow and the sky blood-red. 'Ooh! Aaah!' we all said. I also remember joining the queue outside a caravan. 'Cocaine £1 a line' read the advert, written in felt-tip on a torn piece of cardboard. Taking drugs at that time among those people was commonplace. I remember going to see an acupuncturist and being asked if I'd had any drugs in the last week, and proudly giving a very extensive response: 'Marijuana, speed, cocaine, mushrooms, Valium and temazepam.' It didn't occur to me that if I'd cut out all the substances, I'd have had no need of the treatment for exhaustion in the first place.

I got my comeuppance soon enough, of course. At a party in a big hippy commune house in Muswell Hill, I helped myself to a rather generous dessertspoonful of magic mushrooms preserved in honey. About an hour later everyone was sitting in a circle massaging each other's feet, while I was wandering about the garden having a bad trip. For some reason there was a mattress propped against a washing line. As I rested against it, panicking at the realisation of what I'd inflicted on myself, it crashed to the ground.

After this violent jolt my spirit hovered above my body and couldn't get back in. I went back into the house where they were all in cloud cuckoo land. In my hallucinating state everyone I saw was dead or dying. I saw corpses hanging from ropes, bodies putrefying or being incinerated – ghastly images that I couldn't, even today, say were not real. Finally I was in such a state of terror that I returned to the garden and lay in the foetal position praying to God for salvation. He came up trumps, as He usually does, and I managed to re-enter my body.

Sometimes, just as I'm falling asleep, a familiar wave of fear washes over me and I sit up gasping for air. My soul, having tasted freedom all those years ago in Muswell Hill, is trying to sneak off again. I suspect that if it successfully escapes, I shall die. Keeping my spirit in place until I'm ready to go isn't easy. The caged bird's desire to fly away is a persistent one and I must be vigilant.

I stayed on at the Covent Garden Community Theatre for the next two productions: *Winter Draws On!*, a sketch show in which I played, among others, a paedophile Santa Claus and a faith healer in a kaftan called Gillian Pie-Face, and *Aaaaargh! No, it's 'orrible!* – another children's show, this time about the evils of germ warfare. Jane Janovic and I played Harold and Hiram, two chaps battling over the ownership of an island with an evil countess and her sidekick Cyril Vain, played by Penelope Taylor and Nick Mercer. For any politically aware children, this had deft references to the Falklands War, which was raging at the time. Unfortunately Andy Cunningham, author and director, never got around to writing or indeed rehearsing the ending of *Aaaaargh!*. It just finished rather abruptly with a couple of green smoke bombs, which if the wind was in the wrong direction sent the more asthmatic kids off to the nearest Casualty.

In the rougher inner-city adventure playgrounds, the children were more interested in pinching the props and chucking things at us than sitting quietly watching the entertainment. I still shudder when I drive down the Wandsworth Road and remember 'the riot' we were at the centre of in a nearby park. Who knows why they went on the turn so violently, but as soon as we started the show we were showered with empty cans and ripe insults. And missiles and abuse weren't enough for these little blighters. We had to abandon the show when they charged at us like wildebeest. We chucked the set and props into the van as best we could, sticks and bricks raining down on us, and screeched our way out of there still in costume, thespian refugees fleeing from hostile infant territory. Emergency joints had to be rolled to calm us all down.

Getting a dog wasn't a particularly sensible thing to do at this point in my life, and I made sure I didn't tell my parents about it until after the event. But once I'd had the thought, it became an imperative need and I had felt myself being led, helplessly, towards my unknown companion.

I got Fanny (before we knew she was a Wonder Dog) from the South London Dog Rescue Society. This wasn't a dog's home in the Battersea sense, but an organisation with a list of dogs in need of a home. When I telephoned them, there were only two on the list, both residing in a disreputable pet shop in Eltham. The first dog was grey and sad and lanky. Next to him, housed in a rabbit hutch, was Fanny. She was the last of a litter of mongrels, now four months old, and the shop owner doubted anyone would ever want her. She saw me and threw herself at the wire mesh, desperate, ecstatic. Once I had opened the door there was no going back. What was I doing?

I shook my head with disapproval as I carried Fanny home. I didn't imagine she had it in her to make my fortune and teach me the art of unconditional love. If I'd walked away, overwhelmed with the unfeasibility of practical day-to-day living with a dog in tow, then my life would have been very different, I'm sure. Maybe, as my mother imagined for me, I'd have whiled away the years in some small provincial arts centre. I might have settled down with a charity worker, grown imaginative vegetables in my modest country garden and eventually emigrated to Nova Scotia. In fact, I've made it sound so attractive I rather wish things had turned out that way. Is it too late? Who can say? But getting Fanny was a life-changing moment. I didn't realise at the time, of course. One rarely does.

Lynda the landlady had decided to go around the world for a year and left me and Cathy to look after her cat, Samson, and the flat. Once I got home with Fanny, I looked at her and accepted the inevitable with an amused shrug. It would all work out. I'd see to it she had a nice life.

Fanny was overexcited for several days. She wasn't house-trained and whizzed round in circles in the kitchen. Floor, chair, table, window, bean bag and floor again. Simultaneously she would gently urinate, thus creating a Catherine wheel of dog wee. She was extremely anxious at all times, and would cower at a casually raised hand, and run for cover at the jingle of keys. She would only sleep under the duvet with me, head on pillow, curved back pressed against my stomach. This didn't change for most of her life. She would grudgingly sleep at my feet on top of the duvet if there was a gentleman caller involved, but once the hanky panky had run its course she'd slide slowly up towards me. She seemed to be of the belief that if she moved slowly enough, no one would notice. If instructed to go to her basket, she would go, lie down and then instantly begin a painfully slow mime of a dog getting up. Once upright she'd begin to slowly glide in my direction, eyes half closed, as if battling towards me through a wind tunnel.

Several are they who've reached across for a morning encore only to encounter a hairy six-nippled stomach and a whiff of mongrel. She was very discerning about all the visitors. Positively contemptuous of most, she tolerated some and reserved a deferential coyness with those who were special. She always knew. She'd see them leave, the ones she liked, then watch the door or give me a knowing look. With others she'd refuse even to open her eyes until they'd left. Then I'd get the 'Shame on you!' treatment. (In the fullness of time she was able to assess an audience with the same casual ease. I swear she distinctly rolled her eyes when we played Bangor University, then gave me a look that said, 'You're wasting your time, but carry on if you want to.' I remember that gig. The landlady had locked me out of the B&B because it was gone eleven at night when I got back. I explained that I'd been working and hadn't gone on stage till ten o'clock. She muttered in Welsh as she took the safety chain off the front door and allowed me to scurry upstairs to my dreary room. She was still talking about me in dark unintelligible tones the next morning at breakfast. The other Welsh people looked at me as if I'd been out all night whoring.)

When she was about seven months old, Fanny came on heat. Flushed with sexual desire, she approached dogs backwards in the park. Word got round that there was an easy young lass begging for it in Greenwich Park and the dogs came from miles around. I picked her up and hurried home, salivating horny hounds yelping and jumping at my elbows. Back at Hardy Road I barricaded the cat-flap as smaller canines attempted entry. They stayed out there all night, howling and leaving snail-trails of ardour on the pavement. The next day we retreated to Swindon where a sensible walled garden kept them at bay. The next morning my father got up early for work. Hearing him shuffle downstairs in his slippers to make the tea, Fanny sniffed at my door to go and greet him. He let her out for an early morning wee and took my mother's cuppa upstairs. When I got up later and asked where the dog was, he couldn't remember her coming back in...

We called her for a few minutes before she came wriggling through a previously unnoticed gap, covered in mud and in a state of some excitement. In the distance a hefty black Labrador went on his way, panting. 'Maybe it was just a game of rough and tumble,' said my father hopefully. 'I think not,' said my mother. 'I know that look in the eye.'

As an expectant father I was devoted, spending my dole

money on prime cuts of meat and rubbing Fanny's back. She got fatter and fatter, waddling about the place wheezing, like an inflatable barrel. The vet had a feel round, said she was too young to be a mother really, but it was too late now and as far as he could tell there were two puppies in there and it wouldn't be long.

The next day she only managed a few dozen yards of her walk before turning back for home, looking worried. I woke up in the night to hear Fanny panting noisily. She was squatting just off the floor in the large cardboard box I'd got for her. She was much calmer than I was. Cathy the nurse woke up and took over, doing her profession proud. After a crescendo of panting and quivering haunches and a human-like scream, the first puppy shot out, a large, stumpy, shiny black baguette. Fanny rolled it round with her muzzle, breaking the birth sack and licking the puppy's chest to make it breathe. When that was done she resumed the position and started panting again. Ten minutes later, after another heart-rending scream, the other puppy was born. We watched as she tried to start it breathing, but as it seemed to be taking a while Cathy took over and Fanny looked on. She parted the sack with a perfectly manicured nail and gently rubbed the chest. Eventually it gave a gasp and Fanny took over again.

Exhausted and exhilarated, Cathy and I sat back and reached for a post-natal Benson and Hedges. Fanny began panting once more and we watched to see if it was the afterbirth, but it was a third puppy, soon followed by a fourth. They were all quite burly-looking. All black, although one had a white paw and another a mongrel-like 'V' of white on its chest. Three girls and a boy. We named them Molly, Margaret, Harriet and Wesley.

The afterbirth, when it finally came, was Fanny's reward and she wolfed it down the second it appeared. We averted our eyes and let nature take its course.

After we'd cleaned up the box and settled the child-bride and her embarrassment down on a clean towel, Fanny looked very pleased with herself. She was quite matronly with them, turning them, nudging them, checking and counting them like a baker checking a row of freshly baked scones.

I got a taxi home rather late the next night from the Ship and Whale, where I'd been wetting the puppies' heads, as it were. The driver was rather dishy in a rough South London sort of way, driving with his legs spread impressively wide. I boldly asked him if he'd like to come in for a cup of tea.

'I'm not being funny, mate,' he said, 'but you sound like you're gay.'

'So?'

'So when you say, "Come in for a cup of tea", I think you mean something else.'

'So are you coming in or not?'

Once inside he said, 'Forget about the tea. Where's the bedroom?' I led the way, pulling him by his already unbuckled trouser belt. Afterwards, as he lay naked on my bed smoking an Embassy, I lifted the puppies out of their box and laid them on his tattooed chest.

With four hungry muzzles to feed, Fanny's appetite took on new dimensions. Within a few days the pups' nuzzling became more demanding. Seeing the rate at which the goodness was being sucked out of her, I felt the need to feed the poor girl constantly.

I lived off baked potatoes while the nursing mother feasted on rump and sirloin.

To begin with, the four puppies lay there blindly waving paws about and gently attaching themselves to an available nipple when the opportunity arose. After two or three days this process became more enthusiastic and urgent. By the time they were two weeks old, they head-butted their mother into submission, gorging on her breasts voraciously.

They grew and grew, big wide heads, manic bleary puppy eyes with psycho stares. At three weeks they were a danger to the public. I noticed that Fanny started to avoid them. The devil's spawn were up and marching about by now, as muscular and menacing as a Lewisham posse of teenage ne'er-do-wells. They might bite, they might abuse, they might defecate. Who could predict?

We barricaded them in the bedroom in the interests of domesticity, but every couple of hours Fanny would steel herself and enter the arena. By this time she didn't need to lie down to feed them, far from it. She would stand, back arched like a scared cat, and the four hungry delinquents attacked. Sometimes she could hardly get through the door. I used to go in with her and talk her through it, but sometimes I couldn't bear to watch. Her eyes would quiver and half close with the pain, her rubbery dog lips distort and spasm. These huge, demented feeding machines were eating Fanny alive.

I tried to relieve their demands on Fanny by feeding them powdered puppy milk and solid food as soon as they were old enough. Needless to say, this had a dramatic effect on their faeces.

Until then (as is traditional in the dog world, apparently), Fanny had cleared up after them. With a clean pad of old newspapers and a towel changed twice a day, the new family was no trouble. We all slept in the same room. Fanny would leave our marital bed every few hours for the ordeal of feeding the monsters, and apart from the odd snuffle and squeak there was nothing to worry about. Put the little darlings on tinned puppy food, however, and you're suddenly in the black hole of Calcutta. My room became a sewer. I retched at the sight and scent of them.

It was an awful thing to admit but we both loathed the puppies.

As they grew, they became more thuggish. Wesley, the boy, was the worst. I first saw him slap his mother when he was four weeks old. I subsequently observed bullying, aggressive confrontations, numerable incidents of juvenile sociopathy and even attempted sexual assault. He was a bad 'un and there were no two ways about it. Harriet, on the other hand, had a lovely manner about her, at least during the 20 minutes or so that her appetite was sated. Cheery and adventurous, for the most part. Molly and Margaret I don't remember much about. It was nice of them to turn up. It was amazing how cool I felt towards them and how much I regretted their arrival.

My mind wandered and I started to think about finding homes for the little darlings. After all, they couldn't stay at home with Fanny and me for ever. They had their own lives to lead. There was a big, exciting world out there, and the sooner they went off to explore it, the better. It was a bit like having unsavoury relatives to stay: we'd be polite and ensure they had enough to eat and somewhere to sleep, but whenever they were ready for the off, just let us know...

I put the word out and stuck a card on the noticeboard at Tesco's at Westcombe Park. A charming family responded to the ad, came for a viewing and earmarked Harriet. I said she'd cost £5. The set designer from the Covent Garden Community Centre came and chose Molly. The ticket collector at Westcombe Park said his friend at the next station down the line, Maze Hill, wanted a male puppy, so he was promised Wesley. As for Margaret, I can't remember. Anyway, I knew they all had good homes waiting for them.

At four weeks the puppies couldn't be contained in my bedroom any longer. I called my parents and probably exaggerated the story a bit. I remember my father came to pick us up within hours, bless him, appearing on my doorstep with a worried expression, half-expecting canine Triffids to be entwined around my every limb.

In Swindon we made the garage into the nursery, or Detention Centre, as it came to be known. They were allowed into the garden each afternoon for several hours' association. By now they were a formidable pack. Fanny looked on with distaste as they ripped up the lawn, gnawed at shrubs and showed scant regard for the dignity of the rotary washing line.

Wesley once attacked my 18-month-old niece, Sandy, who was wandering about innocently. He ripped her pink frilly dress and made her cry.

I decided they had to go. Some would say six weeks is too early, but not for Fanny and me.

Off they all went one afternoon within a couple of hours. Fanny didn't so much as glance after them. She gave me look of relief, as if a bad smell attributed to her had finally dissipated and normal service could be resumed. We never heard a word about any of them again. Eventually I stopped scanning the local paper, fearful that Wesley or his sisters had eaten a baby, attacked a pensioner or ripped the face off a postman.

Although still less than a year old, Fanny had a worldly wise air about her now. She hadn't informed me yet, but she had set her sights on a showbiz life.

Unemployed again, I went along to see Andy Cunningham do his ventriloquist act, 'Magritte, the Mind-reading Rat', at a vegetarian restaurant in Highgate called the Earth Exchange. They had cabaret there every Monday night. There was no stage. You just stood in the fireplace and did your turn. You only got paid about £5, but a dinner of brown rice and lentils was yours for the asking. Andy suggested I revive Gillian Pie-Face from the *Winter Draws On!* show. He had a word with Kim, who ran the night, and the next week I did the 'try-out' spot. Ms Pie-Face, as the name suggests, wasn't a serious attempt at female impersonation. She wore a black kaftan, plimsolls, a string of wooden beads and a messy blonde wig. Gillian was an agony aunt, here, she explained, 'to comfort the sick of spirit, the broken-hearted and the world weary.' I had written most of it with a talented young writer called Chris Stagg.

Stave off that nervous breakdown,
Wipe away that tear,
Shun that emotional crisis
Gillian Pie-Face is here!

I've leapt off the page to deal with my public on a one-to-one basis, to get to grips with your problems as no agony aunt has done before, to bathe your wounds with my very own sponge of sympathy... and to plug my new book, *Look Before You Leap*, Methuen Press, £7.50 hardback only. Now, before I start the serious business of the evening, namely solving the many and varied little upsets many of you may be harbouring, I'd like to, if I may, read a specimen from my book, *The Milk of Human Kindness*, Faber and Faber Press, £11.99, hardback only. [Opens book.] Ah, yes, here we are... it's from Head-in-the-Oven, of Thornton Heath.

Dear Gillian,

I am beside myself. Six months ago my wife and six children were killed in a plane crash. I cannot tell you how guilty I feel as it was my first time piloting a plane. How we were all looking forward to it, Margery, I and the little ones. I have even turned to God in my despair and often I ask him: 'Why oh why, God, was there only the one parachute? Will I ever overcome my grief?

Head-in-the-Oven, of Thornton Heath.

And my advice to him was:

> Dear Head-in-the-Oven,
> Some people need something to be depressed about, and go out of their way to find it. Try to get out more and don't wait for people to come to you. They won't. Not if they've got any sense.

The conclusion of the act was the laying-on of hands. 'An uncanny gift I've only recently discovered in my possession.' After a few moments attempting to cure a man in the audience, she said, 'It's no good. I'm going to have to plunge you into darkness.' The kaftan was then thrown over the seated punter, his head at groin level. The effect was of the hapless punter performing oral sex on me behind a curtain. 'Ah, that's better!' said Gillian. 'I can feel the goodness flowing from my tips...'

I was familiar with the material and it didn't go too badly. Kim booked me for the next week and told me of other possible gigs, at the Crown and Castle in Dalston, the Hemingford Arms in Islington and the Pindar of Wakefield in Kings Cross. The alternative cabaret circuit was in its infancy, mostly small rooms above pubs. Three or four acts and a compère performed in front of their friends and a few supply-teacher types, then split the proceedings among themselves. I phoned round and got a few more try-out spots.

Meanwhile, I had some modelling shots done for an agency, and continued to apply unsuccessfully for acting jobs.

The Farndale Avenue Housing Estate Townswomen's Guild's Amateur Dramatic Society was in reality a company called Entertainment Machine run by a worried-looking man called David McGillivray. Their particular niche was the excruciating but hilarious world of amateur dramatics, where sets fell down, incompetent actors forgot their lines and the raffle was more important than the plot. Janet Sate, an actress I'd worked and bonded with at Covent Garden, was on tour in 1982 with their French farce, *Chase Me Up Farndale Avenue, S'il Vous Plaît!* The actress playing Mrs Reece was so dire I was smuggled in to rehearse in secret for a couple of days before she was given the boot and I took over.

Mrs Phoebe Reece was the chairperson of the dramatic society and took her role very seriously, interrupting the play to recall past productions: 'More senior members amongst you will recall with pleasure I expect such extravaganzas as *A Woman's Mission, Cave Girls, It's Miss Wimbush!* and, of course, our big success, *Brown Owl Pulls It Off.*' She also announced, 'After a very heated committee meeting, we've decided to mount our first bisexual production. It's high time we gave one or two of our younger actresses the chance to play with a male member. And I'm certainly looking forward to trying my hand at it as well.'

There were a lot of lines to learn and I was far from ready on my first night at the Prince Regent Theatre on the Isle of Wight. Instead of saying, 'That was a narrow squeak,' I came up with, 'That was a short quack.' I also had a large explanatory speech to reel off in act two which was vital to the plot. My cue came from David, who was playing the part of Gordon. The time came and he said, 'But what shall we do when we get to the bistro and Mr Barratt isn't there?'

'That's your problem,' I said, and promptly left the stage.

Despite all this, the theatre manager Brian McDermot was full of praise: 'Come to the bar and be lionised!' he said after the show. Over drinks I told him about my Gillian Pie-Face act and he booked me. I accepted his offer to do a full evening's entertainment despite the fact I still only had 20 minutes' worth of material. I'd worry about that nearer the time.

David McGillivray, our author and director, seemed to thrive on drama. The tour took us all over the country. The day after my first night on the Isle of Wight we were booked in Irvine in Scotland. Our means of transport – a sad little van for set and actors – broke down in Portsmouth and the AA and British Rail had to pull out all the stops to deliver us in the nick of time. Our performance in Harlech had no business taking place either, when following some hold-up on the Severn Bridge we didn't arrive there until 7.45 p.m. Wild-eyed and breathless, David explained to the audience that there would be a delay until 9 p.m. if they could possibly bear with us. This being Wales, where there was nothing else to do, they waited. Travel-weary and hungry, we began hauling the set into the theatre past bemused punters. Fortunately I had one of my opportune nosebleeds and could only watch and encourage.

Our accommodation was always cheap and cheerful: nylon sheets and candlewick bedspreads. After a show in Cumbernauld, we sat in the lounge admiring the knick-knacks and making small talk with the landlord. When I offered him a cigarette, he said, 'No thanks, I'm a pipe.' Before we retired to our rooms, he asked if we'd like a cooked breakfast in the morning. 'No thanks,' I said, 'I'm a corn flake.'

When the tour finished, I returned to the Isle of Wight to do the one-man show as promised. I cobbled together Gillian, May and Mrs Reece and hoped for the best. It was a disaster, the bemused punters shuffling out in silence after 40 sweaty minutes.

I returned home, back to the dole, the occasional gig at the Earth Exchange my only prospect.

But if work was thin on the ground, men certainly weren't. They were coming thick and fast.

SIX

I met a boy called Mark one evening on the train home from Charing Cross. He lived just down the road. He had a rugby player's face and pale, freckled skin. I didn't fancy him, but he had other attractions. He knew how to enjoy life, and we became sisters, cruising companions and friends. We seemed to go out most nights, but as he was a student and I was on the dole, money was tight.

Here's how it worked. We'd meet about 9 p.m. at the bus stop on Blackheath, each with a £5 note and no more. The bus stop was just before some traffic lights, and Mark would tap on the passenger window of a waiting car and ask the single male occupant if he was driving into town and could we cadge a lift? Once in town we'd skim through the Soho bars, have a drink if anyone offered to buy us one… 'And this is my friend Julian, he'd like a pint of Grolsch too,' kind of business. We'd enter Heaven nightclub, our fiver still intact, either with a free entrance voucher from one of the trashy gay mags or because Mark had somehow wangled us onto the guest list. Inside there'd be more shameless cruising for beverages.

As the evening wore on we might be reduced to collecting the dregs of other revellers' discarded drinks. That's the horrible truth, pain me though it does to reveal it. I think I even stole the odd glass from those frisky enough to take to the dance floor and leave their refreshments unattended. Cheap, I know, and I'm full of retrospective horror and can only apologise. Then it was Pick-up, especially if he had a car, and one could say goodnight to one's sister and leave, flourishing the fiver in triumph for good measure.

Far-from-tantric sex inevitably followed. The earth may not have moved very far, but it would round an evening off nicely. Occasionally there would be an encore. A half-hearted attempt at 'going out' even, but it would always end in stony silences or unanswered calls.

I was obsessed for a while with a man I'd slept with called Henry. He was posh and whisked me back to his Cadogan Square flat in Chelsea to be ravished. The flat was full of antique furniture, but the sheets were dirty – there was a grey mark on the antique linen pillow where he lay his beautiful head. But Henry wasn't interested in an encore and didn't answer my calls. Not good with rejection, even then, I wrote the obligatory poem.

Like the cock on a windless day
Grimly pointing out yesterday's weather,

I am old news.
A motherless goose,
Hatched and blinking by chance at you
Yet having no instinct to beg,
I falter, fret but cannot follow.

Mark chivvied me out of my wistful state by taking me out again. 'Let's go and look for Henry!' he'd say. We never found him, but I was pleasantly distracted by fresh faces along the way. 'Looking for Henry' became our coded phrase for going out on the tiles.

In those pre-AIDS days using a condom was regarded as a kind of weird hygiene-related fetish. The lottery had started but we didn't know. Rumours circulated about a deadly virus you might get if you slept with an American. Bars would fall silent if a Yankee accent was heard. Eyes would roll, backs would turn.

I specialised in Spanish, Italian, Greek and French gentlemen callers. They seemed exotic and lusty, and if there wasn't much joy to be had from conversation, so much the better. Sometimes I'd get exasperated, though, if I said something funny and wasn't rewarded with a laugh. My particular brand of spontaneous comic quip has never stood up well to any form of deconstruction. Any requests to explain my remarks or translate into a beginner's vocabulary got very short shrift.

'You've simply no idea how witty I've just been!' I'd snap.

'Que?'

It was a bit like doing a gig in Chatham.

On Monday nights I usually went to Bangs on the Tottenham

Court Road. It was there I met Siro, an Italian passing through London on his round-the-world adventure. His English wasn't great but he could make himself understood. He wanted sex every 15 minutes, and by Wednesday I could take no more and made my excuses. Before I fell into an exhausted sleep, I wrote down one of his many monologues:

'Portugal, America, Paris, London – I search for love, for happiness, I don't know what. I like to make people happy. In the gay sauna in Boston I let 30 men fuck me. The 31st he call me a slut. I am not a slut. I like to fuck, so I do. I think I give a lot of pleasure. I am very sexual person. You just touch my arm and my prick is jumping bigger. Always it is this. Sometimes I just touch my arm with myself and it is doing it. So. It is the way I am. It is not wrong. Sex is like water. I am thirsty, I drink. Some people drink three or four drinks, some seven or eight. It doesn't matter. I want sex, I have sex. Always I am ready. It is not love, I know this. Sex without love is just water. Sometimes you have water with the gas. This is sex with love. So.'

That's as may be, I thought as I drifted off. But – moral judgements aside – didn't the marathon in the Boston sauna make it difficult to walk the next day and therefore hinder rather than help the 'search' for love?

Another cruising sister was Stephen. Linda and I met him when we took to frequenting the Dover Castle. Gone now, but then a drag pub on Deptford Broadway. Stephen was from Belfast. Twenty-one, black hair and startling blue eyes, full, wanton lips and an arrogant jaw. If you're thinking I put it about a bit, then Stephen made me look like Mother Teresa. Always ready with an anecdote about that day's conquests. 'He was covered in tattoos, so he was, and he came all over the window.' He enjoyed making several dates for the same evening at various bars in Soho so he could decide later which one to grace with his company. He was on the lookout for sex day and night. In the days when train carriages were divided into small eight-person compartments, the journey from New Cross to London Bridge, a good seven minutes, was particularly fruitful. But so were public lavatories, parks or almost anywhere. Stephen radiated charm and sex appeal, and the look was spruced-up barrow boy with a few too many buttons carelessly left undone. 'After dark London belongs to the homos,' he would say.

He always referred to his sex life in terms of 'portions'. 'I've had three portions today already so I won't be picking anyone up tonight,' he'd tell me when we were going out. I had only to say 'Three?' enquiringly if I felt like hearing more. 'I had a portion with John this morning before he went to work, I had my seconds in Charing Cross public conveniences and then I met a man from Glasgow in the Brief Encounter and we went to a derelict building site for sex. That's three portions I've had.'

Stephen divided all of his life up in that way, as if it were so much quiche. There is nothing wrong with this method – you can apply it to anything. At the end of an evening out, Stephen could give you a résumé of what he'd eaten, how many drinks he'd bought, how many were bought for him, how many men talked to him, looked at him, asked him home, gave him their phone numbers. 'I could have gone home with six or seven,' he'd say in a triumphant Belfast twang.

He had a live-in boyfriend called John for a while, but didn't let that stop him. He'd crush up sleeping pills and dissolve them in John's tea, then wait 20 minutes until he'd nodded off before going out. He was suspicious of John, too, and with good reason. He told me he followed him one afternoon. John had gone to a public loo that was a notorious cottage. Stephen waited five minutes then went in. He stood on the toilet seat and peered over the wall into the adjoining cubicle and caught John having an intimate moment, not to say mouthful, with a stranger. 'Coo-ee!' said Stephen.

The Dover Castle featured acts such as the Trolettes, High Society, the Playgirls and a trio called LSD, who were Lily Savage, Sandra, and Doris aka David Dale. Their finale was an appearance as Andy Pandy, Teddy and Looby Lou. Our favourite was Phil Star, a polished and wonderfully vulgar performer, expert at bitching other acts. 'Lily Savage was waiting at a bus stop the other day. She got raped three times and still she never lost her place in the queue.'

When it closed there we could, if we wished, move on to the Ship and Whale in Rotherhithe. Open till 1.30 a.m. and a disco thrown in. Much the same crowd as the Dover Castle, but drunker.

It was here I met Andrew, a car mechanic from Upminster. He had thinning hair and a rather flat face and was a victim of some unfortunate condition that caused his teeth to be black for a good quarter of an inch round the gum region. He wore a very Essex big knitted jacket with frightful leather panels, and cheap underwear from a supermarket. He was very rough and told lies all the time. You always knew when he was lying because his eyelids went into a kind of involuntary flutter and his irises disappeared upwards. An inconvenient physical tick, one might think, and enough to render lying pointless. Seemingly not, in Andrew's case. I enjoyed inducing the lies. I'd corner him about some contradictory information, some fading love-bite not fully concealed beneath the collar of a garish shirt from Upminster market, say, and stand back. He'd sometimes get through a sentence before the fluttering began, sometimes not. When the whopper had been unconvincingly told, he'd fix me with an insolent stare. If I could be bothered, I'd ask a supplementary question and the whole process would begin again.

But I liked him. There was a common gangsterish charm to him. His brother was in prison for GBH, which rather added to it. He would turn up unannounced late at night, park some dodgy motor outside my flat and stagger in drunk, wanting sex and a can of lager. He'd say 'screw' rather than 'fuck' too, which endeared him to me. We 'saw' each other for a while, as they say. We didn't exactly 'go out'. I'm sure you know the difference.

It all ended in tears, I recall, one Sunday night at Benjy's nightclub on the Mile End Road. There was a 'scene'. A few weeks before Andrew had asked for a photograph of me and I'd given him one of my new modelling shots. Anyway, that evening he had a friend with him. I was introduced to the chubby smiling dark man, who nodded a lot in a significant way and looked meaningfully at Andrew. I didn't know what was going on. Later, just before the club closed, Andrew ushered me over to one of the intimate curved couches. A fresh pint of lager for us both.

'What do you think of Sasha?'

'What do you mean?'

'He wants to sleep with you. Will you do it for me? You know I love you. Go home with him and I'll come round later. Or if you'd rather I'll come with you and wait. Do it. I really love you...'

What upset me was the casual nature of the request. So I picked up my pint and poured it over Andrew's head. He didn't dodge out of the way, and the lager, poured with enthusiasm, fanned outwards at 90 degrees, drenching innocent homosexuals, who arched their backs and squealed with indignation. He looked as if he might kill me. I was asked to leave.

The fact that I did not contract the HIV virus during these years is entirely down to luck. I was young and gay and having sex with lots of different men, but I stopped having anal sex. This wasn't a preventative measure on my part, but because I had an embarrassing problem that wouldn't go away. A nasty business: anal warts. It's pointless speculating as to who gave them to me (this is a memoir, not a phone book), but one penis I remember in particular may be the culprit. I met a skinhead type at Heaven who took me back to his south London council flat. He gave me a tab of acid and loosened his braces. We had sex for hours on his bed beneath an open window. I remember watching the night sky lighten, the clouds drift past, dusk and then night again. I thought the trip would never end but I seemed unable to move from the bed. At one point I became enthralled with his penis and examined it closely. Tucked away under the folds of his foreskin were several small, white, bogey-sized lumps. The clouds that floated by the window were now in the room with us, attached.

A month or so later a personal itching problem forced me to get a mirror, spread my bum cheeks and see what on earth the problem was. There were the small fleshy lumps again.

A trip to the STD clinic named and shamed me as the carrier of anal warts. I was mortified, and wrote a poem.

> *This gay life that I lead is now due for inspection,*
> *I haven't gained a lot except venereal infection.*
> *If I have lots of one-night stands and take them lying down,*
> *I must expect a little keepsake, there's so much of it around.*

A weekly treatment of 'freezing' the little bastards ensued, but they seemed to flourish – fertilised, if anything, by their ordeal, and ever increasing. After a while I learned to live with my dark discomfort and re-entered the sexual arena, sternly brushing away any gentleman caller's hand or other body part that sought to investigate my nether regions.

Thus during those dangerous years my sexual activities did not, at least, put me into the high-risk category. That's the only reason I'm still here, I suspect. Anal warts. God bless 'em. They are easy enough to hide, and no one knew. By 1985, however, they had got out of hand, described by one doctor as 'like a bunch of grapes'. I felt like a hybrid baboon. He even took a photograph of them as such 'beauties' were rarely seen these days. I'm probably due considerable backdated royalties by now from some illustrated medical journal or other. He referred me to a specialist and a few weeks later I went secretly to hospital for a few days. The trouble-some blighters were surgically removed, never to return.

I'd been on the waiting list for a council flat since I arrived at Goldsmiths, and in 1983 I was offered a 'hard to let' flat on the Brook Estate in Kidbrooke. Lynda the landlady had returned to Hardy Road, pregnant if you please, so it seemed a good idea to move on. Twenty-seven Ridgebrook Road was my first home of my own. It was a one-room flat with a kitchen and separate toilet. There was no bathroom, but if you lifted up the kitchen counter there was a cunningly concealed bath. I could soak in the bath and keep an eye on my boiled egg at the same time. The only real problem was that there was nowhere to keep your towel. Bottles of shampoo and hair conditioner stood side by side on the windowsill with washing-up liquid and cooking oil. I sanded the floor and my mother bought me a sofa bed. It was rather cosy. I was on the first floor and I trained Fanny to take herself down to the grass verge when she needed a wee.

Being 'hard to let', the flats housed an odd assortment of people who clearly suffered from a number of social problems. The sad old boy next door invited me in one day to admire his new wastepaper bin. 'It's for me little bits of refuge,' he explained. Next door to him was a dirty girl with a cleft palate. One weekend she asked me to feed her cat for her and left me the key. It was unspeakably filthy and smelly inside, and I picked up the cat's bowl to reveal a veritable mound of maggots wriggling on the floor.

Directly below me was a big-boned girl called 'Lesley' who had just come out of prison for stabbing her father. She told me she slept with a knife under her pillow. She knocked on my door one day and asked me to turn my radio down: 'It's getting on my nerves,' she said menacingly, her tone suggesting that perhaps her father had bothered her in a similar fashion. Of course, I never turned it on again. She was quite mad. I heard her shouting one evening, having a furious row. Then her front door opened and slammed shut again. I looked nervously down the stairs and there was a battered yucca plant outside her door, covered in cigarette burns. She didn't even get on with plants.

It was 1983. I never budgeted my unemployment benefit very wisely. When it arrived I went to the supermarket and bought whatever I fancied. When money was running out I ate a lot of baked potatoes. I signed on every other Wednesday at Greenwich unemployment office. My life was full of expectation. My nightly outings to Soho's pubs and clubs were all-important. Surviving on limited resources was a triumph of ingenuity which carried its own sense of satisfaction. Stephen and I managed somehow to save and borrow enough money to go on a week's holiday to Sitges, a gay seaside resort in Spain. We miscounted our pesetas when we arrived, imagining for three days that we were rich. We ate in the most expensive restaurants, guzzled champagne and purchased other stimulants as the fancy took us. On the fourth day, in a rare sober moment, we re-counted our funds and realised our error. There were so many noughts in the Spanish currency that we had mistaken our modest few thousand pesetas for millions. We were left with about £2 each for the remaining four days.

We laughed at our predicament but soon reality kicked in. During the day we went to the gay beach and Stephen tried valiantly to make a new best friend who might lend us some money, but he must have looked suspicious and desperate because, in our hour of need, no one wanted to be our chums. We were constantly hungry. We lived on bread, crisps and water. One afternoon I went for a swim. As I looked back at the crowded beach, I saw Stephen reach into my bag and steal the last of my bread. He tore at it like a hungry hyena, looking warily round as if his food might be grabbed off him by a hungry pack member. I swam back to shore and raced up the beach but it was too late, the bread had all been eaten. Stephen laughed triumphantly, picking crumbs off his towel and eating those too. By the time we got to the airport we were not only hungry but dehydrated. My last memory of that holiday was of us circling the canteen, pouncing on any discarded drink cans. We shook them expectantly. If there were any dregs in there, we threw our heads back and downed the contents. Stephen swallowed two cigarette ends. Karma for eating my bread, I told him.

I applied for a position with Help the Aged, but it was only a half-hearted attempt at getting a proper job. I was far too louche and languid to imagine myself working in any proper sense of the word. At the end of the interview they asked if I'd be prepared to cut my hair, as long hair didn't go down too well with the old folk. I shook my head sadly. Anything but that, unfortunately.

I was always on the lookout for some means of support that didn't involve proper nine-to-five work. Singing telegrams proved to be the solution. The Songbird Agency was run from the front room of a terraced house in Maida Vale by Kara Noble and Sue Holsten. I did some sort of audition and was set to work at once. My first assignment was to tour department stores throughout the country dressed in a top-hat and tails, present a red rose to the top Elizabeth Arden sales women of the year, and read them an encouraging poem in recognition of their achievement. I remember the last two lines of the poem were:

> *Keep on working, keep on graftin'*
> *And best of luck from Elizabeth Arden.*

It was quick, camp and painless, and I enjoyed the work. I travelled round by train, doing two stores a day and staying in cheap hotels. Once, when I'd completed my task in Edinburgh, I was walking down the Royal Mile and an attractive man passed me, turned and smiled, and went into a front door, leaving it slightly ajar. I followed. It seemed rude not to. Up the stone steps and through another open door into his flat. He smiled at me from the other side of the living room, where he was kicking off his shoes and unbuttoning his shirt at the same time. I did as he did. Not a word was spoken. Twenty minutes later I emerged and resumed my walk, laughing at the outrageousness of this spontaneous sexual encounter. I didn't think of myself as a tart – but I wouldn't argue with anyone who did.

Singing telegrams were all the rage at that time and I did lots of them. Tarzan was very popular, so I bought a leopardskin dress from Oxfam and cut it up to make a loincloth. I was also available as a Drag-o-gram (Gillian Pie-Face), Cupid (gold outfit, bow and arrow, popular for Valentine's Day), the Human Christmas Tree (green leotard with baubles pinned to it and green tinsel wig, very festive) and a Nappy-gram (large nappy, big dummy and bonnet, ideal for expectant mothers). I once appeared as Cupid in the Essex County Court, proposing to the Clerk of the Court on behalf of his girlfriend.

The work was plentiful but spread far and wide and I really needed a car. Songbird came to my rescue, lending me a white Honda van to travel about in, the deal being that I also did balloon deliveries for £1 a time. It was a solitary sort of life, but Fanny sat in the passenger seat and we set out each day armed with maps and instructions, diligent in our task. In the back of the van were a helium tank and a supply of balloons, from metallic (longer lasting, more expensive), to your traditional rubber (available in all colours with matching ribbons and a poem), or the ever popular Balloon in a Box: a big, white, mysterious box wrapped in bright ribbons. When opened, a heart-shaped balloon arose, shimmering with glitter and confetti. Attached to the end of the trailing ribbon was a message from the beloved.

Seeing as I couldn't do telegrams without the van, I agreed. Telegrams paid around £12 a time. My Tarzan was very popular and I could do two or three a night. In general it consisted of me turning up at some venue, anything from a rough pub in the East End to a posh 40th in Chalfont St Giles, changing into my loincloth in the back of the van or maybe in the pub gents, hiding my day wear above the cistern. I'd then locate my victim, pick him (I did Gay Tarzan too; no discernible difference) or her up, swing them round, recite a personalised poem with information from

My sisters Beverley (left)
and Frances, with me
in the middle aged two.

Fringe by my mother.

With mother in our grandparents' garden in Stoke Ferry, Norfolk.

Above: With my parents and Nan on the Isle of Wight, the Travolta look seems to have taken hold.

Above: My parents, on their engagement.

Left: My father, PC Clary.

Below: I too would later take down people's particulars.

I took to camping at an early age.

Our trusty Zephyr got us to Spain and back – well, almost.

I was a coxswain for Kingston Rowing Club. (Richard Nelson is resting his arm on my shoulder and, far right, is Grant Watkins.)

Above: Me and my kitten, Pao – who cost 62½p – outside our house in Teddington.

Above: I took Auntie Wyn to see the rhododendrons after her cataract operation.

Right: Posing for the Polaroid with my best friend Nick. We were reading a lot of Iris Murdoch novels at this time.

Me and Linda as Glad and May: my first foray into cabaret.

Me and Neen, the other member of the Goldsmiths
inner circle, looking suitably theatrical.

Still an innocent abroad – early days at Goldsmiths.

Linda and me gratefully accepting yet another chance to dress up.

Me and Noreen. Our correspondence course in romance came to nought despite a grope in a field.

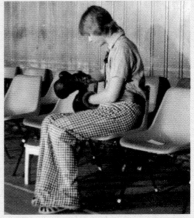

Above: I prepare to defend my choice of trouser, on an ill-advised student expedition to the Edinburgh Festival 1979.

Left: I designed this costume for a character in a Greek tragedy as part of my degree course. The leg is a worry.

Below: An attempt at being a serious thesp. I'm the one overacting on the right.

Above: Outside my first home – a 'hard to let' council flat in Kidbrooke.

Left: The Covent Garden Community Theatre bus – a mode of transport of sorts and somewhere to roll a joint to get you through the day.

Below left: Some of the delightful children we performed for in adventure playgrounds and community centres across London.

Below: A second career: the joys of delivering a singing telegram on behalf of Elizabeth Arden.

Above: My first lover, Miguel, a Portuguese ballet student, took me back to his place in glamorous Dalston.

Above: Visiting Auntie Tess, my godmother, shortly after a bad bleach job.

Right: Fanny and her embarrassment.

Left to right:
Paul (Merton),
me, Addison
(Cresswell) – my
manager and
Philip (Hugh Jelly).

The (cabaret)
artist at rest.
I was very
happy at
Seymour
Buildings.

Writing with
Paul Merton:
my Grayson to
his Hancock.

Too much slap. In character at
Goldsmiths and later as the
Joan Collins Fan Club.

A backstage visit from my grandmother after a show
at the Hackney Empire. She had taken the precaution of
turning her hearing aid off before I took the stage.

King of queens: in New York with Quentin Crisp (below), Australia with Paul O'Grady and Bob Downe (bottom) and doing *Sticky Moments* with Danny La Rue (left).

On stage with Philip and Russell.

Some of the increasingly surreal costumes
I wore, as designed by Michael Ferri.

The gruelling tour of Australia 1992/3. Left: With Philip and Hans. Below: With drag queens during Mardi Gras. Bottom: With an Australian fan and his date.

Christopher. Above: In Tuscany. Left: Where he was happiest – in his dressing gown at Albert Street, Camden. Below: Toward the end, Coney Island, New York City.

In Mallorca with my parents.

Me, Frances and Beverley.

The show must go on. These days I'm no stranger to pantomime.

whoever booked me, maybe sing a snatch of 'I'm The King Of The Swingers', and feed them a banana as salaciously as possible. Being a cut above the rest, our agency prided itself on staying around for 20 minutes to get the party going. I was the life and soul for the appointed time, then slipped out of the door as the conga gained pace. Telegrams were usually delivered in fairly raucous situations, the recipient and their colleagues generally drunk. As things turned out, this work was handy training for comedy clubs a few years later.

The deal with the Honda seemed a good one at the time, but there were days when I'd spend all day doing balloon deliveries in Essex, Wimbledon, Caterham and Willesden, only to collect the paltry sum of £4. A few telegrams in the evening would redress the balance, and after a hard day's work, off I went to the bars and clubs to unwind. I'd leave Fanny asleep in the van and nip into Heaven or Bang to see my friends and try my luck.

It was not the done thing to go home empty-handed. For some reason, I remember sitting on the floor in Heaven's Star Bar, all ripped jeans and tousled hair, more or less waiting for a man playing pool to finish his game and come over. Nothing had been said but an entire dialogue had been spoken with looks and body language. I knew he was interested. I knew he had to finish the game first.

Later back at Kidbrooke, it was a trousers-round-ankles situation. I think the long drive home focused the mind somewhat. Small talk had been exhausted, thighs fondled as we drove along. Once inside the flat there was no talk of slipping into something more comfortable, cups of tea or even turning on the lights. Sexual acts were performed by the illumination of a streetlight, and were all the more memorable for it.

One of the necessary qualities for a camp comic is the overdevelopment of the muscle of aesthetic appreciation. The fact is, I remember the encounter only because the lighting was so filmic. Turns out he was a chef. A self-raising man. I can verify that. His administrations were so encouraging I had the good fortune to achieve an orgasm. We were both delighted for a moment, until the chef decided he wanted me to return the favour. I was thinking more cup of Horlicks and a taxi for Fanny Craddock. The wonder of the moment had evaporated in exact proportion to each thrusting deposit. Left dazed and sober, my sense of politeness went out the window. Suddenly an off-duty chef, infused with chip fat and the whiff of liver, was thrusting his meat in the general direction of my face and declaring with a drunk man's sense of justice that it was his turn now. The Catholic in me did his duty for a while, but my heart wasn't in it and my sense of self resurfaced as my heart rate returned to normal. But the chef was consumed with lust. Snorting poppers with gusto, he slapped and swiped my face with his member. A brief reprise of sexual duty from me did the trick and his knees buckled under the velocity of his ejaculation.

Sleep followed swiftly as it did in those days. No GBH overdose frenzy, no grinding of teeth or sexual dysfunction blighted our pleasure. Just the bleaching daylight, cruel and forthright in its revelations. The chef. Skin trouble, not noticed before. Acrid body odour. Teeth not great.

He was late for work, cursing and punching numbers into

the phone with frantic dread. Fanny looked on with withering indifference. We drove up the Old Kent Road in silence, the chef slapping his legs with anxiety before leaping out of the car at traffic lights near to his alleged place of work. There may have been a 'See ya, mate,' or some such, but I was busy opening the car windows.

The chef has not entered my mind for 20-odd years. But he's an example of the kind of encounters one might engage in at that time. I didn't go out and expect to keep myself nice.

One day the holdall containing the Gillian Pie-Face costume, wig, props and all, was stolen from the back of the van. The thief was probably more upset than I was with his booty. I didn't bother to report it. Gillian was getting on my nerves. I had a bath and thought how I should proceed with the act. Female impersonation wasn't what I wanted to do, but glamour and make-up were. My make-up application had grown particularly extreme, verging on the grotesque.

I jumped out of the bath quickly because *Dynasty* was on. By the time I'd dried myself, all had become clear. I would call myself the Joan Collins Fan Club. Joan was on the cover of every magazine at the time, wearing as much make-up as I did, and her character in *Dynasty*, Alexis Carrington, was the ultimate bitch. Joan's aggressive glamour appealed to me, as did her relentless ability to sell herself. She had a twinkle in her eye; she knew that we knew it was all an illusion, a commercial ruse to earn a fabulous salary with make-up and back-lighting. Image was all. The title 'Joan Collins

Fan Club' was deliciously self-explanatory. My appearance and my putdowns would be justified, and what's more the DSS would never rumble me for earning a bit on the side. Although I was a comedian, my idea was to market myself as a pop star. The Marvin Shark of my youthful fantasies would come to life, the Gay Lusac of the schoolboy cartoons would take to the stage wearing my sister's showgirl make-up, and feather boas would hang from every available limb.

I alerted the handful of regular cabaret bookings I had to my name change, and wrote some new material, which I could brutally if not skilfully weave in with the old.

In mock-evangelical style, I welcomed the audience to a Joan Collins convention and offered to sell them the crystallised remains of Joan's own bathwater scum, tastefully packaged and bottled for their convenience. 'A spoonful of this in your coffee each morning could change your life for the better.' There was also the Joan Collins Vanilla Disco Rub – which doubled as dessert topping and lubricant. 'Imagine the fun you could have at the tea table, or indeed under it.' There was a lot more similar such nonsense. Sometimes the act went reasonably well, but sometimes I left the stage to a mere smattering of 'thank God that's over' applause.

The other acts would commiserate. We were a curious collection of eccentric performers, happy to have found a world where we fitted in: a Marxist magician called Ian Saville, John Sparkes, who the poster promised 'will be chatting to household items', Jim Barclay, who hammered a nail through his nose, Randolph the Remarkable, fire-eater extraordinaire, whose act culminated in the raising of a blue plastic washing-up bowl from the ground with his stomach, and Kit Hollerbach, 'San Francisco's top female comic'. Paul Merton, a comedian who specialised in surreal stories about bus shelters and Marilyn Monroe and used to perform in his pyjamas, suggested I did more audience participation. He came to tea in Kidbrooke one afternoon and helped me write just such a section, called 'The Joan Collins School of Acting – for stage, screen and airport terminal.' This involved me plucking a punter from the audience and giving him a 'vintage *Dynasty* script' to read with me. I was to play the part of Alexis, of course, and the hapless punter was Blake: 'My name is Blake Carrington, but you can call me big knob.'

At the end of the script he had to say: 'I'm a wreck, a ruin and a shrine to despair. There's only one thing that's going to make me feel better and that's to sing that old Roger Whittaker classic "I'm Gonna Leave Old Durham Town" at the top of my voice.' (Roger was another of my fascinations: 'Some people say he's too old for me. Some people say he's too old for anyone.')

Having new material and a proper finale meant I died less often. I was still wearing clothes from the Oxfam shop, but I splashed out on sequins and stiletto heels. Later I progressed to rubber: no creasing and just rinse under the tap when you get home.

Work trickled in and alternative cabaret venues mushroomed. It went without saying that both acts and audiences were left-wing. Overtly socialist comedians such as Mark Thomas, Mark Steel and the musical satirists Skint Video found a ready audience for their anti-Tory material. Even I, whose act had virtually no political content, appreciated audiences that were curious but not phobic about my sexuality. I took to carrying a cassette player on with me, blasting out the *1812 Overture* as my entrance music while I sprinkled confetti over the punters. It was an attempt at bringing glamour to such dingy surroundings, although in reality it meant the front row spent the first five minutes of my act picking bits of coloured paper out of their beer.

I summed up my audience at the time in a poem.

> *Dearest social workers and teachers of all kin,*
> *Dear gingham shirts and readers of Harold Robbins,*
> *Dear late twenties, early thirties*
> *With your unbuttoned collarless shirties*
> *And your little tins with Gold Virginia in...*
> *Dear nest egg for a rainy day,*
> *Dear cottage out in Wales,*
> *Dear children called Germaine after Greer,*
> *Dear housing co-op workers,*
> *Dear Labour Party voters, have no fear...*

Sometimes at these gigs there was no dressing room and I either gave Fanny to someone to look after while I was on, or simply instructed her to wait at the side of the stage. As long as she could see me she was happy enough. At the Earth Exchange, where there was no real stage, I took her on with me and told her to sit in the corner. After a few minutes she started to distract the audience and get titters of unexplained laughter – she was leering at a man at a front table. I picked her up and sat her on a chair and she alternated between looking adoringly at me and disdainfully at the audience.

To keep her amused I tossed her a bit of wholemeal bread. She caught it and got a round of applause. As any applause at that stage of my career was a welcome and unusual delight, I tossed her more bread throughout the rest of my act, and a star was born.

From then on I was to be the Joan Collins Fan Club with Fanny the Wonder Dog. I would throw her choc drops and demand the audience applaud her, then throw them to the crowd. 'See, it's not as easy as it looks!' Her impressions were next. If you whispered in her ear she slowly raised her head: this was Tower Bridge. With a red wig she was Sarah Ferguson, the Duchess of York ('complete with facial hair'). Lift her gums to reveal brown teeth and, hey presto, she was the Queen Mother.

She did films too. A green soldier's hat: *The Dogs Of War*. A shower cap: *Psycho*. But Fanny's main gift was to stare at the punters. Particularly rowdy ones. Perhaps it was her protective instinct towards me: she could silence a heckler with one glance and stare him out for the next 20 minutes before turning her back with body language of unmistakable contempt. Her timing was always spot on.

This, then, was my life for a couple of years. Between the comedy circuit and the singing telegrams, I survived. The latter made me fearless. I could deliver a telegram in a rowdy pub or at a drunken party no matter what the obstacles. I learnt my way round London in the Honda van, became expert at extracting a tip on top of my fee, and after a year or so earned a reputation on the circuit as a reliable turn.

My disastrous gigs became fewer and there were more and more calls for bookings. I grew my hair long; shoulder length, bleached and tonged into a spiky cross between Rod Stewart and Tammy Wynette. Off stage I wore ripped jeans and studded belts with a black handkerchief tied round my neck, a rock'n'roll gypsy look, and called in at gay pubs and clubs after work to meet Stephen or Mark, adept at finding my man for the evening, and Oscar winning when it came to ejecting him the next morning.

I didn't analyse my lifestyle or my prospects much. For those few years, ambition was bubbling under the surface, but I didn't seriously imagine cabaret gigs were a stepping-stone to anything more lucrative or exciting. I had stopped applying for acting work after a miserable Theatre in Education tour with Buster Young People's Theatre. (I'd been miscast as a blokey bloke, doing a dreadful play four times a day for a pitiful wage and having to turn down cabaret gigs into the bargain.) As the Joan Collins Fan Club, I could make an asset of my mannerisms and voice, aspects of my performance that were criticised in the theatre. It didn't feel right to me to suppress them. Why should I? I could write my own material, arrange my own bookings and direct myself. It was a wonderfully self-sufficient lifestyle.

What I liked best about it was the utterly trivial nature of my 'job'. I was paid for speaking the thoughts I'd be having anyway, for criticising hairstyles and holding up punters' grubby coats for everyone to ridicule. I purposely nipped in the bud any material that might be construed as having 'meaning'. Anything that smacked of resonance was undesirable. I was lightweight – that was the whole point of me. JCFC was about choc drops, glamour, mild humiliation and gentle laughter, nothing else. I deliberately set out to create my own world where I was the norm and the audience were the outsiders. What's more, they were to feel privileged to get a glimpse of my superior environment. Their lives, I declared, were dreary by comparison with mine. I was kind to let them in but scornful of them once they arrived. My satisfaction in all this, and probably my psychological motivation, was a reversal of all I had experienced at school. I would be vindicated. I would be applauded for the very things I was once victimised for.

Whether or not it worked this way varied from show to show. A lot of factors could spell ruination. It's never been a watertight act; failure was always a sniff away. I might go on too late and the audience would be too drunk to enter into the conceit. The p.a. might be dodgy so they couldn't hear properly. My self-confidence (always fragile) might evaporate, or Fanny might not be in the mood and leave the stage. I might go too far in picking on a particular individual and sympathies for one of their number could cause the audience to turn on me. The act on before me might go down a storm, in which case the audience were laughed out and willing me to die for the sake of some variation.

There was a flurry of excitement in 1984 when I was asked to appear on a television show called *Live From the London Hippodrome* and be interviewed by Janet Street-Porter. Dusty Springfield was the star turn. I can't remember much about it, except that the van broke down en route and Sue Holsten from the singing telegram agency spent the evening fending off the clampers while I rehearsed. I was shown to the seated area where the interview was to take place, to find it was all wet. Apparently Dusty had had a tantrum and thrown her gin and tonic around. I was thrilled to sit on such an icon's spilt beverage. I was only on air for a fairly uneventful three minutes and no one at all seemed to have seen me, so after a few days had passed and I'd had no phone calls offering me highly paid bookings or more TV work, I went back to the telegrams and the circuit.

Bigger and swisher venues began to do alternative comedy nights, and more comedians and more punters were attracted to the circuit. Jongleurs, Banana Cabaret, The Comedy Store: work was there almost for the asking. Quite a few comics ran their own clubs, with varying degrees of success. Malcolm Hardee ran a club called the Tunnel – so called because it was right by the south-east London side of the Blackwall Tunnel – in the back room of the Mitre pub. It was always well attended, a rowdy well-oiled crowd waiting for the inevitable moment when Malcolm would get his genitals out, which he did most weeks. He was quite rightly very proud of his enormous testicles. A man fell asleep in the front row once and Malcolm woke him up by pissing on him. Paul Merton and John Irwin ran the Room Above a Pub cabaret in Wimbledon, although not many people seemed to come. I played there in June 1985 for £7, my share of the door takings. Usually you took home a percentage of the box office, never knowing in advance what your fee would be. I didn't mind this, as the money was always fairly divided and no one was making huge profits.

In April 1985 I worked what must have been my first seven-day week, and my earnings were as follows:

Monday – Earth Exchange, £15.
Tuesday – Word of Mouth Club, £10.

Wednesday – Pindar of Wakefield, £17.

Thursday – Rosemary Branch, £9.

Friday – Jackson's Lane, £50.

Saturday – Finborough cabaret, £25.

Sunday – Xenon's, Piccadilly, £50.

I was the only camp act on the circuit in those days. No one else dressed up apart from me, and other comics looked on bemused as I painted my face and pulled on my tights. Fanny rested in the empty suitcase prior to her performance, stepped on once by an apologetic Patrick Marber, in those days one half of an act called the Dross Bross. I'd found a gap in the market and I had novelty value, if nothing else.

Susan Sontag in her 'Notes on Camp' was moved to write that camp is 'a feat goaded on, in the last analysis, by boredom'. Who knows what she was talking about, but from time to time boredom and then depression crept over me. When the dark cloud descended, my life seemed tiresome. I only got up in the morning to walk the dog, otherwise I wouldn't have bothered. I trekked round London with Fanny and a suitcase trying to entertain a few dozen members of the public in charmless pubs and clubs. I enjoyed the chase when cruising a man, but post-coitally I was under no illusions. My existence was vacuous and lonely. There was no point to it. I sometimes felt like I had deliberately fashioned an existence that would starve my soul.

But I gamely carried on, diligently keeping a journal for a week or so, reviewing my own performances with a critical eye.

Saturday 9 March. Pranksters cabaret, Southampton University

Shameful. Lifeless and uninspired from start to finish. Mitigating circumstances might be that I was deaf in one ear and the audience not a sophisticated one, but I didn't rehearse and was overconfident until the moment I stepped on stage. Before my first sentence I heard a 'fuck off!' and many people walked out while I was on. Extremely embarrassing in front of Arthur Smith, Jeremy Hardy, Podomofski and Berni Bennett.

Sunday 10 March. Room Above a Pub cabaret, Prince of Wales, Wimbledon

Fine. Did some improvising as soon as I came on, prompted by the tape not coming on ('What is this? Amateur night?'), then delved behind the curtain and found a fridge and pulled out an empty packet of Dark and Golden ('Rather like this place: empty'). Did a lot of touching and walking around. Had 3 stooges: Sebastian, Hermione and Trevor ('I could almost be in Hampstead!'). All went according to plan. Hadn't rehearsed.

Friday 15 March. Bangor University, North Wales

Audience quiet but good-natured, as opposed to disinterested. Necessary to move in close and prod them about a bit. Did well to pick on the union secretary and ask if he was the college stud. Asked a group of rugby players, 'Are you six individuals or three couples?' On the whole it was confident, if not inspired. What you might call satisfactory.

Saturday 16 March. MacClachlans cabaret, Hemingford Arms, N1

Very good. Lifted by the presence of Linda and Charles Miller, BBC. Got myself into a speedy, hyper mood before I went on, which worked, so that I interrupted myself all the time. Kept referring to some poor man's extraordinary ears, then another man's mouth, someone else's nose, etc, and built up an identikit picture of an Islington punter.

Sunday 24 March. Xenons, Piccadilly

Got quite carried away and did half an hour instead of the specified 15 minutes. A lot of heckler stoppers including, 'Did you forget your broom?' Put most of the new ending in, about the JC School of Acting, but bottled out of getting a punter up for the finale. Next time. Shouts of 'More!' which doesn't happen often.

Sunday 31 March. King's Head, Crouch Hill

Good, but a regression in that I didn't include any of the new stuff this time, and still didn't do the new ending although the time was ripe. Had a very friendly stooge called Ian and made the most of that. Timing good.

Sunday 7 April. Tunnel Palladium, The Mitre, SE10

With the usual crowd of hecklers it was necessary to keep

the laugh lines coming, so there was much chopping and changing to keep them at bay, which I did. Did the new script, too, at last, which works really well. Unfortunately I'd already used half the jokes in it, which was silly. Sweated buckets and was indeed emotionally drained.

Thursday 11 April. Rub-a-Dub Club, Sydenham, SE26

A good night. Took my time and did half an hour. One punter was persistently talking to his friend so I asked what they were talking about. 'I'm trying to find out if you're any good.' Shut him up on my third attempt. Commented on the large number of quiffs in the audience. Did new ending. Went very well.

Friday 12 April. Donmar Warehouse, Late and Live

For BBC and friends I excelled myself. Constant ad libs, including, 'Did we get up the wrong side of the slab this morning?'

Saturday 13 April. Not the Camden Palace, NW1

OK. Nosebleed started as soon as I did, so that threw me somewhat and according to Linda I had my glazed expression on. New ending but punter refused to sing 'I'm Gonna Leave Old Durham Town'. Should have it on tape in case.

What I didn't know (and how could I?) was that things were about to change. Moves were afoot, a TV channel was in the making, a programme being conceived that would change my life for the better, bringing me the excitement and adoration that eluded me. Fate was about to stir things up for the better. Had I known, I'd have grinned and borne it. Farewell south-east London housing estate, farewell gigs above pubs, and farewell anonymous gay cruising. For a while, anyway.

SEVEN

*'The worst thing about having success is trying to
find someone who is happy for you.'*

BETTE MIDLER

Over the next few years my life seemed to improve in a series of leaps and bounds. Whether this was due to some beneficial astrological alignment I cannot say, but I was grateful for each happy change. There was a positive progression at work, each step seemingly connected to the one before, as if I was a character in a film, the plot of which was racing towards my fulfilment. The first area of my life that destiny took charge of was my location.

As we know, I was residing in a one-room council flat in deepest south-east London. I had kept the local kids at bay on the Brooke Estate with the occasional free helium-filled balloon, but local youths were not so easily won over. They had eyed me suspiciously from day one, and when they saw me emerging from the van one afternoon in my Tarzan costume, their dark mutterings denoted trouble ahead. They did the only thing possible and tried to kick my door down. When this failed they poured sugar into my petrol tank.

The next morning a letter arrived from the Seymour Housing Co-op in Marylebone informing me that they now had some vacancies and would I like to come for an interview? I had registered with them several years earlier and forgotten all about it. The co-op was fabulously located in Seymour Place, W1, and consisted of about fifty flats clustered round a charming communal garden, secure and safe behind a big, dark-red iron gate. When I went along and explained my plight they were most sympathetic, and within weeks I had moved in. I loved it so much there I thought I would never move out again. Flat 21 was another studio flat, but bright and sunny. A pillar in the middle of the room separated the bed from the living area, and it boasted the luxury of separate bathroom and kitchenette. The fortnightly co-op meetings were fun, my neighbours were cheery and I was a five-minute stroll away from Hyde Park. I gave up the balloon deliveries and the Honda van.

It was a few weeks after this that I went into hospital and had the anal warts forcibly removed. My personal comfort, inside and out, was complete. I thanked the Lord.

Ye Gods now seemed to be turning their attention towards my career. I joined an improvised comedy workshop run by Kit Hollerbach at The Comedy Store, which improved my confidence when messing about with punters during my act. I had plenty of work and was able to declare myself officially self-employed. In 1985 I did 144 gigs, and in 1986 the number had risen to 195. I became very business-like on the telephone, arranging my bookings and negotiating my fee. I was now one of the stalwarts of the comedy circuit, but apart from the listings magazines I received little media attention. I wasn't yet labelled 'limp-wristed camp comic' by the tabloids. But people were starting to take interest. I became fashionable, in a cultish, underground sort of way.

The Times wrote: 'His timing is impeccable, his tongue razor-sharp, as he satirises anything from Joan Collins to surrogate motherhood. Fanny the Wonder Dog, his tiny honey-coloured mongrel, sits deadpan at his side throughout.' *Time Out* did a spread on me with nice big colour pictures. 'In such celebrated but frankly dingy venues as The Comedy Store, possibly London's most famous underground car park, Clary seeks to create a world of glitter and glamour... but his main aim is to insult the audience,' wrote Malcolm Hay. I liked the way he finished his article: 'If you want to catch the act, my best advice is don't sport a Marks and Sparks jumper or a centre parting. One other thing – watch out for the smile on the face of the tiger.' I sent it to my parents with a note: 'Here's a little light reading which might make a welcome change from the *Telegraph*...' I was anxious to impress them. They had never seen my act. They knew I wore make-up and a lot of black rubber and I wondered if they thought it was far more sinister than it really was.

Family was very important to me. I phoned my mother every few days and went home every few weeks with my dirty washing, accompanying mother to church on a Sunday morning. My sisters were both married and nephews and nieces featured. At Christmas and Easter we all gathered together and cards were played, the same catchphrases passed down from one generation to the next. One Christmas Auntie Tess played cards for 16 hours with only the briefest of lavatory breaks.

These were happy, carefree days. Fanny and I trotted off to work with our trusty white suitcase, on a Saturday maybe squeezing three gigs into the evening: The Comedy Store in Leicester Square at 8 p.m. and midnight, and in between a dash across Soho in full slap to the Chuckle Club, run by the aromatic Eugene Cheese.

We travelled about a lot too, to university gigs or provincial comedy clubs. Sound systems that crackled, dressing rooms that stank, punters who didn't listen and doormen who refused to let dogs on the premises were all everyday obstacles. But we went anywhere that wanted to book us, and stayed in grim B&Bs where necessary:

16 December 1986

Fanny and I have to laugh sometimes. We find ourselves at the Chatsworth Guesthouse in Bristol, a small terraced house. 'No Vacancies' sign proudly displayed in the window. The concierge is old with a cough.

The decor in our twin room is a symphony in pink. Three walls ice cream pink, the wall opposite me salmon. There is a grey-and-white speckled carpet with root-like squiggles of black, red and blue. On top of this between the beds is a brown mat, elaborately patterned with darker brown rings and sunset red small, medium and large squares, each of which is afflicted with the root problem first noted in the grey carpet. Curtains are red faded to orange with large hand sized daisy chains from top to bottom, filled out with smaller white freesias. (And nets of course). Matching duvet covers in maroon and purple floral effect with differing pillow slips: pink and white nylon. The under sheet is nylon with suspiciously rubbery under cover. There are two chairs, a wardrobe, a small chest and a small black and white television.

The fire instructions suggest: 'Attack the fire if possible with the appliance provided.' The remaining feature of the room is the sink with cold (true) and hot (untrue) running water.

I also had an interesting sideline going as a member of a pop group called Thinkman. The record producer Rupert Hine, together with the lyricist Jeannette Obstoj, had created a nifty album about media hype called *The Formula*. To market the album they plucked three likely-looking young actors from the pages of the actor's directory *Spotlight* and passed us off as musicians. Together with Rupert we were Thinkman.

The three of us sat bemused in Jeannette's Connaught Street living room and listened as she rolled an unfeasibly large joint and explained that the con we were about to pull on the music industry was all in keeping with the concept of the album. We were each given new names and assigned a musical instrument. I was Leo Hurll, keyboard player. Andy was bass guitarist and Greg was to play drums. We were given fake biographies to learn and driven to a warehouse in Battersea where we were given lessons in miming our instruments. 'This is mad!' we three would whisper to each other when Rupert and Jeannette weren't listening, but as they were paying us £150 a day to enter into the fantasy, we just went with the flow. We wondered what on earth we were getting ourselves into, but a stylist dressed us in expensive designer clothes and we dutifully turned up to film a big-budget video. There was a huge industrial set: cameras, photographer, make-up artists, record company executives, catering trucks – it all seemed to be happening for real. The champagne and joints helped things along. On set and off we were referred to by our new names. We learnt the lyrics and bashed away at our (unplugged) instruments as we mimed:

> *It's an interview*
> *But it's a second take*
> *There's a questioner*
> *But your mind's at stake.*
> *Let's break down the formula*
> *Let's switch off the set*
> *...and be glad we finally met.*

Then at the end of the day we were thanked and returned to our own, mundane lives, pop stars no more.

A few months later Jeannette called to say we were in the German and Canadian charts and were required to fly to Europe to do press and television appearances to promote 'our' album. I cleared a few days of cabaret shows out of the way, assumed my Leo Hurll persona and off we flew on a whistle-stop tour of Germany and Belgium. We sat on sofas to be interviewed on serious music programmes, reeled off the fibs from the fake biogs and took to the stage, 'playing' and pouting to excited girls who called out our names and threw soft toys at us. We were then bundled into a people carrier with blacked-out windows and whisked to the airport to fly off to the next city and repeat the proceedings all over again. If we had dinner in our posh hotel at the end of the day it was with a number of top management from the record company who had all swallowed our collective lie, and so the charade had to be kept up relentlessly. There was one tricky moment when a Belgian suit pointed to the piano in the corner of the restaurant and asked me to play something. I was so immersed in being Leo I almost agreed. 'Shall I?' I said. Rupert glared at me, Greg sniggered. After an awkward pause I decided on a pop-star-like response and said, 'Nah. Fuck off,' and everyone laughed nervously. 'Girlfriend trouble...' Rupert explained to the suit.

We had three or four trips abroad like this. I loved having a secret other life. It was all so bizarre. No one really believed me when I said I was a German pop star called Leo Hurll. I had to produce press cuttings and photos to prove it. Thinkman produced a second album a year later, but by then I was on the verge of my own big break and had a manager who wasn't inclined to let me go. Leo Hurll left the band under mysterious circumstances. A few German schoolgirls wept into their sauerkraut.

On the circuit night by night you never knew who you would be working with, so you would check *Time Out* to see who it was going to be. The quality of your evening ahead depended on it. If it was Paul Merton, for example, you knew it would be a laugh. 'Kissed any men lately?' he'd ask in mock disgust. Paul was always very willing to help me write new jokes, despite the fact that my innuendoes and music-hall style of performance were a million miles removed from his own carefully honed act. He has a mind that can slide into any comic genre, and year after year he slipped me handfuls of gems that stood out as funnier and cleverer than any of my own offerings. If I wasn't getting many laughs, I'd race ahead to a 'Paul' section, sure in the knowledge that a couple of his lines would get me back on track.

Each year I lured him to my flat where for a couple of French fancies and a cup of tea he'd help me rewrite the audience partici-pation spot. He made sure I laughed from the moment he arrived, delivering a line as I opened the door. Once he came in limping: 'I tried being homosexual the other night and put me back out.' On another occasion I opened the door and he said, 'I've followed your career with a bucket and spade.' We adopted roles with each other, his Hancock to my Grayson. For comedy purposes I was as dismissive of his hetero world as he was horrified by my homo exis-tence. We even went on stage late one night at the Pleasance in the midst of a well-oiled Edinburgh Festival and told alternate lines of our acts, each delivering the other's punchlines with withering disinterest. For example:

Me: 'Who does your hair for you?'
Paul: 'Is it the council?'

Paul: 'My father always said, "The only bombs you've got
    to worry about are the ones that have got your name
    on them." That really upset the neighbours—'
Me: 'Mr and Mrs Doodle-Bug.'

For one of my later tour programmes I asked Paul to write an account of our early days. He wrote:

I first encountered Julian in 1983 when we were both performing in a small vegetarian restaurant off the Archway Road. Julian was halfway through his act when he suddenly spotted me as a potential victim.

'And what do we have here?' he said.

'I'm the next act,' I whispered.

'Are you indeed?' replied Julian. I could see that he was in somewhat of a predicament. Should he obey the ethics of professional courtesy and move on to someone else, or should he take the piss out of my jumper?

He moved on. Inevitably we became lovers.

Julian, along with Fanny the Wonder Dog, soon found cabaret work trickling in. Even in the early days Julian was fond of making a grand entrance. He was the only act on the circuit who played a music tape to announce his appearance on stage. For a while he used Beethoven's 9th Symphony but as this was over an hour long the audience became understandably restless. Soon he settled on Tara's theme from *Gone With The Wind*. Many's the time I've heard that evocative tune flowing through some polytechnic's battered old sound system as Julian emerged into the spotlight scattering confetti into the first three rows.

Around this time Julian and I moved into a charming cottage and converted it into a railway station.

Also from this period I remember Julian demonstrating just how far he would go for the sake of a joke. We were working in Guildford and Julian was walking amongst the audience when something in the distance suddenly caught his attention. He strode down the central aisle of the theatre trailing the microphone lead behind him before settling in front of a rather red-faced student with close-cropped hair.

'And what's your name?'

'Simon,' said Simon.

'Ladies and gentlemen, Simon spent an hour and a half combing his hair tonight.' Pause. 'And then he forgot to bring it with him.' Julian then turned on his heel and walked the 30 yards to the stage.

The *Dynasty* script had been a highlight of the act but was now past its sell-by date. One year we wrote a *Doctor Who* sketch. I was to be the doctor and a man and woman from the audience were to be hauled on stage to play my assistant Maureen and a Dalek.

Maureen: Doctor, doctor, where are we?
Doctor: Look out the window.

Maureen: We're in the middle of an alien landscape where
there's no sign of life as we know it.

Doctor: We must be in Haslemere.

Maureen: Haslemere?

Doctor: Yes, Haslemere, Land of the Daleks.

[Enter Dalek.]

Dalek: You are all my prisoners. Will you come quietly or
shall I turn the stereo up?

Maureen: Has anyone told you you look just like Rod
Stewart?

Dalek: You have ten seconds before I shoot my load...

... and so on. In 1987 Paul Merton and John Irwin wrote a series
for Radio 4 called *The Big Fun Show*. I was invited to join the cast,
which included Josie Lawrence, Neil Mullarkey and Tony Hawks.
Paul recalled:

The idea was that Julian would feature in a long sketch
every week playing some kind of authoritative role, rather
than a camp caricature as is so often the tradition in light
entertainment. One particular exchange still brings a smile
to my lips. The scene took place in a restaurant.

Julian: Now, what shall I have to eat?

Josie: The Chef's Special?

Julian: I know that, but I want my dinner first.

For the Edinburgh Festival, acts who got along together would
join forces to put on a show. In 1985 I played at the Comedy

Boom, a pub-basement festival venue, with the cheery Jewish comic Ivor Dembina and the musical double act Skint Video. This was a success, and the following year, back at the same venue, I wanted to combine forces more and maybe attempt something along the lines of a traditional showbiz finale. Barb Jungr and Michael Parker were favourites of mine – a jazzy, folky duo who had been on the circuit almost as long as I had. Steve Edgar was a subversive comedian whom *Time Out* described as 'an urban Puck, dedicated to disruption'. We called our show *Fourplay*. Together we wrote a couple of songs. 'Dream Home' was a vision of ultimate tackiness.

> *I live in a dream house, a modern-day home,*
> *I've got concealed lighting and a push-button phone.*
> *I've a plum flock lounge with an alcove in green,*
> *And a thick pile carpet in rich tangerine.*
> *I've a coal-effect clock and a ladyshave broom,*
> *A microwave telly and nonstick vacuum.*
> *I've tinted double-glazing which is twenty-four hour,*
> *And over my bath I've a teasmaid shower.*
> *I've got dolphin-head taps for my low-level sink,*
> *And a flamenco lady in rouched satin pink.*
> *I've got my dolls of all nations behind glass in the cove,*
> *And a coney-ette rug in deepest dark mauve.*
> *Hand-painted Tupperware with real marble effect,*
> *And Venetian glass rabbits which I like to collect.*
> *I've got pastel-shade cushions all scattered about,*
> *And foam-filled cavities inside and out.*

There's bronze-tinted mirrors the length of the hall,
And a hologram of Jesus on the porch entrance wall.
I've basketweave fire tongs – they're just for show,
And Melvyn Bragg's novels for those in the know.
It really is a dream home…

The lyrics were difficult to remember, unfortunately, and most of the time I lost the thread after a couple of lines and said, 'Well, I'm sure you get the general idea.'

On stage one night in Edinburgh my rubber shorts split and to cover my embarrassment I made a bit of comedy business out of it. After the show a scary-looking local punk with home-made anarchy tattoos on his arms (and, as it turned out, on his chest, too) offered to fix the shorts for me with a bicycle repair kit. His name was Michael Ferri and as I chatted to him it became apparent that he had lots of mad costume ideas. What was more, he was about to travel south to start a two-year course at the London School of Fashion. It was a fortuitous meeting: the sort of clothes I wanted I couldn't find in any shop, and Michael was making clothes no one dared to put on. The first things he made for me were a helter-skelter dress, a red chiffon cape and a silver spacesuit. There would be no more Oxfam outfits. For the next few years my image was in the hands of Michael Ferri, an industrious shaven-headed anarchist from Scotland. He would expose my nipples to the world, and his imagination would not be stifled by any stuffy TV executives who threw their hands up in horror at what I was planning to parade myself in.

Back in London I was doing a show at Jongleurs in Battersea one night when word went round that Geoff Posner, director and producer of *Saturday Night Live*, was in, sniffing about for potential guests on the second series. The show, hosted by Ben Elton, was a live mixture of music and comedy and had been a big hit on Channel 4 the previous year, elevating several comics from the circuit to greater things. I knew they had seen me before and passed me by, so I assumed my act was too risqué to make it onto TV. But this time it was different. Jo Brand (then working as the Sea Monster) and I were just what they were looking for.

I was booked for a slot on 7 February 1987. It was recorded at the LWT studios and we went along in the afternoon to rehearse. We were on the show with The Communards, Harry Enfield as Stavros, Phil Cornwell and Meatloaf. Fanny wasn't too fazed by the cameras, which was a relief, since her behaviour was becoming increasingly neurotic. For about a year she had had a phobia of lamp-posts, unusual in a dog. When walking down the road she would flatten herself against the pavement every few yards whenever we passed one. In a car or bus, when the fearsome lamp-post situation could occur every few seconds, she recoiled and bobbed her head repeatedly. What brought this behaviour on I never knew, but luckily there were no lamp-posts in the studio.

In the dressing room I piled on the make-up and squeezed into my rubber several hours early. I was in a state of terror and seriously considered slipping down the back stairs and running away. I felt sick and sweaty as a researcher led Fanny and me down a corridor to the studio. Just before I was on, Stephen Fry and Meatloaf were doing a sketch and as I waited my turn I seemed to go through the fear barrier, and a sudden feeling of calmness washed over me.

'Hello, punters. There's nothing I like more than a warm hand on my entrance.' Because the studio audience were all standing by the stage it was not unlike any other gig, and I quickly spotted just the person to pick on: a thin, smiling boy called Colin. 'Look at your horrible jumper! What a pity the shop didn't have your size...' We messed about for a while, Fanny caught her choc drops and did her impression of Fergie, then it was all over. I got the idea I'd gone down rather well when I got home to find 30-odd congratulatory messages on my answerphone. Then Geoff Posner asked me to go back on the show two weeks later. I got loads of bookings, agents offered their services, journalists wanted to speak to me, Fanny was recognised in the park. Those seven minutes on live television suddenly seemed to be having enormous consequences. For the first time I felt a little bit famous. So this is how it works, I thought.

Addison Cresswell was a well-known figure on the cabaret circuit. As a promoter and manager he ran a company called Off The Kerb productions from the front room of a converted old bakery in Peckham. He presented himself as a Jack the Lad, not to be messed with, affecting a rough south London accent. In fact, he was the well-bred son of the dean of Goldsmiths College, where I had spent three years, and had honed his entrepreneurial skills as entertainment officer at Brighton Polytechnic, managing to turn the subsidised student union into a profitable set-up. A year younger than me, he had blonde hair and angular good looks. He swaggered around, prodded you in the chest with his pointed finger and had the habit of sometimes staring at your throat when talking to you, as if contemplating taking a bite out of your oesophagus if you didn't agree with him. His eyes darted about the room, as if every conversation was a furtive drug deal. He was impressive, irritating and endearing in equal measure, his bluster and machismo clearly a beard for a sensitive, insecure soul who simply wanted to be loved.

Everyone on the circuit had an Addison story, and his faux pas and malapropisms were legend, even then. 'I'm like a bull at a china gate,' he said of himself. 'I've got the Mazda touch...' I was familiar with his terrier-like personality because he ran the Comedy Boom at the Edinburgh Festival, where I had appeared for the last two years. As my career gathered momentum he also booked me for some better-paid, better-organised gigs on the circuit, such as the Albany Empire. He always amused me, discussing appearance fees as if he was a barrow boy selling you a cut-price pound of apples. A somewhat sleazy but reputable agent called me one day to say if I'd sign to him and take his advice to tone down my act, he could guarantee me lots of TV work. I asked Addison what he thought I should do. 'Don't touch him. I'll manage you, if you like,' he said. And so he did. For the next 15 years. The fateful meeting took place at a pub, the Sun Inn on Long Acre in Covent Garden, on Monday 13 April 1987. He rather thrilled me with his instructions.

'You don't do nothing from now on without my say-so. No gigs, no interviews, no nothing unless I give you the green light. All future enquiries you refer to me, get it? You don't go to the dentist, you don't even cross the road unless I tell you it's OK. Understood?'

It was a bit like having a very possessive boyfriend. He let me do the bookings on the circuit I'd already agreed to, but he stood in the wings glowering. 'You're too good for this place,' he announced as I came off stage at one of the quainter venues. 'It's so quiet in here. You could hear a mouse drop.'

He soon took me away from all that and by June I was playing three sell-out nights at the Hackney Empire, supported by Paul Merton, Harry Enfield and Randolph the Remarkable.

Paul Merton:

Not only were these shows a professional triumph for Julian, but I believe they also meant a great deal to him on a much deeper level. After years of working with inadequate sound systems and poorly constructed stages, in the days when a box of confetti was a special effect, Julian had at last found an audience that shared his vision of another kind of world, a magical world of glitter, glamour and blemish concealer. One moment from those first Hackney Empire shows remains with me still. As we stood in line and took our final bows, I noticed Julian saying quietly to himself, amid the rapturous applause, 'Thank you, thank you.'

These were the first shows my parents came to. 'Thought we'd better come and see what all the fuss is about,' said my father. 'Very nice,' said my mother, 'but please don't ask us to come again.' On the written page this looks unkind, but she was joking, acknowledging the significance of the occasion. That initiation was good for them, I think, as they've been to see me many times since. My sexuality has now been well and truly demystified for them, and indeed everyone else. I've never worried about upsetting them: they're fairly thick-skinned and we do, after all, share the same sense of humour. There was only one time when I faltered. I was performing at the Playhouse Theatre and I had booked a box for my parents, my grandmother and Auntie Tess and Uncle Ken. The older generation were in their late eighties. The box there is right on top of the stage and just before I came to a particularly graphic section, I saw them all sitting there in a row, glasses glinting at me. I took a deep breath and sallied forth.

'I didn't know I was gay myself until last Thursday week. I was just getting out the bath when I suddenly thought – do you know what I feel like? A great big cock up my arse.' It was the sort of line that sorted the men from the boys, usually causing a collective intake of breath and a delayed laugh. (Paul O'Grady was in that night, too, with my favourite drag queen of them all, Regina Fong. 'We could not believe what you'd just said,' recalled Paul. 'Regina nearly passed out!') I nervously glanced at the box and thankfully they were all laughing, apart from my grandmother, who was smiling happily: she'd taken the precaution of turning her hearing aid off before the show began.

I needed to expand my act as a matter of urgency. Addison was booking me into larger and larger venues where my fee would be considerably more than I was used to. I could no longer get away with my usual hit-or-miss 20 minutes. Songs would be a good filler, I thought, so I put the word around for a pianist. The fact that I couldn't sing was neither here nor there. A posh friend of

Neil Mullarkey's called Dobbs offered his services, as did an ex-Cambridge Footlights musician called Russell Churney. Dobbs had cheekbones, Russell had dimples and a whiff of Rick Astley about him, and after some rumination I opted for Russell. Kim Kinney from The Comedy Store helped us rehearse, and we soon resurrected 'I Wonder If My Mother Ever Knew' from Glad and May days, and a strange song I wrote the lyrics for about an incestuous pederast, inexplicably sung in a West Country accent. It was called 'Was That A Robin I Saw Bobbin On Your Finger, Uncle Tom?' ('Or was it just a little piece of fluff? And why was you a huffin' and a puffin' like you was, and snortin' like you'd just been sniffin' snuff?')

Kim Kinney used to choreograph Soho strippers years before and his directions were along similar lines: 'Pout and sashay! Swing those hips, Julian!'

Russell soon settled into his role as a stooge. He was to be known as 'The Lovely Russell with his Fabulous Upright'. Russell's heterosexuality alone gave me plenty of material to work with. I introduced him as 'the straight I bait – the only known heterosexual in the world of showbiz today – apart from Judith Chalmers'. He had that slightly irritating, lazy self-confidence about him that Oxbridge types often display, but that was a minor matter and easy enough to live with. 'You've got lovely eyes, Russell. Goat's eyes. You'll make someone a lovely yoghurt one day. Are you hot under these lights, Russell? Maybe this will cool you down...' And I threw a glass of water over him.

Spare the rod, spoil the pianist, was my philosophy. And anyway he enjoyed his moment of mock indignation. The more we worked together the better he got. Russell quickly memorised my act and I could turn to him mid-sentence in a blank spell and he would rescue me.

Prior to Edinburgh that year we played three nights at the Purcell Rooms on the South Bank. Proper stage and lights and a Steinway grand for Russell to tinkle on. I called the show *Uncanny and Unnatural* after another song I'd written with Jungr and Parker:

> *Something strangers noticed as they peered into my pram*
> *Uncanny and unnatural, that's what I am.*

I did my best to live up to the new expectations people had of me. Some new material, daring new impersonations from Fanny, stylish costumes by Michael Ferri, a recorded announcement for my entrance and a glitter ball twinkling above me. (Glitter balls have featured in my stage shows ever since, despite the fact that they've crashed to the ground on three occasions over the years and I've narrowly missed what would be certain death. But what a way to go!)

But I note from my diary of that time I wasn't particularly pleased with myself.

6 August 1987

Must be more sure of myself. No good being wishy-washy, is it? Brassier, in fact. Too low on physical energy, too calm. Be more affectionate towards the audience.

Interesting to note how completely I ignored my own advice. I've never gone in for self-confidence and I often find it rather off-putting in others. For better or worse my lethargic ways, off stage and on, have become something of a trademark. As for being nice to the audience, it's not in my nature. An air of amateurishness has come to be expected of me. No one quite knows if I'm going to make it to the end of the show. I was particularly forgetful in those days, possibly due to the vast amounts of marijuana I was consuming before and after the shows. That was where Russell came in handy.

'Where am I, Russell? Who am I?' He could always be relied on to set me back on course. And then be told off for being a smarty-pants. Reviewers in Edinburgh that year noted the fact. 'The whole act is surprisingly hesitant and unprofessional, with Clary seeking desperate prompts from his long-suffering pianist, the Lovely Russell,' wrote Charles Spencer in the *Observer*.

But there were forces at work whatever the critics wrote. People came and clapped and talked of me to their friends, who then came to see for themselves. The amoeba of popularity was multiplying. Despite my lethargy, despite my hesitancy, poor memory and poorer singing, the snowball of fame was rolling down the hill, getting bigger and attracting more attention than was seemly.

Meanwhile in a place called Manchester their chief of police, a bearded hulk of a man called James Anderton, was making some unpleasant homophobic remarks. Gay men were 'the spawn of Beelzebub' he announced, and the AIDS epidemic a direct result of their unnatural practices. Homosexuals were 'living in a cesspit of their own making' – you get the drift. Such unsavoury views from a pillar of society quite rightly caused a storm of protest and I was as incensed as anyone. Fear and ignorance about AIDS seemed to be particularly prevalent among police forces across the nation in those days. There had recently been a raid at the Vauxhall Tavern in south London where 40-odd policemen piled through the door wearing latex gloves, as if merely touching a homosexual might lead to infection. The pretext for the raid was the sale of poppers behind the bar. Lily Savage was thrown down the stairs in full drag but managed to kick an officer in the back. 'The best fucking strike of my life!' The next series of *Saturday Night Live* (now moved to Fridays) seemed as good a place as any to respond. Paul Merton and I wrote a sketch called 'Police Constable Fan Club'. I had a glamorous uniform made and a fluffy pink truncheon.

Evening all! They said it could never be done. They said I'd never be a bobby on the beat, but *quelle surprise*, I'm wearing Marigold gloves and I've got a truncheon in my pocket. Need I say more?

I've only been in the force two weeks and already I'm president of the Shiny Helmet Club. And could I introduce you to Fanny of the Yard – now a fully qualified police dog. She's a sniffer dog. Well, she's got a bit of a cold.

It's a hard life. It's not all flat feet and whistles, you know. They wanted to send me on a dawn raid the other morning. I said I'm sorry but you won't see me before half past ten; I don't have my porridge till nine and I'm not leaving the house without something hot inside me, not for anyone.

But I've got a very understanding boss. I'm James Anderton's personal assistant. I've got the whip marks to prove it. I've certainly earned my stripes. We've got pet names for each other. In private I call him Jimbo and he calls me the Spawn of Beelzebub. He's a hard man but I quite like that.

Now I'm here tonight because the police want to improve their image. We seem to have lost touch with the young people of today. You don't trust us and you don't respect us. So from now on any young person, or YP, placed under arrest will not automatically be beaten up in the back of the van, but instead will be given a nice cup of herbal tea and a fudge finger. Interrogations will now take place in the station sauna with the detective of your choice, and all High Court judges will answer to the name of Shirley.

So what's new?

I was invited back on *Friday Night Live* a few weeks later and decided to do my version of The Shangri-Las' 'Leader Of The Pack'. I had first performed this at the Hackney Empire a few months before, at the suggestion of Steve Edgar who was now with a band called The Howlers.

In Shadow Morton's original anthem a teenage girl has to tell her boyfriend (Jimmy) that her parents have demanded she finish with him. He screeches off on his motorbike and has a fatal crash. She vows never to forget him. The plot remained the same in my version, but there were one or two lyrical modifications. In my version Jimmy and James Anderton became one and the same.

> He was the Leader of the Pack but now he's gone. Well he's dead, let's face it, he was killed in that terrible accident. I'm the Leader of the Pack now, and a much better job I think I'll make of it. I don't drink and drive, which Jimmy certainly did, and I don't actually have a motorbike, but I do have a Sierra Estate, which is much more comfortable: the boys can all fit in the back, which is what I like, and we can travel around together as a group, instead of some kind of threatening, machismo convoy, getting separated by traffic lights and junctions and that sort of thing. He was the Leader of the Pack but now he's gone. Good-bye, Jimbo.

Stephen overheard two men in a pub discussing my performance.

'Did you see that Joan Collins Fan Club on *Friday Live*? He was spaced out of his head.'

'Oh yes, I've seen him a couple of times. He's always like that.'

Someone from 10 Records, a subsidiary of Virgin, was watching and within days I had a record deal. My Thinkman bandmate Rupert Hine produced the single, and 'Leader Of The Pack' reached number 47 in the charts. We might have done better, but I'd got Stephen in the video and he licked an ice cream too suggestively for the network's liking and it was banned before midnight.

Ho hum. My follow-up single was 'I Was Born Under A Wandrin' Star'. Its meagre comedy value stemmed from the fact that I sang in an unexpectedly low, gravelly voice. It featured lots of clippety-clop noises, and references to Dobbin the horse, a feature of my live act at that time: 'Here's your nose bag, Dobbin. Fresh hay soaked in amyl nitrate.' Before the singing started you could hear me say: 'Hold up here a while, Dobbin, and I'll spread my ging-ham tablecloth out over that grassy knoll and fumble in my ruck-sack for my banjeleylee.' I think we sold about five copies. I went on Phillip Schofield's radio show and he played it and enthused in his kindly, professional manner. I got ready to leave while the next record was being played. Off air he gave me a concerned look. 'You don't really expect it to be a hit, do you?' he asked.

'Well, no, I suppose I don't,' I said. And that was that.

Back in television-land, a producer called Michael Hurll was putting together a new Saturday teatime game show called *Trick or Treat* for LWT. It needed two presenters and, as the title suggested, contrasting ones. Chalk and cheese, was the general idea. He'd settled on Mike Smith as one; a harmless, genial man, the male equivalent of his wife, Sarah Greene. But who to pair him with? The pilot with Nicky Campbell hadn't worked. (I could have told him that.) Daringly, Michael thought of me. The show itself was a rather flawed concept: I'd pick preselected punters out of the audience and Mike would give them money tokens they could swap for keys, which may or may not lead to a new hi-fi (treat) or a tin of baked beans (trick). One week the excited contestants were promised a caravan for the final star prize. When the curtain finally went back, a stuffed camel was revealed. I didn't understand it either. Anyway, my main job was to chat to the audience, which I quite enjoyed. I knew the show wasn't very good, but I was just doing what was asked of me. My transition from late-night TV shows to kiddies' teatime caused alarm in some circles.

'TV BOSSES WASH OUT GAY JULIAN'S FOUL MOUTH,' screamed the now defunct *Today* newspaper.

'Gay sex gags by gender bender Julian Clary have been AXED from TV star Mike Smith's game show,' said the *Star*.

'SMITH'S TRIP OR TRIPE DISASTER,' said the *News of the World*.

It seemed to get worse each week. Some sort of former football person called Jimmy Greaves who had downgraded to become a 'TV pundit' chimed in on a live *TV-am* talk-in: 'He asked people in the audience if they'd picked up a bit of trade. He's a prancing poof!'

'GREAVSIE JIBE AT TV POOF,' reported the *Sun*.

Mike Smith gamely defended me: 'I'm going to do a show called *Small-minded Bigotry* and Jimmy's going to star in it.'

I'd had no dealings with the tabloids before and was bemused by all the fuss. Surely they were mad? 'Outrageous drag artist Julian Clary shocked showbiz last night when he appeared on TV wearing MAKE-UP and a crushed velvet suit' (*Sunday Sport*). I ask you. The nonsense all rather peaked when I said on Michael Aspel's chat show that reformed alcoholic Greaves 'must be on the bottle'. Not a particularly kind or interesting comment you might think, but enough to get me on the front page of the

Mirror: 'GREAVSIE IS PUT THROUGH TV'S MINCING MACHINE.'

I wasn't thrilled, but Addison was. 'You made the front page, my son! You've caused a right Ferrari!'

Soon enough, of course, they change the attack. Tabloid hacks collude to create a drama out of nothing in particular, then question the worthiness of the subject they selected, turning to bite the languid hand that fed them. 'Who gives a toss about Julian Clary?' asked Linda Duff in the *People*. 'Gender benders are a thing of '84. Make-up on men is kind of passé, is it not?' I could not have agreed more. This kind of bite was toothless, tabloid gums nibbling painlessly.

The public made their feelings clear, too, if we consult the LWT duty officer's report, a written record of people's telephoned comments. Twenty-two people rang up after the first transmission. 'This is disgraceful.' 'This isn't fit for family viewing.' 'Mr Stein of Dagenham is not happy with Joan Collins Fan Club on the show.' 'The co-presenter is shocking. Why not have a woman?' 'Mr Thomas Crayford has three young sons and finds the gay presenter distasteful.' 'The gay guy is not in keeping with family entertainment.' 'A Yorkshire viewer thinks the producer should be sacked for employing a gay.' 'Merseyside viewer disgusted and sickened by the gay on the show.' But they weren't all so bad: 'Caller started to watch this programme but had to give up because she was suffering from severe visual disturbance brought on by the dazzling costume worn by Joan Collins Fan Club.' My most mysterious message, though, said: 'Julian mentioning South African fruit was unnecessary.'

I rather specialised in making television interviewers uncomfortable and never quite grasped the 'chat' element of chat shows. I often wished I was somewhere else. Such thinly disguised indifference wasn't helped by my insistence on having only my right profile towards the camera, purely for reasons of vanity (the left profile is inferior). This was fine if the interviewer was situated on my left. If he was on my right, I barely glanced at him. I was all for ignoring inane questions and chatting to the studio audience instead.

In 1987 Gary Glitter interviewed me on *Night Network*. Some of his questions made no sense at all. He said that comedy tours were as big as rock and roll shows used to be. 'Is this because the rock and rollers aren't funny any more?'

What was there to say? 'That's a bit high-brow for me,' I said. 'You're new to this interviewing lark, aren't you?'

He struggled on. 'Who had the idea for the act? Was it you or Fanny?'

'I did,' I said. 'Fanny is just a dog.'

I dreaded most of these interviews, although someone like Terry Wogan, who had improvisational skills and wit, could be more fun.

On *The Last Resort*, Jonathan Ross's first question was: 'Why the Joan Collins Fan Club? Where did the idea come from?'

'Let's start with the obvious,' I said rather ungraciously. 'The idea came from wherever ideas come from,' and turned to stroke Fanny.

My boredom was usually obvious. For these shows they want you at the studio four or five hours before you go on for your six minutes on air. You are greeted at reception by an overeager researcher and confined to a windowless dressing room to await your moment. Maybe the researcher will painstakingly walk you across the set explaining that you enter here and walk to the vacant chair like so, as if you might head straight for the fire exit or take your seat on cameraman four's face by mistake.

But the pendulum of good fortune swung relentlessly on in the right direction. With or without my cooperation. What I needed was a show of my own, late night on Channel 4, and a proper boyfriend. The time was right for both, and they were just around the corner.

EIGHT

Some day I'll find you,
Moonlight behind you,
True to the dream I am dreaming.
As I draw near you you'll smile a little smile,
For a little while, we shall stand
Hand in hand.

Noël Coward

When asked if he had any regrets in life, an elderly John Betjeman said: 'I wish I'd had more sex.' If I make that claim in my dotage, somebody slap me.

As fame gradually crept over me, I became aware that anonymous gay cruising would soon be out of bounds. People would stare for the wrong reasons. I might be scandalised in the Sunday papers to the embarrassment of my family and the detriment of my thrilling career. I didn't want that. The night before the first transmission of *Trick or Treat*, I took myself to Hyde Park after dark and had a 'portion' behind a tree with a shadowy figure simply because I knew it might be my last chance to be so reckless. He turned out to be a bit peculiar, as it happens.

'We're both going to go to hell for what we've just done!' he hissed at me, as fearful as if we were standing on the precipice of Satan's fiery cauldron.

'You speak for yourself,' I said, and rearranged my clothing.

I recall travelling home with Fanny on a crowded tube after an innocent stroll on Hampstead Heath had produced unexpected carnal results. People were looking down at her with unusual disdain. I reached down to give her a reassuring stroke on the back and came into contact with the sticky wet ejaculate of my surprise afternoon husband. I hurriedly produced a tissue to wipe my hand and the dog's back, but Fanny's expression – that of a duchess whose husband has just farted at a royal garden party – remains clear in my mind.

It was not dissimilar to the expression on the gasman's face when I opened the door to him early one morning after a night of passion with someone called Augustino. I thought he was offended by the sight of me in a frayed kimono. It wasn't until I closed the door after him and glanced in a mirror that I realised a now dry, flaky residue from the previous evening's activities was spread in expressive jets from forehead to chin, like a jet stream in a clear blue sky.

I found sex in all its variations a reassuring and exciting pastime. Apart from the odd, painful infatuation, true love eluded me, and what you've never had, you don't miss. I'd heard talk that with your soulmate, sex (or love-making as it would then be called) could be elevated to something deep and spiritual, and I looked forward to that elusive, apocalyptic moment, but meanwhile the endless variety of available cock would have to do. I had never quite got the hang of relationships. Even now I don't think I'd pass an A-level in the subject. I might scrape through with a GCSE grade D but only just. I've been told I'm manipulative and selfish by those who have attempted a lasting partnership with me. Well, pardon me for living. I thought the whole point of having a boyfriend was so you could manipulate him. What fun!

But I accept that I'm wrong about that. As for selfish, I went out with someone once whose persistent selflessness drove me to distraction. Every time I asked what he wanted to do he said, 'What do *you* want to do? I'm happy to do whatever you want me to do.' Very kind I'm sure, but neither of us was happy because happiness meant doing what the other wanted to do and we weren't sure if we were doing it or not. A bit of selfishness and plain speaking all round might have saved the day. We couldn't even bring ourselves to split up for ages because we weren't sure if that was what the other one wanted. It was exhausting. I didn't have the energy. Bring back the revolving door and the endless variety of men.

Not that my choice of one-night stands has always been satisfactory. There have been bed-wetters, wallet-lifters, wart-infectors, crab-carriers, colostomy-bag owners and worse. That's just the law of averages. Here are some of the gentlemen callers that I can recall: the Brazilian scaffolder, the Geordie scaffolder, the Irish pick-pocket, the Greek Cypriot drinker, the bald Brighton leukaemia victim, the Chinese sex worker, the Australian blackmailer, the Dutchman, Henry from Chelsea, Andrew the car mechanic from Essex, Emmanuelle – illegal Albanian immigrant, nice Craig and nasty Craig, Miguel the ballet dancer, Tony with low self-esteem, Christopher the dead boyfriend, Jacques the Frenchman *avec* wind, the Nigerian taxi driver, Max the Birmingham lawyer, the Cardiff band bassist, the boy from Hove youth hostel, the Dutch nurse, the man from Madrid who pronounced me 'magnifico!', the air steward in Gran Canaria, the bed-wetting Dubliner, the bed-wetting bouncer from C.C. Blooms, the West End chorus boy, Henry with the dirty sheets, Morgan the Organ, the Spanish hotel worker, Augustino – inventor of the kangaroo game, boy in striped top on holiday in Gran Canaria, his friend, the Swiss flight attendant, THT man, former RUC man with real bullet scars and colostomy bag, Pop-it-in Pat, large man with nice eyes in Rio de Janeiro, Rio man with skin complaint, Chris at university, the Canadian actor, the newsreader, the Texas chef, Prince Charming, an Asian gentleman, a Chinese gentleman, Brisbane martial arts expert boy, Sydney Glenn, two Toms, Angel of Majorca, doctor in a waistcoat in Key West, Palma man with one eye, Roman car driver, prematurely bald Adelaide boy with hairpiece, Thai boy, Sensible Ian, R from Gibraltar.

There were more. Any past conquests scanning the list for their own description and not finding it should not feel inadequate. The omission is no reflection on their performance. It's just that I forget. Lord knows, there are those who are included who have no business calling themselves homosexual at all. Let's just leave it at that, shall we?

It's no wonder I'm always tired. And it's no wonder the night I met Christopher I hadn't the vaguest idea I would fall in love.

But I like the fact we met in a nightclub called Paradise. The Catholic in me hopes that this will be where we meet again – if the contents of this book don't prevent my entry.

My guardian angel had been doing her job well. The boxes for location, career and finances had all been firmly ticked in the last few years – only personal happiness remained. Christopher was 26, he had black hair, brown almond eyes and an Essex accent. He liked Dionne Warwick, Diana Ross, Dawn French and Julie Walters, and claimed to have once seen an old lady tumble head first into the freezer at the supermarket when she reached in for a bag of frozen peas. He would laugh helplessly if anyone tripped up or slipped over. He was outgoing and friendly and without any queeny pretensions. When you looked into his eyes you saw his soul.

We dated for a while before we became official boyfriends. I was more smitten than him initially. I knew we had made a connection, that there was something different about my feelings for this particular man. But then he disappeared. My phone calls weren't returned and there was no sign of him. I felt sad and love sick. True love, so long in coming my way, was being thwarted and I had no idea why. I went off on the *Mincing Machine* tour and wrote a song called 'Dropped Me Like A Brick', which I sang each night draped in my Cloak of Sorrow.

Any port in any storm.
I thought your love would keep me warm.

You kissed me on the cheek,
But you were gone within a week.

Six months later I spotted him on the dance floor at Bang night-club and tapped him on the shoulder. He explained that he had been in hospital with pneumonia, but was now better. There in the nightclub, shouting over the music, he explained that the pneu-monia had been the first sign he'd had that all wasn't well. Although he looked fine and as handsome as ever, he didn't just have HIV, he had full-blown AIDS.

Never mind about that, I said. Perhaps they'll find a cure. We picked up where we left off. Then late one night he turned up unannounced at Seymour Place. It was late and he was tipsy. I buzzed him in through the gate, opened my front door and stood in the middle of the room waiting in my dressing gown. A minute later he flew through the door and into my arms. He was breath-less and desperate to tell me how he'd had a revelatory moment: he loved me. He'd been out at a bar in Islington where all eyes had been upon a devastatingly handsome young man. To everyone else's chagrin, the man had approached Christopher and proposi-tioned him. Christopher panicked, said he was popping to the loo but ran out of the bar and caught a taxi to my place. 'I love you. I love *you*!' After that he never left.

Sticky Moments was a game-show parody dreamt up by Paul Merton. We were sitting in the dressing room at Jongleurs discussing my prospects. *Trick or Treat*, for all its faults, had at least paved the way for me to get my own TV show and we had a meeting arranged with Seamus Cassidy, commissioning editor at Channel 4. A game show was the perfect set-up for me to mess about with punters. 'You can take away points for wearing beige, humiliate the poor bastards all night, then give out rubbish prizes. The winner gets a lift home,' said Paul.

Seamus agreed, but there were a few hoops to jump through first before he'd allow us to create our own production company to make the series. The whole point of this was so we could have control over all aspects of the production and editing process. On *Trick or Treat* the liberal use of dubbed laughter on shots where clearly no one in the audience was laughing at all was irksome. I also wanted to pick the contestants out from the queue where the audience was waiting to enter the studio. This hadn't been done before and was obviously risky as they might not be wacky or extrovert. But to my mind this was just an extension of what I'd been doing for years on the cabaret circuit and I wanted to trust my instincts. But the main problem was that our proposed new company – Wonderdog Productions – had never made a single programme and had no track record of any kind. Seamus was understandably nervous about handing over vast sums of money to such virginal idealists. But Addison, with his bulldog determination, argued on, and after we secured John Henderson, a reassuringly experienced and charismatic director, as both a shareholder of the company and director of the series, we were given the go-ahead.

We set up offices in Noel Street in Soho, printed up stationery with Fanny as our logo, and set to it. Various people sat behind computer screens all day doing who knows what, runners scurried about offering everyone tea and coffee and being generally keen to please, and our producer, the fertile and constantly lactating Toni Yardley, oversaw the proceedings. Michael Ferri made me some outrageous costumes, the like of which had never been seen on British television, and Anne Tilby designed a set so camp and brightly coloured there was some worry that the cameras might spontaneously combust when filming it.

Meanwhile, Paul and I sat upstairs in the boardroom writing the scripts for the ten forthcoming episodes. The six contestants were to take part in several rounds, starting with 'True or False' and culminating in a *Generation Game*-style playlet, and a final round where they had to stuff as many cream cakes into their mouths as possible. At no point could they ever hope to get a question right. All the questions were just set-ups for gags, and the awarding of points was entirely at my discretion. This way I could ensure that the best-value punters made it through to the end. For example:

Question: Which L is King of the Jungle?

Answer: Lionel Blair.

Question: Which L is the most important ingredient in a
marriage?

Answer: Lager.

Question: Which L would you urinate in?

Answer: Luton.

Question: True or false: all condoms are individually
numbered.

Answer: True. You've obviously never unrolled one far
enough.

Question: Tony Blackburn: true or false?

Answer: False, obviously.

Question: Complete the quotation – 'Is that a pistol in your pocket...?'

Answer: Or is your penis engorged with blood?

Question: Complete the quotation – 'Cupid, draw back your...?'

Answer: Foreskin.

A more elaborate game involved the blindfolded contestants searching in a laundry basket for a simple household object, which turned out to be Bernie Winters. After a short chat about which panto he was in that year, he read out a riddle which, in the style of Ted Rogers's *321*, was a clue to a mystery prize:

> *You may find yourself in foreign climes*
> *And although you may feel like revving up*
> *Be careful you don't get sunstroke*
> *And end up in a sea of despair...*

After some speculation about exotic holidays and fast cars, I decoded the riddle for them: 'You may feel like revving up: that could mean a car, but rev is also short for reverend, so revving up could mean dressing up as a priest, which could mean an 18–30s holiday in Majorca. If you take the letters of Majorca and add 15 more you have enough letters to make the sentence: "Get off the table, Mabel, the money's for the beer." Beer means alcohol, alcohol means whisky, whisky means gin, gin means a rowing boat.

Rowing boat, punt. Punt, Oxford. Oxford, Cambridge. Russell went to Cambridge, so you've won Russell!'

At the end of each show I wound up the proceedings by singing a song from my growing repertoire, accompanied by Russell with Barb Jungr and Michael Parker. My glamorous assistant was Hugh Jelly, in the real world called Philip Herbert, an old chum from the circuit where he worked as Randolph the Remarkable. His function was to assist and agree and read out the scores after each round.

We knew we had a hit on our hands after the first few recordings. John Henderson created a jolly, carefree atmosphere in the studio and set me loose to do my thing. Recording was rarely interrupted for any technical reasons. Audience, contestants, crew and performers were all happy and it showed. When it was broadcast even the critics liked it. Paul and I did go on *Right to Reply* to defend the show against two rather lame viewers who, it turned out, had only watched five minutes of the show before they complained. Just prior to the recording the producers had sat them down to watch a video of the entire show. Much to everyone's chagrin, they discovered they rather liked it so there wasn't much of a heated debate after all. Channel 4 commissioned a second series.

When he returned from a holiday to Africa, Paul's behaviour started to become a bit strange. He'd march in circles round the office during meetings, then lie down on the floor and try to calm himself down. He spoke rapidly and excitedly, ideas and thoughts fighting for expression. It was amusing for a while, and as Paul had always been eccentric and excessively imaginative no one took much notice. But I could see he was getting worse by the day, bewildered by his own thoughts. The strange mixture of anxiety and wonderment soon resulted in paranoia, most of which centred round the Freemasons. He was sure they were watching him at all times. When some workmen built a canvas hut outside his flat, he was sure this was just a flimsy cover for their spying activities.

Eventually his girlfriend at the time, Julie Balloo, took him to the Maudsley psychiatric hospital, where it was discovered that the antimalarial pills he had been taking were the primary cause of his malaise. He was there for some weeks and I visited him several times. Once he passed me a note. It read: 'The lunatics have taken over the asylum. Get me out of here.' It was a grim, scary place, but I knew he needed treatment and was probably in the best place. Nevertheless, I felt duty-bound, as a friend, to respond to his plea for help. I had a word with his doctor and it was agreed I could take him out for a few hours.

That night there was an incredible gale-force storm blowing. As we drove through Dulwich the car was almost lifted off the road, and tree branches swung menacingly overhead. We found a restaurant but on the next table an American woman was talking loudly. After ten minutes Paul could stand it no more and asked me to take him back to the ward. It would be a few more days before he was able to cope with the real world again.

I was 30, newly famous, bank account swelling nicely. Since I was a teenager my ambition had been to live in Camden Town and drive a Citroën 2CV. I could now afford to do both, so I tore myself away from Seymour Place and bought the ground-floor flat at 5 Albert Street, Camden Town in north London. It was long and narrow, laid out like a railway carriage, with bedroom, bathroom and kitchen-diner leading off the hallway. Through the French windows was a small patio garden featuring an established vine. It was something of a love nest. Christopher and I curled up on the new Chesterfield sofa with Fanny and counted our blessings. The pendulum of my good fortune was now at full swing.

Christopher worked at the Marks and Spencer headquarters in Baker Street doing something with computers but because of his illness he was able to 'retire' with a pension.

We went on holiday to Portugal where we swanned about wearing matching pastel shorts (like you do when you're in love) and people-watched the package-holiday folk for our entertainment. At our hotel we met a couple called Mr and Mrs Plank. Their name amused us no end. 'Here come the Planks,' we'd say whenever we saw them waddling towards us. They were both barely five foot tall and none too bright. 'They're as thick as two short Planks,' said Christopher.

Every few weeks he'd go to the Middlesex Hospital for blood readings or scans. The results were never encouraging so we just took no notice. He was given more and more pills to take, got thinner and slept a lot, which Fanny loved as there was always someone warm to curl up with. We'd get up most nights and change the sheets because his night sweats were torrential. At this time the first series of *Sticky Moments* had just been broadcast and I was rushing about doing interviews and chat shows and the like. Christopher came with me when he felt like it, but often I'd leave him and Fanny sleeping, putting a Post-it note by the bed with a mound of pills, instructing him when to take them. For some reason the ritual was I'd kiss them both 15 times before I left.

He had a lot of baths. He would slide silently in and lie there motionless. It used to bother me that I never heard him splashing about. I would sit next door and imagine him lying there thinking about his illness. A healthy, carefree person would splash, I thought. Was he looking through the clear water at his failing body, imagining himself as a corpse? I wished the scientists would hurry up and find a wonder drug that would make him better. We didn't talk about him dying at all. We never cried. Maybe we both only thought about it during these silent baths.

I had some shows to do in Dublin and Christopher came with me. Homosexuality was illegal there at that time and when I asked at the check-in for a double room, the receptionist said it wasn't their policy to give double rooms to two men. I looked at him in disbelief.

'I am a gay man here to perform at the Gaiety Theatre. Tonight I shall be interviewed on the Gaye Byrne show. Give me a double room now!'

His face darkened and he handed me a key.

'Now,' I said loudly to Christopher, 'let's go upstairs. I'm desperate for a fuck.'

I remember committing myself to Christopher one time when he was in hospital for a lumbar puncture. We were sitting in the day room talking about him coming home. Somehow the conversation got on to where exactly his 'home' was. Although he'd been living with me in Albert Street, nothing had ever been 'said' officially, and he still had 'Reach View Court' as the address on his medical records. I said I wanted him with me, I wanted to look after him. 'I will see you through this' are the words I remember saying, gravely, eye to eye, hand in hand. It was almost ceremonious. He immediately went to the nurses' desk there in the ward and had Albert Street registered as his home address, and came back looking happy.

There was a merciful respite for six months when the doctors put Christopher on steroids. He was his old self, full of beans, if a little high and relentlessly jolly. We flew to the Maldives for ten blissful days. We swam in the clear warm sea, met up with two amusing florist women in the bar in the evenings, slept in each other's arms and generally carried on like a honeymoon couple. But after a few months the steroids were stopped on account of his bone-marrow readings or some such jargon. We didn't choose to go into too much detail. But he slept a lot again after that.

As with most people who get success in Britain it was decided around this time that I should have a go at America. Addison announced that we were off to New York to play a venue called the Ballroom for three weeks. It's not there any more, but Eartha Kitt had entertained there, and other music acts had. It wasn't known for its comedy. Christopher came too.

We stayed in a big brown flat in Times Square and slept opposite a huge ugly portrait of Ethel Merman. Christopher broke out in red angry lesions on his face and coughed all the time. He came to my opening night nevertheless. There are some things Hide the Blemish cannot conceal and there were concerned looks and grave whisperings all around. Quentin Crisp came and wrote a complimentary review, saying 'Julian Clary wears as much make-up as the human face will allow.'

After that night it all went a bit quiet at the Ballroom. I remember playing to eight people one evening, and they were hoping for a jazz quartet, not buggery jokes and some English queen rifling through their handbags. There weren't many laughs. I went off stage for a costume change, leaving Russell playing a loop of 'Leader Of The Pack'. Why don't I just go home? I thought, and so I did. As I walked down the road I could hear Russell's voice singing ' Leader of the pack, but now he's gone, Leader of the pack, but now he's gone...' over and over. Russell ground to a halt eventually and then called it a day. It was for the best. I'm not really sure if anyone noticed.

We tried to get some hospital treatment for the various ailments Christopher had but after a few initial questions, when our (rather foolish) lack of medical insurance became apparent, we were directed to another hospital and then another. Eventually we came away with a prescription as long as a weekly shopping list. I doled out eight pills of various shapes and sizes for Christopher's breakfast in bed. Down they went and he smiled and laughed. Three minutes later they came up again, projected with consider-able velocity at Ethel. Red, yellow, orange. 'Everything's coming up roses,' said Christopher and laughed again. We went to Coney Island that day and had even more fun.

When we got home to London we both knew there wasn't much time left. We didn't say it out loud. It was obvious. He coughed and slept and sweated. I was off doing TV shows and inter-views, leaving pills by the bed as Christopher and Fanny snuggled under the duvet. I'm aware in retrospect of a kind of panic neither of us acknowledged. We just carried on from day to day and talked sometimes about going on holiday somewhere warm and sunny. I didn't really think he could go far from hospital. His blood readings and cell counts were grim. But we went to Majorca in early June and stayed in a rented villa in the north of the island, far from anyone, surrounded by lemon trees and accompanied by Christopher's mother, Yvonne.

Christopher coughed all night by now, and I got irritable from lack of sleep. We kept a bucket by the bed and looked with suspicion at the morning's booty, sunset red and alarmingly fleshy. Yvonne commented on how thin he was each morning, but then he went to bed and we lounged about the pool and planned the evening meal.

One morning I emptied the bucket and went out to the swing on the terrace with some pills for Christopher. 'Look at my leg!' he said. I knew then it was the end. It was ominously swollen from the knee down and an angry blue and yellow. The rest of his body was so thin and concave it looked like some kind of anchor. Christopher smiled down at his naughty body, but didn't manage a laugh. Who knows how he felt.

I broke through the shutters of the off-limits room in the villa, where I'd previously heard a phone ring, and called an ambulance. I left some money and a note, I remember, explaining there had been an emergency. Yvonne went to do her hair and put diamante earrings on.

In a Palma hospital they examined him wearing surgical gloves. Removing his mask the doctor explained to me that 'the disease has entered its final phase…' No one could believe Yvonne was his mother, she looked so young and glamorous. 'You must try and get him home.'

We couldn't get a wheelchair at the airport, so I whizzed Christopher through sitting precariously on top of a luggage trolley. He had full slap on. There is some airline rule about being 'fit to fly' and we didn't want some jobsworth refusing to let us on board. We made it and as the plane climbed higher the coughing went into a whole new gear. I passed the tissues and slipped the bloody lumps into a plastic bag. 'Is it the flu?' asked the stewardess. 'Kind of,' I said and Christopher's eyes twinkled at me.

Sue Holsten was waiting for us at Heathrow and took us straight to the Brodrip Ward at the Middlesex Hospital in Goodge Street, where familiar nurses greeted us at the door with a smile and a gentle tut in the direction of the patient. We were both relieved, we knew he needed some special looking-after now. But how marvellous that we went on that ill-advised trip, I think today. Christopher had seen the sea and felt the rays of a warm sun one more time. More importantly, he'd done what he wanted.

The next ten days were all taken up with visiting and sleeping. For a couple of days they thought he had TB and the door to his room had warning signs on it. We had to put on masks and plastic aprons before going in to see him. In fact, he had all sorts going haywire in his body, but there was a growth in his lungs that was winning the race to kill him. Yvonne and I had a rota system, but no one was under any illusions. Least of all Christopher. Occasionally I left him to go for a cigarette in the smoking room. The oxygen mask made it difficult for him to speak, so he either wrote things down or mimed. He wagged his finger at me, pointed at me and then at himself. Smoking kills. His notes I keep rolled up in an orange pot by my bed. They say: 'I am missing you xxxx.' 'Will you still love me tomorrow?' 'You are always on my mind.' 'Chris loves Julian.' And, 'Eternally yours, x.'

As the days passed he was moved progressively nearer the nurses' station, a sure sign, if any were needed, that he wasn't getting better. One day I arrived to find him in the prime spot, right opposite, forever under their professional gaze of compassion. A sort of booth with half-glass walls so the nurses can see in. That's the dying room. Whenever I pass the hospital I glance up at the window. It's on the first floor at the angle of the building nearest the main entrance and I wonder if someone is in there, breathing their last breath at that very moment.

The morphine supply went in via his neck and I think there was some kind of dial whereby he could regulate his own supply of pain-killing oblivion. I don't think he was mean with himself.

The last night he kept trying to tell me something and I kept trying to understand. It went on for hours and in the end I did something rather unsuitable for the occasion. I pretended I understood, just to give him some peace. His anxiety at being unable to express whatever his last thoughts were before passing on was too much to bear. But I feel bad about it now. I'd like to say now that when I'm speaking my last, no one is to say, 'Oh, yes dear,' until I've made myself crystal clear.

Soon after that his breathing settled into a slow shallow rhythm. Everyone got ready. But death didn't come. Eight hours later my stomach rumbles were spoiling the tranquillity of the scene and I slipped out of the room and over the road for scrambled eggs in a greasy spoon café. Twenty minutes later as I hurried along the corridor I was met by a nurse. He'd gone and I hadn't been there. But I shouldn't feel bad. It's often the way. Sometimes people don't want to die in front of anyone, she said. I went in to see him and put a circle of flowers around his face. I couldn't bear the thought of body bags and refrigerated drawers, so I asked them to leave him lying in state for three hours. Ideally I wanted three days, but I knew there was a queue for that room.

I said goodbye and thank-you to his doctor, Michelle. I was surprised at how upset she was. I thought they just wrote in the time of death and closed the file, but she cried real tears. 'He was so lovely,' she said. I met her by chance at the theatre a few years later, and although we only exchanged pleasantries, we both had tears in our eyes.

The funeral was on a very hot, sunny July day. We went in Sue's Saab convertible with the roof down. Me, Frances, my mother and Sue driving, all dressed up. I suppose it looked like a glamorous outing, four people from the King's Road off to the country for the day with smoked salmon and vintage Cava in the boot. I didn't cry although I sweated a lot, torrents from forehead, back drenched and trickles down my trouser legs. Alternative tears.

His clothes stayed in the wardrobe for years. Sometimes I'd lift a sleeve and get a whiff of the Dead Boyfriend. Yvonne took away his shoes, I remember, sorting out pairs to give to his friends. 'He'd want them to have something to remember him by.'

Two days later I met up with Paul Merton to start writing a sitcom for Channel 4. We wanted to call it either *The Man from Uranus* or *Meet the Rent Boy*, but by the time it went to air it was called *Terry and Julian*.

It felt a bit disrespectful, writing buggery jokes at such a sombre time. Should I not have been at home crying and wearing black?

'The thing is,' said Paul, always economic with his words of wisdom, 'you can only think about one thing at a time. At least for the hours we're writing, you can't be miserable.' And, as always, he was right. Writing buggery jokes is the perfect therapy for the bereaved. Gales of unseemly laughter were soon coming from the open window of our office in Noel Street. Whenever I became slightly pensive, Paul would do something funny, like shout out of the window to the workmen on the scaffolding opposite: ''Ere, Bert, send up my underpants, would you?'

Two days after burying my lover I was laughing all day long. It was life affirming.

I had a 'real' communication with Christopher some years after he died. I was depressed, stoned and listening to Dionne Warwick's recording of 'Heartbreaker'. I was missing him and felt that he was missing me. I thought I heard him calling me, forlorn and desperate for my physical presence. It wasn't as if he was just in another room or another town, he was in another world, behind glass, through the mirror. I only mention it because it was one of several such experiences I had for a few years. They have always been quite distressing because try as I might I couldn't comfort or reassure him. I gave up smoking dope.

But maybe it was these experiences that made me try something regrettable. About eight years after he passed away I went along to see a psychic in his surburban semi one winter evening with my friend Penelope. He was in great demand and we'd booked months in advance. We arrived at an ordinary semi-detached house. A porky man sat at the door with a money tin on his knees and charged us £25 to go in. I handed over £30 and waited for my change but the tin was snapped shut. We went into the garden and about 20 people stood around, mostly pale worried-looking women. The atmosphere was hushed and expectant. Eventually we were directed to the 'Spirit Lodge', little more than a roomy garden shed at the end of the path. Inside a hodge-podge of chairs, some comfy armchairs, some of the wooden school vari-ety, were arranged in a rough circle. The porky man arrived and explained that the psychic would soon be with us. The seance would take place in complete darkness and we were sternly told not to make any sudden loud noises as this could put the medium's life in serious danger. After the build-up in came the star attraction, right on cue. Obviously he'd been listening outside the door.

He sat in a vacant chair that was really more of a throne. He strapped himself in with plastic ties around his wrists and ankles, explaining this was necessary in case of convulsions. The lights were turned out and we sat in pitch darkness. We then sang a rous-ing chorus of 'She'll Be Coming Round The Mountain When She Comes' – to summon the spirits, apparently.

First he 'channelled' Charlie, a twelve-year-old boy from Victorian London. He began to speak in a cockney falsetto: 'My mum's a lady of the night but she's still a lady.' Charlie mentioned various random names from the Other Side, until a punter whis-pered their recognition. The general drift was that they were 'all right' and no one was to worry. Next up was Dolly, a former music-hall artist who had committed suicide on the jagged edge of a baked-beans tin. She was raucous and theatrical and also brought messages from the dead saying all was well.

When she left there was a pause. From the nasal tones and the greeting, 'Oh 'ello, it's Kenneth 'ere...' I gathered we were to believe Kenneth Williams was in our midst. So far I was prepared to go along with all this nonsense. It was vaguely amusing as a naff cabaret, but I was disturbed by the quivering responses of the assembled punters who'd handed over their cash in the belief that they really were getting an audience with their dearly departed.

But it was to get a lot more unsavoury. Suddenly Kenneth's voice changed to a breathy whispery sing-song. 'Hellooo! It's Christopher! Julian, I love you! Thank you for looking after me! Thank you! I love you!' I felt spidery fingers stroking my cheek. Although I was incensed by the impersonation, at the time I just said a curt 'Thank you' and brushed away his hand. How low can you get? Pretending to be dead people for money? As it turned out this was his finale. Once again we were asked to sing-a-long-a-psychic, this time to 'When The Saints Go Marching In', although I'm quite sure the choice of song is irrelevant. As I worked out later, this is just to stop us detecting the noise of our medium getting in and then out of his plastic ties. As this was going on I felt a chair leg dig into my calf and when the lights came back on, there he was, in a state of collapse from his exertions, the chair in a different part of the room. We sat in bleary-eyed silence while Porky Man untied him, near collapse from his supernatural efforts, and ushered him out of the shed with the delicate reverence accorded to the Turin Shroud.

We, the paying public, then filed silently out. As we slipped through the side gate I saw him, Britain's premier psychic, smoking a Benson and Hedges in the kitchen, a healthy bulge in his top pocket, no doubt the £500 he'd conned out of us. It wasn't until I was back in the car that my indignation surfaced. Why had I gone along with it? Why hadn't I exposed the con for what it was there and then? How dare he pretend to be Christopher, or anyone else's dearly departed?

I had felt the need to close this chapter with a moving epitaph to my dead boyfriend, such as: When I think of Christopher now I feel a warm glow, as if I'm basking in his presence although that is gone forever, on this earth at least. His eyes are alive, hovering in front of me, glorious amber fireworks of adoration, his aura swirls around me like a cashmere wrap fluttering in the breeze of an unknown existence. His mood is always benign, the gentle euphoria of an angel, banishing shadows and illuminating all that is dark and confusing. I know he is always there, I only have to call. It's just like the movies.

But I think it sounds a bit crass, don't you? The mourning homosexual secretly loving the tragedy of his bereavement, making sure he has a faraway look in his eyes at all times. His own pose and posture more important to him than any real depth of sorrow in his soul. His relationship with the dead the only one he can keep alive.

The dead don't snore or leave you for another. Nor do you bump into them unexpectedly when you are out on the town with someone else. In many ways, death is the ideal ending. There is a lot to be said for it.

NINE

Three letters to Nick.

5 Albert Street
21 March 1992

Dear Nick,

Ola! I've been to Paris, if you please, with Ivan
Massow, though there was no hanky panky. Probably
because I've just enjoyed a brief 10-day affair-ette with a
young American called Tommy. He was delightful: very
small and Italian-looking, with a body that was no
stranger to the gym. He's gone back to Chicago now,
which is probably just as well: a transatlantic lover is the
only type I could cope with, I fear, but it was a pleasant
distraction.

Meanwhile, I've just got a part in a new Carry On film – *Carry On Columbus*, which will be fun I should think.

Probably as a result of pawing young Tommy's washboard stomach, I've joined a gym myself: a swish one, of course, behind Liberty's, and I have a personal trainer called Dave, a kind of gladiator with a cockney accent. I did my first workout today and couldn't help but get very camp-faced with all the serious body-builders. It annoyed them no end, I could tell, when I cried 'O-er! Which one's for my laterals?' There was much grunting and clanging of weights. Dave was amused, although he does refer to his girlfriend in every other sentence, I suppose in case I try to corner him in the sauna. Physical exertion is the only thing that gets me going and lifts the gloom of bereavement. It started with the Y-Plan video, then Jane Fonda and now the gym. Who knows where it will end?

Love Julian x

Pinewood
6 May 1992

Well hello,

Here I be trussed up in doublet and cod piece (chips are off) in dressing room 82 of F Block. Over on stage E a life-size reconstruction of the Santa Maria awaits me. Maureen Lipman is currently carrying on there, along with Richard Wilson (with whom I share a cabin...), Jim Dale, Alexei Sayle and Jack Douglas.

It's a laugh being here. Pinewood is a bit run down and disused now, but it still has a whiff of former glories – ghosts of Messrs Hawtry and Williams follow you through the ornamental gardens.

A minibus full of minor celebrities collects me at 6.20 a.m. and by 7 I'm in the make-up chair, tended to by Sara ('a collection of miniature Toby Jugs can look very attractive'). There's much sitting around, of course. I simply have to create mischief to pass the time. Now I'm known as 'the grass' – not for any drug-related incidents but because Sara Crowe (famous for the Philadelphia cheese adverts and for upstaging Joan Collins as Sybil in *Private Lives*) puts additional blusher on in the privacy of her dressing room after she's been to make-up, and I told on her. She also had two glasses of wine in the canteen the other lunchtime and I told again. It's all lots of fun unless you get trapped in a corner with Jim Dale who likes (nay, insists) on telling you about his Broadway triumphs. He's more fun if you get him onto Kenneth Williams anecdotes, but that's not always an easy transition to make.

I also flirt with the extras; poor souls sat around on bales of hay for three days, waiting to be called. Two lovely Greek brothers and a muscle man/boy from Madame Jojo's.

I find it very all-consuming. There's no life outside of filming. I just go home to sleep and on a good day, water my patio, which is ablaze with geraniums.

I play Diego, the prison governor, an 'amiable, vague, somewhat camp character' as the script puts it. Michelle Pfeiffer wasn't round so they gave the part to me. The dialogue is as you'd imagine. After water is discovered in my cabin I rush up to the bosun and say: ''Ere, I've just had a leak in the hold!'

Bosun: 'Well, next time do it over the side.'

After three takes my mind begins to wander and I say, ''Ere, I've just had a leak over the side.' Fortunately our director, Gerald Thomas, saw the funny side. He's very gentlemanly and smartly turned out at all times. On bank holiday Monday he wore casuals, though.

'I'm afraid I can't work with corduroy,' I sniffed, indicating his perfectly pressed beige trousers. He obligingly moved out of my eyeline.

So between *Carry on Columbus* and the patio, that's my life until we finish on 29 May.

My mother, if you please, said she was going to enter some playwriting competition about homelessness for the *Independent*. Or rather she said she'd tell me her idea and I could write it. I think not. They're in Majorca at the moment with Grandma, Auntie Tess and Uncle Ken. They're all getting older now. Uncle Ken's just had new teeth fitted. They'd worn away on one side where he'd stuck his pipe for the last 70 years.

To finish here's a good story from Sara Crowe. One day while rehearsing for *Private Lives* she wore a big diamante brooch. Joan Collins enters and says: 'Darling, what a gorgeous brooch! On anyone else it would look expensive.'

That's showbiz. Lots of love,

Julian x

5 Albert Street

22 June 1992

Well hello,

Sorry there were no more missives from Pinewood. I think it was the day after writing to you that I slipped on a cable and fractured a bone in my foot. I had an attractive limp until a week ago, to say nothing of the constant pain. Still I got a basket of fruit out of Gerald Thomas (not a claim many could make) and they got Peter Gordino to double (feet only) my flamenco dance. It's all over now and quite a blur it all seems.

All in all the five weeks were a hoot. Sara Crowe dated, fell in love with and then announced she was going to marry Jim Dale's unsavoury son Toby. Everyone smiled politely when the announcement was made. (Toby being 26, fairly witless, grubby, Jack-the-lad sort.) I said to my make-up artist, while the pretence of 'how lovely' was still being maintained, 'I'm just wondering if he's good enough for her,' in the manner of a powdered aunt at the hairdresser's. 'I'm glad you said that,' whispered Miss Monzani through gritted teeth as she reshaped my eyebrow. So within minutes we'd spread the word that really we weren't delighted at all. In fact, we rather hoped poor Sara would come to her senses. 'She's on the rebound,' I said. 'So is he,' said Miss Monzani knowingly. But we must wait and see.

Anecdotal highlights were Bernard Cribbins telling us how he got stung on the bum while 'going at it' with his wife on the sand dunes in Cornwall. Bernard's obsession with shooting, fishing, trapping and pest control can probably explain his strange Womble phase.

I've just re-read *Mapp and Lucia*, hence the E.F. Benson-ish tone. In fact, I read it by the swimming pool in Mykonos. Had two hilarious weeks, with Patricia McGowan (1st week), then Ian Shaw (middle) and Philip (last week). Highlights from Patricia were her eccentric Scottish phrases, thus 'Have you got a hangover?' became 'Have you got a dangly donger?' Ian Shaw was good fun. Found a piano bar in town and he nightly took the place by storm. (Sometimes he sang, too.) Then Philip arrived and it all got very camp. We rather forgot ourselves in the Santa Marina swimming pool, when Philip was teaching me the crawl. (A stroke I've never mastered.) The hushed and snooty atmosphere among well-to-do Americans and Germans was rudely shattered when Philip, at the triumphant moment when I achieved the crawl for the first time, shouted, 'That's it, girl, you've got it!' We also did lots of Palare: 'Vada the lallies on the omi-polone at the bar.'

Mykonos is, of course, the gay capital of Europe, so what the provinces are like I can't imagine. It's a surprisingly tacky collection of gay bars full of international hairdressers.

We met some funny Americans. 'Hi, my name's Harry, I'm a singer-songwriter from California and I'm also a good fuck.' Or, 'I'm here for a life-changing experience.'

Romantic highlights were a Frenchman called Marcel and a boy whose name I can't remember who came from somewhere like Egypt but who definitely wasn't English or American.

It was quite a tiring holiday for someone who went away to rest. All that vadaing and those Metaxa Colas are all very well, but the next thing you know the sky is turning purple and the dawn is upon you.

So I've been back a week or so and quite exhausted by it all. *Terry and Julian* starts churning into action in August. Gawd help us. That's me more or less up-to-date. My grandmother isn't well still. Her hip hurts and she keeps forgetting if she's had her lunch or not. M and D thinking of building a granny annexe onto their house. My patio is a riot of colour and Tommy from Chicago is still a regular feature by telephone.

Friday is the anniversary of Christopher's death so I feel decidedly turbulent in the emotional department. Started a new course of therapy with my therapist. Now I lie down with my eyes closed. Gets to the nitty-gritty faster.

Our office in Noel Street is just around the corner from your place of employ so maybe we could meet up one day? It would be nice to see you.

I hope life is amusing,

Lots of love, Julian x

Russell and I had been on an exploratory visit to Australia before, but by 1992, *Sticky Moments* had appeared on their television screens and had rather taken off. Always ready to party Down Under, they made the weekly transmissions into social events with barbies, tinnies and fancy dress. As soon as the series finished, it was repeated. When we went to Australia and New Zealand in 1992 it was for a 62-date tour and a TV special called *Brace Yourself Sydney*. The timing was perfect. I was newly famous and I was all the rage. Fanny went to stay with my parents and spent five months looking expectantly out of the dining-room window for my return.

On my last night in London I went to visit Stephen. He was ill, and in the familiar Brodrip Ward. He slipped his jeans on over his pyjama trousers and we went to a bar. The next thing I knew he'd bought three Ecstasy tablets from someone and was swallowing them ceremoniously before my very eyes.

I arrived in Australia ahead of the entourage to do a few weeks of publicity. Gaynor Crawford was in charge of this department and she would hire an entire hotel corridor and install journalists in ten adjacent rooms. I was thrust into each room for exactly ten minutes, hoicked out mid-sentence when the time was up. One day a visit to the Melbourne Positive Living Centre appeared on my afternoon schedule. Before tea or cakes could commence there was a photo-opportunity to deal with. The photographer said, 'Could we have a shot of you chatting to someone living with AIDS?' An amicable young man with the relevant qualifications volunteered and we settled ourselves on some chairs and pretended to chat, oblivious to flashbulbs and zoom lenses. But the photographer wasn't happy. 'Could we have the PWA lying on the bed and Julian with his arm around him?' The PWA and I exchanged weary glances.

We were playing large theatres for several weeks in each city. *My Glittering Passage* was a big theatrical extravaganza, with 18 costume changes, set and props and special effects. Apart from Russell and Hugh Jelly, we employed a camp backing singer called Michael Dalton. Technical matters were sorted by Helen Jackson, or 'Helga, the lesbian in the wings' as she became known, and Grazio Abella. There were producers, tour managers, sound lesbians, stage managers and a tattooed lighting boy called Damo.

The performances got under way in New Zealand. For those not in the know, Kiwis pronounce 'a' and 'e' vowel sounds as if they were 'i' which can lead to some misunderstandings for the untrained ear. During my first show in Auckland I asked a couple where they met and they said 'tricking'. I naturally assumed they were prostitutes. In fact, they met up a mountain with nothing more interesting than a haversack on their backs.

In one of their splendid restaurants after the show, Mr Jelly ordered cock-a-leekie soup and asked the waiter if it had real 'cock' in it.

On such a gruelling tour we needed our creature comforts about us. I had nine suitcases. Mr Jelly had a collection of fluffy toys, which he added to each week. By the time we reached Brisbane in Australia he had more than a dozen: kangaroos, koalas, lambs, emus and Tasmanian devils. But disaster awaited on the baggage carousel. The holdall they travelled in had split, and the heads, limbs and beaks of Hugh's various surrogate children were scattered among the suitcases. 'It's my own fault,' he sobbed. 'The bag wasn't big enough … there was a teddy bear overdose.'

Paul O'Grady had warned me that a Cloud of Evil hung over Adelaide. Even on the drive into town from the airport I sensed something fruity in the air. I felt a strange sexual ache in my loins that remained for the duration of my stay. People in the streets have a look of readiness about them, some vague, dark, slightly unsavoury desire shining in their eyes. You can imagine groups of Adelaide folk meeting in barns at night in deserted fields and performing strange gratuitous acts on each other, children and animals. Vada-laide, we called it, on account of their staring eyes. Indeed, there had been a recent spate of kidnappings there. Teenage boys bundled into vans and driven off, only to be discovered dead, defiled and decomposing in some remote ditch months later.

It was warm but threatening rain when we arrived. This didn't stop the hotel receptionist saying, 'Beautiful day, isn't it?' with that glazed Adelaide look in her eyes.

I nearly let it pass but couldn't. 'Well, it's cloudy,' I said.

'I like clouds,' came the dreamy response, and she beamed at the fountain as it tinkled in the foyer.

We went out to play that night and I was chatted up by a gay couple in their early twenties, one blonde, one dark. They invited me back to their place for a threesome. Always ready to try something different, I said yes. I had sex with a lot of Australian men in my time. It saved talking to them. After a confusing hour or so of tangled limbs and surprise manoeuvres, we were all tired and dozing off. The blond boy, resting across my chest, then prodded me awake and said, 'I've got something to tell you.' Predicting his next sentence I arranged my face into a sympathetic expression. But he didn't speak. He reached up to his head, got hold of his public schoolboy fringe and pulled it. With the unmistakable growl of Velcro, he removed his hair and plopped it on the bedside table. He was a complete baldy.

We had been greeted rapturously in each city, but on our first night in Adelaide I was aware of some disruption at the back of the stalls. We carried on regardless, and it wasn't until after the show that we learned there had been no less than three fights in the auditorium. Police had been called and were taking statements from the injured. At the stage door I met a woman with a horribly swollen eye who had been punched by a man when she told him off for talking homophobic nonsense. A boy called Scott had been kicked to the ground and was in shock.

Later we went to wind down at a gay club called Cloud 9 where the staff were recovering from an attack by six local queer-bashers. They had stormed in an hour earlier wielding broken bottles; two bouncers were having their injuries attended to in hospital. The bar staff served us drinks with bandaged heads and hands. Punters were few on the ground but we stayed and watched the show – two drag queens and three boys in cut-off shorts doing rather well to a Madonna track. Whether all this nastiness was a nightly occurrence in Adelaide or had simply erupted in my honour I couldn't say, but my performance certainly inspired strong opinions one way or the other, as the next day's review testified.

'Derivative, insulting, patronising and pathetic drivel,' wrote the *Sunday Advertiser*. 'Julian Clary is the most embarrassing, inept and unfunny comedian you'll ever have the misfortune of seeing.'

The matter didn't end there. The next night I was featured on Channel 10 news, where they read bits of the review and filmed indignant punters coming out of my show kissing their programmes and me signing autographs. I rang my mother to tell her I was on the news.

'Why?'

'Well, I got a bad review...'

We were packed out, of course. In the next week's *Sunday Mail* letters page, a headline declared: 'ADELAIDE THEATRE-GOERS HAVE THEIR SAY! The only drag is your critic.' Ten letters were printed, all saying nice things about the show. Printed between them in darker lettering was a reprint of the original review.

There was small-scale weirdness too. One night after a pleasant evening chatting to one of the Sisters of Perpetual Indulgence, called Sister Whip Me, Beat Me, Call Me Louise, I returned to the hotel at about 1 a.m. The receptionist told me a gentleman had arrived an hour ago claiming to be a member of my party and asking if he could wait in my room. 'His name was Mr Hammond, about 55, wearing a blue shirt.' I knew no one called Mr Hammond and had invited no 55-year-old men up to my room.

Perhaps he was also known as 'David Pervis', someone who phoned me at the hotel every few hours and whose calls I always refused. 'I don't know anyone of that name,' I had said to the operator. 'Ask him to leave a message.' Within minutes, cryptic typed messages were being slipped under my door, saying 'Lift your game' or 'Be careful tonight'.

One night before the show he manifested in person in my dressing room. He just walked in and said, 'I'm David Pervis. May I shut the door?' I said no, he couldn't. He was about 50, badly preserved, swaying slightly and with wicked, watery eyes that spoke of madness, perversion and violence. 'Do you work in the theatre here?' I asked, having clocked the dubious eyes and been further alarmed by the clinging, clammy handshake. The answer was no and he settled down on a chair, looking at me triumphantly as if I was a long-lost son or a pleasant fabric he was thinking of covering his sofa with. Just then Helga arrived with a photographer. 'This man must go!' I said and Helga did some strong-arm lesbian work.

I never established if Mr Hammond was David Pervis, as the next day we moved on. As we drove out of Adelaide I could see a thick bluish-black cloud hanging low over the city. I knew what Paul O'Grady would have said.

We were all tired out by Christmas and in need of our week off. I had a painful ear infection and was on a course of antibiotics. My rather wonderful surprise gift from our promoter Adrian Bohm was a week's holiday in a luxury villa on the island of Orpheus on the Barrier Reef. It was a beautiful island: palm trees, cocktails, snorkelling outings to see the underwater coral and multi-coloured tropical fish. Unfortunately my doctor had given me strict instructions not to get any water in my ear. I sat on the beach and listened to others snorting in wonderment through their snorkels. It was a bit like being in a sauna but unable to take your towel off. And there were mosquitoes to deal with.

26 December 1992, Island

How anyone can stand living here with these wretched mosquitoes, sand-flies and so on is a mystery to me. I'm bitten to buggery and have just had a tantrum with my can of Rid – spraying a harmless and rather beautiful moth for no reason, other than it was visible and slow enough to catch. It's flapping listlessly on the kitchen counter as I write. I'm rather hoping it will recover and fly off home to its babies, full of tales of the evil punter in chalet number nine. Some other flying nuisance has just dived into my Champagne and sizzled to its end. A relative's revenge.

My watch mysteriously gained two hours today. I went down to dinner at what I thought was nine o'clock, full of questions about how come it wasn't getting dark at the usual time only to be told by a waitress setting napkins in a deserted dining room that it was only 7 p.m. My guess is the girls who serviced my room played a trick on me, tipped off by the lunchtime waitress who was clearly put out by my 2.30 p.m. arrival. Although I just wanted a salad and apologised, I guess it elongated her shift a bit and by resetting my Rolex they thought they'd buck me up a bit or at least make their point. Can't think how else it happened. It was two hours fast exactly.

On a desert island all by myself I have time to think.

Reaching for a cigarette as I dined alone tonight, I suddenly realised the significance of the date. Christopher died exactly eighteen months ago today. Made me pause. Seems such a long time ago, but it isn't really.

There have been three significant lovers since then. Tommy (Chicago), Hans (Amsterdam) and Josh (Perth). An interesting geographical triangle if nothing else. Josh is foremost in my mind, almost an obsession, but I remember when the others were too. And I'm reading Adam Mars-Jones's *Monopolies of Loss*, which is making me philosophical, seeing my life in terms of a short story (or series).

Josh 18, me 33 – he on the threshold of physical maturity, me on the threshold of decline, hanging on by means of expensive moisturiser and sit-ups.

But Christopher, lover, friend, soulmate, meaning of Life and Death, is there all the time, in the foreground and the background.

And later...

Feeling a bit sluttish now.

Just spoke to Hans for the first time in a week and he sounded all sleepy and sweet and pleased to hear from me. It felt cosy and familiar and reassuring. With a little prompting from me to 'say something nice' he said he still loved me and said he hadn't done 'naughty things. And you?'

'I've been a good boy,' I lied.

Didn't eat much dinner as I wasn't hungry and I'm feeling fat. My hands constantly wander down to the midriff bulge, or when I'm alone grip the purses of flesh above the hips. Go they must! Exercise, less eating, more gym and less alcohol for me. Oh yes!

Why is cruising such an important part of gay life? I was day-dreaming just now about sporting my new tan at 3 Faces [Melbourne nightclub] and even when I think about Josh coming to Melbourne or, in my more loyal moments, Hans coming to Sydney, a part of me feels deflated because 'it', that cruisy, hunting, ravenous twinkle, knows that it will not be able to come out and play. It's positively odd. That peculiar instinct is only ever happy and sated for about 20 minutes at a time, when contact has been made but the 'kill' not yet secured. It's a kind of hormonal surge. Similar to the fight-or-flight adrenaline rush. Its sexual identity coursing through the body, highlighting all innate powers of communication towards sex, sex, sex.

Sometimes wonder if Josh is a rent boy. A nasty queen with bad breath whispered in my ear one night, 'I think you should know the boy you've been, er, seeing is interested in, shall we say, the financial side of things...'

So perhaps when Josh dashes off in the mornings to

retrieve his car that's parked somewhere it shouldn't be, he's actually in a hurry to service some old trout.

I don't know, but I want to. I think we must take into account that the informant was so unsavoury with a manic laugh and a ridiculous ponytail. Silver and greasy, it looked as if it could have your eye out when he swung his head around in Munchkin-like mirth. On my last night he sidled up to me again: 'I hope you've enjoyed Perth and the, er, various pleasures we have to offer...'

After the holiday, the tour picked up again in Melbourne. Addison paid a visit. On New Year's Eve we did two shows back to back at 7 p.m. and 9 p.m. at the Universal, a sweat-box theatre. As I came off stage dripping with sweat he said, 'You think it's hot here, mate, you want to try it in there,' heaving a thumb in the direction of the auditorium. 'Well, where do you think I've just been?' I snapped. This is a fairly typical exchange. That night at 3 Faces he started earholing me, talking conspiratorially and quickly about business and who's who. The night's phrase was 'coming out the woodwork'. 'I don't trust that John Pindar. I don't forget. Three times he turned us down for the Melbourne Festival and now you're big news he's coming out the woodwork.' Or: 'That Hocking and Wood – no sign of them last year, when you were at the Comedy Club. Now you're making them lots of money they're coming out the woodwork.'

I called Stephen. He was at home in Deptford having discharged himself from hospital. He sounded very ill. I asked him how he was. 'I'm dying!' he shrieked. 'I'm a full-blown AIDS boy now. In my heart of hearts I think I'm dying. I'm sick of being ill.'

Don't let anyone ever tell you that fame comes overnight. There is a time when you buy into it. You see what lies on the horizon and you either go towards it or away from it. And once you decide to go towards it, it's like a panther chasing a three-legged gazelle. Fame is in your sights and you have but to run. There it was, wafting before me like gladioli in the breeze. There was no excuse not to grasp hold.

For all its drawbacks I recommend fame if it comes your way. You get paid more, it's a tonic for your self-esteem, people are nicer to you and it makes life more interesting. It helps if you have a particular talent of some description. I imagine if you are a *Big Brother* contestant people just want to thump you.

But you have to watch out once you are famous. Weirdoes, for example. A sewage worker from Yorkshire wrote to me for years. Curly, babyish writing in green ink, telling me how disgusting and perverted I was in descriptive, some would say arousing, prose. A disturbed teenager from Newcastle told me how fervently she wanted to cut off her breasts, this alarming information written on the reverse side of a Marks and Spencer's ready-made meal cardboard cover. She completed the missive with a review of the said meal. ' A little salty, but the creamy sauce was delicious.'

Which is not to say that all fans are such a worry. A dozen or so regulars started to appear at the stage door. When on tour I couldn't help but notice that the same faces would wave me good-bye at the stage door in Sheffield, for example, and be there to greet me at the venue in Derby when I arrived to sound-check the next afternoon. Soon the front row was completely occupied by the same girls. They didn't laugh when everyone else did as they had heard it all a dozen times before, but if I strayed, even momentarily, from the script, they all fell about.

They came with us on whole tours. First there were 'the Billericay girls', Helen, Elaine and Sharon, teenagers from Essex who loved the camp, fancied Russell and were prepared to sleep in skips to catch a glimpse of us. Each night, if 2,000 people were transported to camp heaven, I was high and happy. But there were nights when the fragile bouquet of camp, improvised and musical nonsense received a more modest response. The faithful were there come what may. I always felt reassured when I saw them.

For a year or so I almost had pop star status. Girls screamed and grannies parodied desire. Women of a certain age altered their breathing when I hugged them. Mercifully this died down after a while. A more mature, less tactile collection of women now come to see me. Some have been around so long now I follow their lives with almost as much interest as they follow mine. But not quite.

10 January 1993. Melbourne

A review in the *Sunday Age* describes me as 'fast as quicksilver'. Come again? Mind you, another review mentioned my 'taut frame', which, for someone obsessed with their midriff bulge and given to cheap champagne and brandy binges on alternate nights, was very pleasing. Hurrah for another theatrical illusion, say I.

Hector [a friend of mine] arrived yesterday and we met up at 3 Faces for a post-show rave. Well, too much to drink and a late-night visit to the Peel [a seedy pub], which was tragic. Made me think of going to dinner at his place once when Christopher was quite ill. He laughed all the way there because we were going to 'Hector's House'.

It was lovely to see a face from home. What's more, he had a present for me of two Valium. So I breezed through the evening on one, took the other when I got home, and before you could say Rex Mossop, I was boohooing down the phone to a very sober Hans in Amsterdam.

'I'm lonely, I miss you, our relationship can't survive the separation' was the general text and produced a number of 'sweethearts' from Hans and vague talk of coming out to see me. The state I was in rather concerned him I think, but he asked, 'Have you taken a pill?' and in that nursey-like way said the right things and told me to go to sleep. That's the trouble with these nine-hour time differences. People aren't on the same wavelength.

I had met Hans, a Dutch nurse, the previous summer while on a weekend break in Amsterdam. He was tall and lean with long Ali McGraw hair. 'I am very beautiful,' he informed me, 'I get a lot of attention in the bars.' In fact, I'd put him in the show, telling the punters nightly how his orgasms were the eighth wonder of the world. 'We're talking volume (Wellington boots) and we're talking velocity. I've had to board up the windows.'

When I announced my extended trip away, I asked if he would come and visit me. 'Twenty-four hours on a plane? Fuck off!' he said with typical Dutch forthrightness. Now, following my distressed call, he managed to take some time off work and I arranged a ticket for him. Discussing the arduous flight a few days later I explained there was nothing much to do on a plane but eat and sleep. Hans said, 'But I am sure that the food is much better in first class.' Of course it is, but I'd booked him into economy. Next day I phoned my agent and arranged an upgrade.

Hans had no inkling of my infidelities. When our conversation moved on to Michael the backing singer's shifty new beau, Hans said, 'But you look at Australian men differently. You have me to compare them to. I put everyone in the shade.' We both laughed but then he said, 'No, but really, it is true,' and we both laughed again. For different reasons.

31 January 1993. Melbourne

Hotel full of Sydney queens here for the Red Raw party tonight. They were out in force by the pool. One was heard to say to the other as they looked me over: 'Nothing to write home about.' 'I thought I'd lost a contact lens,' said the other.

Later I went for a drink with Mark Trevorrow, aka Bob Downe, and the others. Again I was perused by two clearly unimpressed queens. One leaned across to ask, 'Are you enjoying the tour?' I said I was, thank you. 'You're looking very tired...' said the other. 'That's because I am tired,' I explained. They retreated, po-faced, but not quite out of earshot. 'Arrogant, isn't he?' said one. 'Yes. And look at the ugly people he's with!'

I turned to Mark. 'I'm not arrogant, am I?'

Mark said, 'No. And I'm not fucking ugly!'

Later still, just to round the evening off, a punter approached me and said, 'Hi, Julian. That man over there says he'll suck my friend off if I come and speak to you.' God Bless Australia. We ended up in a club called 'Hot Cock for Men'. Unfortunately there was only luke-warm cock left, but somehow we managed.

It was good to finally get to Sydney and check into my favourite hotel, the Sebel Townhouse. Hans arrived. I went, shaved, showered, waxed and tinted to meet him at the airport. He came to see the show on his first night but wasn't overly impressed. 'We had this sort of show 20 years ago in Holland,' he said dismissively. He endeared himself to the rest of the company, though, who appreciated the fact that he was having none of my nonsense. 'Shut up, arsehole!' he said during a company visit to the Blue Mountains. 'I've never heard anyone say that to sir before,' said Philip, incredulous.

'He doesn't adore me the way Christopher did,' I complained to Michael one night in the dressing room. But then I didn't love him with such gusto either. In fact, love was hardly mentioned. It didn't seem appropriate, somehow. Sex was of the grabbing, biting, scratching variety. One night we tried toe sucking and something different with a mouthful of Champagne. But there were too many rows, too much sulking.

14 February 1993. Sydney

Armistead Maupin is in town. Staying at the Sebel, in fact. Sent me a copy of *Forever the Moon* signed 'Happy Valentine's Day from a devoted fan'. That was a highlight.

'We don't seem to get on very well,' I said to Hans as we made up after the umpteenth row. He disagreed. 'I think we have a lot in common. We're both very intelligent.' And so modest, too, I could have added but plumped for: 'Are you intelligent?'

'Of course. Very,' came the inevitable reply.

When Hans departed for Amsterdam, I felt a mixture of regret and relief. All was not well with our relationship but it would have to wait until I was back in the real world. For the last dates of the tour we transferred to the bigger, better State Theatre, and I wanted to enjoy the moment. Our first night there was a little fraught, however. Audio equipment was late arriving and the lighting truck suffered a puncture, so the sound check took place amid traumatised technicals shouting things like: 'I need a barn door on number four NOW!' as they climbed shirtless up ladders. And that was just the lesbians. After the show a herd of Sydney VIPs, including arts editors, reviewers and assorted gay glitterati, invaded our backstage area. I wore a forced smile and poured them cheap white wine. Once they left we discarded the cheap plonk and cracked open the Laurent Perrier.

15 February 1993

Scurrying through Kings Cross [in Sydney] after the gym wearing a hooded sweatshirt and dark glasses, I encountered Mr Jelly. He nearly strolled past me. 'Didn't recognise you!' he laughed as we did the theatrical kissy-kissy business by the fountain. 'Your disguise is marvellous,' he said admiringly. 'It was only the walk that gave you away.' For the remainder of my journey back to the Sebel Hotel I study manly walks and attempt to alter my own accordingly. By the time I'm home I'm waddling like a horserider with piles. Oh, sod it, I think to myself, and mince in my usual fashion through the foyer.

Two days after the tour finished we were to begin filming for *Brace Yourself Roger*, and the Wonderdog troops were already gathering; producers and researchers were holed up in a suite at the Sebel, barking into walkie-talkies with that hard-faced television attitude, devoid of sincerity and only really concerned with their own status and prospects. It all felt vaguely like vultures circling, in that I wasn't 'theirs' until the tour had finished and filming began. Then they would swoop.

More upsettingly, Grazio had a terrible accident. He was in hospital with horrific burns to his face, hands and legs after a box of pyros exploded as he was setting up for the show. He was unrecognisable when I went to visit him in hospital, hands encased in plastic bags full of soggy cream, his face swollen like a football and eyes peering at me from puffy balls the size of oranges. What price camp comedy, I thought? He suffered, and suffers still, so that I may feel the meaningless pleasure of glitter falling gently on my head at the end of my second act.

16 February 1993

Grazio seems a lot better. His face is still bandaged, lips are blistered and fingers are black and brittle but you can see his eyes, familiar and reassuring. He's fighting jolly hard, but you can see that the realisation of what has happened to him and the constant pain are beginning to get him down. Skin grafts seem to be in order.

Philip and I took to frequenting a seedy club called Bottoms Up in Kings Cross, full of rent boys, lorry drivers and transvestites. It was presided over by Monique, a big-boned gal dressed in white. Hair wafted over her head à la Quentin Crisp, face cracked and caked, she had amazing eyes, slightly bulbous and unblinking, which she'd fix on any intrepid fan seeking an autograph. 'That'll be nine dollars,' she said, menacingly. When the resident midget said hello she said, 'I was wondering where I'd find a stool to sit on.' She would peruse the room and point people out to me: 'She's a nice queen, he's a low homo.' I liked her until she began a prolonged invitation to dinner, suspiciously punctuated with the information that 'there will be no one there, only us. I know after all the hassle of autographs you've been through that you just want to rest, one, two, three.' I said yes but meant no.

I phoned Stephen often to see how he was doing. 'I haven't had a bite past my mouth all day but that's because I'm twisted.' He'd suffered three days of vomiting and diarrhoea since he drank a bottle of holy water someone sent him from the Nile. He had a Spanish boyfriend but had taken to faking his orgasms. His body was failing him but he was finding ways to cope. I admired his inventiveness: 'I just thrash around while he grunts and groans, then grab half of his spunk and cover myself with it. Either that or I pretend to come and then grab a towel straight away and wipe myself although there's nothing to wipe away.' I asked him if he could come when he was by himself and he said no. He'd borrowed a porno film and got no results. 'There's nine films on this tape and normally I can't get through the first but I sat through the lot without a twitch!'

9 March 1993

Asian waiter delivered my room-service Sebel burger and fries.

'I didn't know you hate me,' he said.

'Pardon?'

'You always have salad. I didn't know you hate me.'

It took me a while but I finally understood; he didn't know I ate meat.

Our final show of the tour took place on the eve of the Sydney Lesbian and Gay Mardi Gras (not forgetting transgender folk too), where I'd been invited to lead the parade down Oxford Street, waving at the crowds from the back of a decorated float.

After the interval my entrance music began and I headed towards the stage and fell over. Over the swelling violins of 'Tara's theme' from *Gone with the Wind* I heard the crack of my arm breaking. There was nothing to do but go on.

'I'm in terrible pain. I've just broken my arm,' I said.

There was silence as the audience waited for the punchline.

'No, I have. Really. Look, I can't hold the microphone with my left hand. Helga, have you got any painkillers? These bastards don't believe me, but it's true. They think it's part of a comedy routine.'

Helga trotted on with some Nurofen. I was desperate for a laugh by now, so I spat them out and made Helga bring me more. I struggled through the show, wincing through painful costume changes when I had to twist and turn my arms. I went straight to hospital afterwards, where my arm was plastered with festive pink plaster.

The next day I waved my damaged arm at half a million Mardi Gras revellers. By that evening's party a rumour was sweeping Sydney. 'Is it true you broke your arm fisting someone?' I understood the basic mechanics of fisting, but it wasn't something I had any desire to try. But I'd like to meet the sphincter that can snap a bone. Nevertheless the mental picture of me fisting someone amused me and I resolved to think of a fisting joke and use it when the opportunity arose.

TEN

I have a poet's mind but a poor exterior,
What goes on inside me is superior.

STEVIE SMITH

One of the advantages of becoming famous is you can make unreasonable demands and people go along with them. It's almost expected of you. I, for example, refuse to travel in a maroon car. Agents and tour managers have been alerted to the eccentricity. It's only because that colour vaguely reminds me of school uniform. It's not a serious aversion, I don't break out in hives at the sight of such a vehicle, but no one dares to say, 'Don't be so stupid,' so it becomes a vital requisite of Mr Clary's transportation requirements. There are others. I prefer my driver to be a lactating mother; they seem to drive more carefully and never exceed my 80-mile-per-hour speed limit. I like to travel in the front passenger seat with my hand curled casually around the handbrake. This way I can create my own emergency stop at any time. On tour in the

Terago minibus there is also the 'No Trade In The Van' rule. Backing singers and chorus girls are wont to pick up fans and are often understandably keen to transport them home for sexual shenanigans. Michael Dalton would invariably drag some floor-sweeper back to his hotel after our post-show disco outings, and I really couldn't be doing with the small talk and the whiff of bleach in an enclosed environment. Call me old-fashioned, but the rule was created and rigorously imposed.

It was during our five-month tour of Australia that I decided I could no longer pack my own bags. Every week, sometimes every few days, we were on the move and the endless folding, zipping and buckling was too much for someone in my position. The task fell to Helga, the lesbian-in-the-wings tour manager. She would arrive an hour before departure and dutifully fold, squeeze and roll my scattered possessions from around the current suite into the tasteful selection of matching Louis Vuitton suitcases. When the day of our longed-for return to the mother country finally dawned, I didn't mince my words with Helga. 'Hurry up and pack,' I said. 'Get me out of here. I've had enough of Australia!' I missed my family and friends. The relentless sunshine and partying were getting on my nerves. As was the acidity of some Australian queens: 'Back in Australia again, I see... Things not going too well for you back home?'

I wanted to see the grey skies of home, I wanted to mix with my own sort, moan about everything and absorb some fine British apathy once more. Another day of jolly Aussies and I would scream. When my sundry bags were all piled neatly by the door for the porter to collect, Helga, the ultimate in efficient lesbionic tour management, asked the obvious question. 'Plane ticket and passport?'

'Yes, yes!' I said and produced my ticket within seconds. It took a little longer to realise that my passport had already gone back to the mother country in the side pocket of a suitcase I'd sent ahead with Addison.

I lay on the bed having a panic attack and took the Valium I'd been saving for the journey home. After a few phone calls from a determined Helga, the British Consulate opened its doors for me, even though it was a Sunday afternoon, and clutching my temporary passport I was whisked across the tarmac on a buggy to catch my plane with seconds to spare. Had I been an ordinary Joe Public I'd have missed it, been forced to do things like queue up and get paperwork stamped. It doesn't bear thinking about. As I relaxed in first class and perused the extensive menu, I thought how marvellously Helga had dealt with the crisis and how grateful I was to her. Everyone should have a bull-dyke problem-solver at their disposal. I wanted to let her know I appreciated her sterling work, but unfortunately she was back in economy and I couldn't be seen there. I got the air stewardess to deliver a complimentary bag of nuts.

My mother said recently she thought my life would grind to a halt without the support network of cleaners, gardeners, beauticians, managers, agents, personal assistants and personal trainers I employ. She is right, I suppose, but having made the choice not to have anything to do with the practicalities of day-to-day life, all these minions are vital to my well-being. I don't want to empty bins, poison slugs, discuss fees, pay bills, post letters or book train tickets. Assisted living suits me and leaves me free to spend my days thinking up buggery and oral jokes. It's what the public would want. Anything more mundane than walking the dog or watering the plants, and reality might raise its vulgar head.

Safely home at last, there was no rest for the wicked. *Aspel*, interviews and meetings, not to mention the unfinished business of Hans. Tours require publicity, as did almost anything it seemed. I recently came across an interview schedule prior to my *Camping at the Aldwych* run in 1991. In three days I did interviews with the *Ham and High*, the *Independent*, William Cook (writing a piece on 'Life After Thatcher'), the *Pink Paper*, Steve Wright in the Afternoon, John Sachs for Capital Radio, *Dogs Today* magazine, BBC Radio 5, Cathy McGowan for BBC News South East, John Dunn for Radio 2, *Loose Ends*, *Box Office* on Channel 4, LBC and GLR. Plus photo calls. I tried to be friendly and chatty but it didn't always pay off. I made sandwiches and everything for a *Guardian* journalist once, only to be described (on Christmas Eve, too!) as 'exotically packaged mediocrity'. The nerve! The only hint I'd had that she was capable of such bad taste was the earrings she wore, which looked like salvage from a recent car crash. She was all smiles when she left. *Dogs Today* were far more amiable, even writing to me afterwards and asking me to host their show. They were undertaking a nationwide search for the best singing dogs. The show was to be called the Paw-O-Vision Song Contest. Sadly I was too busy.

26 March 1993

I said to H: It's only in the throes of passion that I love you. When you're being Dutch and I'm being English, I can't be bothered.

H: I enjoy being with you and I KNOW that you enjoy being with me. I know that.

Stephen arrived by taxi from the Brodrip Ward and sat fidgeting while I cleaned out my wardrobe. From five carrier bags full of old clothes he only rejected two old pairs of boxer shorts and a JCFC T-shirt. 'It's like Christmas!' he said. Dropped him back off at the Middlesex and he wheeled his booty in on a wheelchair. We'd had a frosty moment earlier when he cast his eye at Christopher's urn on the patio and said, 'You should have a shrine built for Christopher,' and I said, 'Thank you for your opinion.' I liked to see the urn out there, battered by the seasons. Earlier he said, 'I never really liked Christopher and he never liked me,' which was true enough, but the constant references to Christopher as a kind of gauge to his own deterioration annoy me. 'At what stage did Christopher's hair fall out?' was one.

29 March 1993

Stephen has moved into a single room at the Brodrip Ward. Not because his condition suddenly deteriorated or anything, but because he saw it was empty and fancied it.

He went out today and bought a fish tank and three fish. He was sitting in bed smoking a joint when I arrived. In fact, it was the same bed I slept in head to head with Christopher one night towards the end, the night when the nurse slipped me a bottle of Valium.

'I'm going to treat this place like a hotel. I'm going

to come and go as I please. I'm going to buy a houseboat. I'm going to take an intensive driving course, so I am. I'm getting my self-confidence back. I refused laser treatment today, I'm not ready for it, I'm just up and about again.' He raves on and on, determined to achieve so much in so little time. Then he starts attempting profound phrases I think he imagines will be remembered after he has gone, like: 'Life is beautiful. Every day is a new beginning.' I sit in embarrassed silence most of the time and talk about the patio plants.

Hans and I had a more conclusive conversation about our relationship. Neither of us can really end it just for the reason that it's impractical. So we've decided to hang on for a while and see what happens. 'Maybe we'll have a row or something a bit more conclusive,' I offered helpfully.

'Perhaps we won't,' he said. I felt a shiver down my spine.

The UK leg of the *Glittering Passage* tour got under way in April. My new tour driver was a nervous young man called Toby. On his first day he walked dog shit through my flat and soon found himself on his hands and knees with a bowl of disinfectant and a J-cloth. He became known as 'the Poo Man' – not ideal for the self-esteem of a 21-year-old straight boy. The spaceship set took two men to operate it, and Steve and Keith, two south London non-theatricals, took on the task. One day Philip asked them: 'You boys strictly down-the-line heteros or do you delve at all?'

After the Brighton gig, cast and crew retired to the bar at the Grand Hotel. Andy Cunningham, who had directed me back in the days of Covent Garden Community Theatre, came with us.

'Such a nice outfit you've got,' he said to me.

I casually brushed my clothes and said, 'Oh, thank you. It's just something I threw on.'

'No,' whispered Andy. 'I meant nice people you're working with.'

Hans came to visit but the situation wasn't helped when I had a phone call one morning from Josh in Perth informing me he was in contact with the *Sun* and ready to sell his story. 'What story?' I asked, lying in bed with Hans beside me. 'I'm 18. That's illegal in Perth,' he said triumphantly. I hung up, but Hans wanted to know what the conversation had been about, so I told him. The next day I came clean and told him about my other infidelities.

28 April 1993

This Morning with Nick Owen and a heavily pregnant Anne Diamond. Just before we went on air at 10.30 a.m. I was sitting on a sofa with Jilly Cooper, who turned suddenly and touched my hand. 'Are you all right?' she asked, concerned. Worried that my hangover was showing through the make-up, I said, 'Yes, I'm all right. I'm only half here, really.'

'Sometimes', she said, 'you think you're over something and then you realise that you're not.' I realised she was referring to Christopher and bereavement. But there was no time to continue the conversation. Suddenly cameras were rolling, Anne and Nick were showing their teeth and Jilly and I were making merry between a cookery item featuring stewed apples baked on butter-soaked bread and Claire Rayner helping the nation with their relationship problems.

I managed a good joke. Viewers were asked to phone in with tongue-twisters in response to a German student who needed help with his English lessons. 'I've got something a German student might like to get his tongue around,' I said. Nick and Anne just stared at me. There was silence, so thinking the camera might still be on me I widened my eyes and shrugged at them. Then the pause ended as Jilly shrieked with laughter. The show went on and on and on. My final appearance was a 90-second item with the Chef of the Year. 'Have you ever stuffed a chicken?' I asked him.

I hear that Addison refers to me, Philip and Michael as 'the Handbags', which might be offensive if it wasn't funny. The other day he greeted Keith the technical by saying. 'Tour going well, mate? How's your arse?'

The next day we arrived in Oxford to do our gig at the Apollo, only to find the city centre sealed off due to a bomb scare. We sat in Fat Jack's for four hours, until we realised we'd have to cancel. I called Addison. 'Oh my Gawd. Why does it always happen to me?' he said from his office in Peckham. We passed the time talking to the gay Australian waiter. 'I really admire you,' he said. 'Making all that money just for being camp.'

My relationship with Hans did not survive the tour. I was in Margate when I called him. 'In my country, if love is not fed it dies,' he said. I went for a post-show walk along the seafront and felt suitably desolate. Feeling miserable was an interesting mood change, after the hilarity of tour fun and japes and the high of being applauded and lionised every night on stage. There is a self-consciousness, sometimes, about despondency. (There is with me anyway.) As I took my melancholy stroll I could almost have been auditioning for a remake of *The French Lieutenant's Woman*.

Becoming famous plays havoc with your emotions, and because you are famous people will scrutinise your emotions much more than they ever did before. You are being looked at more than is normal, so it stands to reason that you are also being analysed. The Sydney queens who said 'Nothing much to write home about' would not have passed the comment had they not recognised me. They would have kept their thoughts to themselves. And while your ego is suitably massaged by the nightly confirmation of the public's love for you, the stakes are higher. You think if you make one false move the adoration will be withdrawn. The game will be up. If they didn't make as much noise in Southampton as they did in Glasgow, you might think it's your fault. You don't always put it down to regional clapping variations or theatre acoustics. And if it hadn't been for public demand you would not have been on tour and tired and emotional in the first place. Your worst fear is that it will stop. What if your next tour, your next performance, TV show, interview or joke is not received as favourably as the last? All will be lost.

What if I don't want to do it any more? All this was just the low after the high, you understand, but I don't think my reading material at the time helped.

6 June 1993. Margate

I'm reading Frankie Howerd's biography so career dives are on my mind. Failures of all kinds, all round. I'm trying to convince myself that I'm by myself because I want to be, but it isn't working.

I fancy a change of lifestyle. I could take a year off. I could change management, social scene, house and lover. I could finish the tour and see if I'm quite as hysterical about things then.

There is a trajectory to fame. We see it all the time, most commonly with pop stars who suddenly hit the big time. Self-esteem and insecurity battle it out. Modesty and disbelief give way to arrogance and self-delusion. I have been guilty of both, snappy and demanding with friends and fans alike. There is a period when the basic courtesies of human interaction do not seem to apply to you, the famous person. If luck is on your side this will all level out and you can make your apologies before too much damage is done. But we must bear in mind that those around a famous person often don't conform to normal patterns of behaviour either. The whole business of day-to-day living is suddenly topsy-turvy: you're not exactly behaving in a normal way, but neither is anyone else. It's hard to know how to behave. I used to leave my fans waiting for hours at the stage door. 'The longer they wait, the more they love you,' I used to repeat nightly, as if it were an ancient Chinese proverb rather than an unnecessary test of loyalty. Nowadays I'm there before they are, offering a selection of sand-wiches and a flask of tea. For my next tour I'm thinking of offer-ing a free T-shirt to the first five to arrive. In TV terms, of course, one's career goes through a number of phases from 'Accept no offers. You're too good for that!' to 'How lovely to be asked! I'll take anything!'

I clearly didn't endear myself to Ivan Massow. We met in 1991 in Heaven. He decided he wanted to be my friend and I went along with it in a half-hearted sort of way. We went for a drive down the A40 in his Aston Martin, and had a glam weekend together at L'Hotel in Paris. I treated him with shocking indifference. This, of course, made him all the more eager to please. But I couldn't take him seriously because he was a Tory. As an obstacle to friendship that was a bit like being a convicted paedophile, decorative though he was. He came to the launch of my coffee table book *How To Be A Real Man* at Madame Jojo's and I arranged to meet him at a bar across the road after I'd finished schmoozing some journalists, but there was a bomb scare in Soho and we were locked in at Madame Jojo's for several hours – an unfortunate predicament at the best of times. I didn't much care. This being the pre-mobile-phone era I was unable to contact him. The next day a stern letter was delivered by bike. Ivan (self-made multi-millionaire) clearly felt the need to assess our friendship in writing.

Dear Julian,

It has been fun getting to know you and I think that by London standards I have at some stages got as close to you as anyone. I have found you a rewarding friend on the whole but very difficult at the same time. It frightens me when I invest energy and respect which is unrequited and with you that was so often the case... I don't think I have ever really let you down in the ways you that you have done so with me. The trouble is that I make excuses for you and never really say anything when you simply don't turn up. The truth is that it has made me feel more and more worthless to you, which is why I have been slipping away.

I couldn't believe it when you left me in that pub the other night. It was an example of just how cruel you can be and it upset me almost to tears because you made me realise just how worthless I am.

I am not the wonderful 'Julian Clary' and never will be. But I work very hard and have a life which I am, like you, very proud of. I am brilliant at what I do, as you are at what you do. I have never denied you that compliment, which you have never paid me... anyway, please excuse this last little luxury of saying goodbye. I'm a bit sentimental about things like that.

love Ivan xxx

We have made friends again since, although we had a good six-year break. In fact, in a recent magazine article Ivan claimed me as one of his best friends. Apparently we speak on the phone at least five times a day! Good Lord... whatever do we find to talk about?

A similar 'farewell' letter came my way from a fan called Susan.

With a bit of detective work she discovered my home address and was sitting on my garden wall one day when I emerged. I told her, quite reasonably in my opinion, to 'Fuck off, and don't ever come back'. She didn't take it well...

> Last night I emerged from a dream that began at the Civic, Leeds on May 11th, 1989. I saw, for the first time since that evening, how things really are. Thank you for being so straight with me. It's time for change, time to move on, maybe. So it's no more crazy trips just for a smile and a kiss. I think what I'm trying to say is – you may not see me quite so often waiting at stage doors. There are people in my life who have gone without love and attention for too long. Yes, they are the ones who really matter to me. So, Julian, I'm letting go just a little bit and giving myself and my life some time. I'll be seeing you. Take care.
>
> As ever, Susan

10 June 1993

Les Dawson died today. Very sad. His daughter was only born in October. They kept on about his 'funny face' on the news. Bit more to him than that, I thought.

Wrote and dispatched a completion letter to Hans, which I think makes me feel better. I said I didn't like the loose ends of our relationship fluttering about in the breeze. It was a friendly enough letter; I didn't have the knives out. Even hoped we could be friends one day. Miss him though. Keep thinking, I'll give the Dutchman a ring, then remember – Oh! It's all off.

Cheered myself up by going to the Black Cap for a drink with Michael Ferri and promptly met a hilarious Greek Cypriot with Marxist leanings called Mikos. He's an unemployed welfare worker and said, 'I want to be the saviour of the underprivileged!' He's hilarious. When asked to explain the difference between a wasp and a hornet, he said, 'A wasp is a mother but a hornet is a mother-fucker.' He's only just left, and I'm in a very good mood.

13 June 1993

Played the London Palladium. Friends, family and punters galore in.

Up and out of bed again as I can't sleep and was having potted shrimp fantasies. Luckily I had some in the fridge. There's a whiff of Greek Cypriot about the duvet which I'm rather enjoying.

I'm fed, watered, nourished and I even have the warm glow of the recently traded about me. Now all I need is rest and gym tomorrow afternoon. The end of *My Glittering Passage* is in sight... Soon will start looking at houses as it's time to move from Albert Street. The local kids here are a worry. As I got in the car today a seven-year-old screamed, 'Stay away from me, you fucking poofter!'

Bernard Bresslaw dead too. Heavens!

20 June 1993

Didn't get to my last-night-of-tour party until 12.30 a.m. Was having champagne with Lily Savage and Bob Downe in my Palladium dressing room. Sir Ian McKellen had gone by the time I arrived. Addison was frantic, drunk and wired. In no time he had my head in an arm lock and in a loud fierce whisper was telling me how he 'loved me to death'. Then Mikos arrived late and we sat with a competition winner from Kent who didn't know who to make eyes at first. That was the third night for me and the Greek Cypriot. Might even give him my phone number if there's a fourth.

After the British tour finished, Philip and I decided to go on holiday together to a Greek island. We booked a package holiday to Thassos. It was cheap and cheerful, a bit like us. Philip calls me 'sir' on stage and off. Having been working together for so many months we easily slipped into our on-stage personas when confronted with 'punter alerts', as we called them. There were so many requests for autographs and photos that we became quite skilled at warning each other. 'Punter alert approaching from the left, sir!' Philip would gently inform me, and sure enough a woman from Stoke-on-Trent would be walking determinedly towards me clutching a camera. 'Sorry to bother you while you're on holiday, but do you mind if we have a photo?' We nearly always said yes, and then a flurry of requests would ensue, those too polite to ask before suddenly emboldened by our cooperative manner. We only refused once, when we were dozing on the beach and a man boldly poked Mr Jelly awake and said, 'Do you mind...?' as he waggled his Instamatic. 'I was asleep! Go away!' said Philip.

My holiday reading was B.D. Hyman's 'candid' biography of Bette Davis, and for a while I took on the personality of that wonderful actress. I found the book stupid – a jealous daughter's dreary monologue – but hilarious gems of Bette's behaviour shone through. Thus 'Jesus, brother!' became my new catchphrase, and when a cheery Mancunian asked if I was enjoying Thassos, I said, 'No. Jesus, brother!' I did, in fact, quite like it but it was tourist land, and fiercely straight, too. Its saving grace was Lisa, a big bright girl from Kidderminster and our rep, who said, 'What are you like?' all the time and told us the holiday reps referred to us tourists as 'the Billys'. There was also Tim, a penny-wise but good-value theatre director, there to unwind and soak up the sun and Metaxa. In fact, he directed Sara Crowe and Joan Collins in *Private Lives*.

One day we hired a Fiat Uno and caught the ferry to the mainland, in search of some fun and gay life. We braved the heat and mad Greek drivers and settled eventually at the ABC Hotel in Thessaloniki. That evening we went to a bar called Tabou and I met Yiannis, who spoke very good English and had a big nose. I knocked a few years off and told him I was 29. 'I'm older than you,' he said. 'I'm 30!' After more chat and finger entwining we moved to his car and he drove me up a mountain to the 'place of a thousand trees', a sort of Lover's Lane forest where we had marvellous sex in the back of his car, complete with condoms, wet wipes and simultaneous orgasms. 'If you lived in Greece, I would fall in love with you,' he said. He complimented me on my sensual performance. 'Usually the English have sex as if they are taking something from the fridge.'

A cucumber, perhaps.

30 June 1993. Thessaloniki

The door clicks shut and Yiannis takes his leave. On this, our third night, we graduated to the hotel room. A sober encounter this time and frankly without the Metaxa and the forest and the stars it wasn't as exciting. The long lingering goodbye and brooding Greek eye contact were trying.

'You will remember me?'

'Oh yes.'

'As what?'

'As my Greek lover.' Funny, I've got one of those at home.

My uncanny knack of booking into noisy hotels hasn't abandoned me. Each morning at 8.30 a.m., drills, hammering, shouting and smashing have woken me from next door. Renovations. This morning when I rang reception to ask them to stop they said I could move rooms. I said, 'I'd have to get up and pack first!'

'Then the noise will continue.'

We returned to Thassos and Lisa our rep made us spaghetti Bolognese and fruit salad. Later we met Tim at Blue Bar. After several Brandy Alexanders and four complimentary vodka/schnapps concoctions from Stefan the waiter, Philip went home while Tim and I drove to

Club Bolero. There we tucked into Metaxas and watched Greek boys. Stefan appeared and Tim asked him, 'Where are the men who like men?' He wasn't sure how to handle such a direct approach.

Tim went to the toilet and a Greek boy approached me: 'You go with my friend?' I said. 'Yes, OK,' and off we went in my 'auto', Tim abandoned, me off on an adventure. He was called Something-opolis and was 20. Fortunately he drove (as it were). First we went to Island Club, then home to Limeneria, stopping en route at a charming Greek church for unorthodox sex.

'You AIDS?' he asked.

'No,' I said with grave expression.

After a while we got out of the car. 'Moment,' he said, and flipped me over a raised flowerbed for some attempted Greek penetration. It wasn't happening there so he settled for something less strenuous. He stretched out on the paved surround to an olive tree, not 20 feet from the church entrance and whispered, 'Yes, baby...' I looked up from my task, saw his face twitching with lust, the full moon reflected in the sea, the sacred place of worship and the olive tree and thought: I am so glad to be me.

On our last night we dined at Palomo's restaurant. The waiter, alerted by a family having chicken in a basket, asked if I was a television star. I nodded. 'Are you Luke Perry?'

'Photographer alert!' said Philip as we emerged through the Green Channel at Gatwick airport, and indeed he was right. As the photographer did the clever walking backwards trick he flashed away, while I tried to cover the mosquito bite on my cheek and the love bite on my neck with my one available hand.

'Can I ask where you've been for your holidays?' enquired a young pup of a reporter.

'A package holiday in Thassos,' I said.

'How was it?'

'What are you like?' I answered.

18 July 1993. Albert Street, London

Another weekend featuring Mikos. Yesterday he said, 'You really like me, don't you?' He made it sound like an accusation. He asked about my wedding ring so I told him about Christopher. He picked up my hand and kissed the ring. 'That's for Christopher,' he said.

Later that night, post-coitally, he said, 'You can certainly take a good battering.'

When I return from the land to which he transports me, I lie there murmuring with pleasure. Tonight we found out he'd been mistaking this noise for a request for more. We'd both been too polite to do anything but oblige the other.

We were awake again at 5 a.m. Mikos was having a panic attack. Eyes searching the room, he was full of fear for five minutes and I did my best to calm him.

I went to visit Stephen this afternoon. He was glad to see I had a smile on my face. 'I've got KS on mine,' he said. He's sick of being sick. He's sorry he's so strong. But he was chatting away at his normal pace.

One never knows exactly when or how things start to go awry. Life is rarely plain sailing from one year to the next. The pendulum swings. Contentment is fleeting. We are centred and serene one day, our judgement unwise and our mood fractious the next. The HIV virus that lurked quietly in Stephen's blood took years to make itself known. A passing thought, planted innocently enough by a casual remark, may erupt months later in serious mental disorder. We must be careful what we say and how much gravitas we give our thoughts. The universe is always listening. One evening in the Laurel Tree pub, Mikos said, 'Have you worked out what game I'm playing yet?' There and then I had the thought that he would leave me soon and this would break my heart. The thought came and went, but I remembered it and called it back. Learn to disregard negative thoughts and the rot cannot set in. I didn't know that then. I toyed with my imagined abandonment like a cat with a sparrow.

28 July 1993

'Don't worry about Mikos,' said a sleepy Stephen on the phone after I voiced my fears that I will end up getting hurt. 'Just use him, then throw him out like a dirty dishcloth.'

8 August 1993

Well, a Mikos-free evening, which is quite a rarity. I've been working on some scripts and he's at home in

Turnpike Lane with no electricity because someone forgot to get the key recharged. 'I'll have to go to bed early and have a long wank,' he said.

'Whatever helps you sleep,' I said.

He's been here all week and quite a joy it's been. He says 'You LOVE it!' in cod north London accent after sex and says people are 'well shaggable' when we're out and about. We took Fanny to the park and he ran about shirtless while I felt like an elderly uncle chaperone. Not that he's childish. Quite full of angst and self-doubt maybe, but bright, perceptive and funny too. He chuckles a lot and says I put a smile on his face. I cry 'Don't leave me!' whenever he gets out of bed for so much as a cigarette. He gets drunk and forlorn and regresses to a one-year-old. We make furious, passionate love at all hours and my legs tingle constantly. We don't have heavy talks about our relationship.

Money is a somewhat hilarious disparity – he doesn't have his bus fare home and I receive a cheque for £58,000 from Addison.

11 August 1993

I think I have piles, and I'm not talking about my bank balance. Mikos has gingivitis. So with various orifices off-limits and no kissing advisable, it's a wonder we're both still smiling.

When your subconscious is planning a nervous breakdown, the right location is important. Camden Town, as my chosen place of residence, made me happy. I knew I needed to stay right there. It was imperative for the virus of negative thoughts to flourish that I be winkled out of that safe house. The conscious mind must be persuaded. Darker forces alone cannot visit estate agents and contact solicitors on your behalf. I had been looking at bright, sunny flats near to my bright, sunny railway-carriage flat in Camden. 'For the same money you could have a whole house if you'd only move a couple of miles further north...' said a cold-eyed man in a suit from Hotblack Desiato, estate agents in Parkway. He slipped a photograph of a smart if rather gothic-looking Victorian detached house across the desk: all turrets and towers, teetering on the corner of a junction. 'Where is it?' I said, unsure. 'Holloway,' he answered, brightly. It was just the location my subconscious was looking for. In a moment of madness I made an offer.

12 August 1993

All set to move to 9 Middleton Grove, Holloway, on September 8th. This is my dream home and I lie awake at night fantasising about living there.

Stephen is home in Deptford and I went to visit him. He wanted to drive to Hayes to see a houseboat but when I got there at 3.30 p.m. he was in his dressing gown kneeling in front of an aquarium getting in a tizzy about the pump mechanism.

'I don't want to go to Hayes any more. I want to go to Battersea,' he announced, but in the end he spent the afternoon having a tantrum with the pump and complaining about the instructions. His cleaning lady was there and his neighbour popped in. His fridge was full and he offered me Madeira cake, walnut cream slices or apple turnovers.

I'm reading Kenneth Williams's diaries. Fascinating. He could survive for months on a flirty greeting from a tasty road-worker. Times have changed!

Have been invited to speak at a therapists' conference. They want to know how my counselling at the Red Admiral Foundation has helped me deal with Christopher's death. I was just going to bed when that old Joan Collins Fan Club line came back to me: 'How to turn personal tragedy into lucrative image building.' Have to say no.

Lovely to see Paul Merton yesterday. I don't just like him, I love him!

'What are you looking at?' he said.

'You!' I replied. 'I haven't seen you for a year!'

'That's no accident,' he said.

15 August 1993

Fidelity has not been one of the topics of conversation with Mikos, so bugger me if he doesn't go and sleep with someone else. His Thursday night out had involved speed, alcohol, the Black Cap and staying the night at X's.

'Was there hanky panky?' I asked.

'There was a certain amount,' said Mikos.

'What, exactly?' I asked.

'I shagged him.'

My upset after that was quite unexpected. Mikos somehow made it seem like an act of kindness. Poor X, ex-boyfriend, sick, pleading and his birthday too... why, a Catholic priest would have had difficulty refusing.

'Don't blow me out for this,' he said.

'The thing is,' I said, having an idea, 'it changes the way I feel about you.'

'What do you mean?'

'I mean it makes me not fancy you any more,' I lied.

That was quite a bull's eye: wounded to the marrow he was, and I let him suffer for quite a while before I retracted it with first-degree physical contact that put paid to the lie.

On Saturday we didn't discuss it much but took Fanny to Kenwood where we wandered through the dappled trees stealing the odd peck and pressing legs together discreetly on the lawn. A choir and orchestra were rehearsing for the evening's open-air concert, so moving arias and Mozart opera music was seeping through the trees.

'Sometimes when something is too perfect you just want it to stop,' said Mikos. I had a painful rectal twinge by way of agreement.

Saturday evening, as I put the finishing touches to roast chicken, potatoes, courgettes and peas, he came into the kitchen and shat himself: sudden unannounced diarrhoea. He shuffled out clutching his behind. Then he felt cold, then hot, then sleepy. I ate my dinner, put his in the oven and put his soiled trousers into a pre-soak wash.

26 August 1993

Saw Stephen on Tuesday as he's going back to Ireland 'to be looked after'. I don't think he'll be back and I think he's got his doubts too. Fear of dying made him cry on the phone. He asks me a lot of questions about Christopher and how he handled it. I could only reassure him that morphine would be on hand if he was in any distress at all.

Went to see the Chinese State Circus with my mother. Mother caused a laugh in the seats around us during the snake girl's act. Watching as she contorted herself into all sorts of amazing shapes, my mother said in a loud whisper, 'I can't even put my tights on.'

2 September 1993

Had a lovely five days at the Edinburgh Festival filming 'Best of Edinburgh' TV thing. It was a painless experience. The highlights were Jenny Eclair ('I went to the countryside and came on. There was nothing else to do there'), writing the links for the show with Paul, and Simon Fanshawe's attempts to organise a 'Fags on the Fringe' dinner party. Didn't go as I'm not… on the fringe.

Peter Cook rang to confirm I'm going to the relaunch of *Derek and Clive Get the Horn*. 'There will be two photographers at the party,' he said.

'Well, I'll try and keep my trousers on then,' I said.

'Well, no, don't,' said Peter. 'Nothing comes free in this life.'

7 September 1993

Last night in residence here. Boxes are packed, cupboards cleaned and memories disturbed. Cards from Christopher, backstage passes, postcards, etc. Various bits and pieces from the last four years locked away in drawers or put on shelves to be kept, and each capable of transporting me backwards in time.

Mikos is sleeping off his exertions. I sit, legs up on the kitchen table in my usual place, listening to the hum of the fridge for the last time. I packed Christopher's urn. Mikos carried it in from the rain and it sits resplendent in its very own box, which I've just noticed is from Portugal! Duoro, Murca. Wine, I think. Just packed his Filofax and chest X-rays in the Box of Memories. A candle is burning in the window under the Portuguese terracotta shade.

Had fun last night at the *Derek and Clive Get the Horn* video launch with Peter Cook and Dudley Moore. Every face was a fascinating one. Mikos asked Ronnie Wood's wife if she'd ever been unfaithful. 'Never in 16 years,' she said. 'When you've had the best, why spoil it?'

Now was the time to come to my senses, but I didn't. Leaving Camden Town was unwise. I would not be safe outside of NW1. I would not be happy elsewhere. The lid would be lifted. The universe could do nothing to protect me. I would be sorry. A part of me knew this. I was going against nature. I sensed this, but didn't act on my suspicions. Would that I had. I can hardly bear to relive what happens next. If instinct had been adhered to it would never have occurred. Writing this down for you to read is like watching a video recording of your loved one's suicide. I have to keep covering my eyes. ' Don't do it!' I want to scream at myself. But it is too late. The fatal step had been taken.

ELEVEN

'What stars fear most is the death of their fame, and most
would rather be infamous than go back to anonymity.
The worst thing you could possibly say to a star
would be, "Didn't you used to be famous?"'

TRUMAN CAPOTE

The day I moved to 9 Middleton Grove, London N7 saw relentless torrential rain. Mikos, by coincidence, had moved into a
flat round the corner, so he and his flatmate came to help unpack.
Everything was soaked and muddy. It felt damp and cold. Later
that night local youths chucked some gravel over the wall and it
clattered menacingly on the conservatory roof. Fanny looked up,
but she was deaf and didn't bother to bark, just gave me her 'told
you so' look.

29 September 1993. Middleton Grove, N7

I have a tradesman at the rear. A plumber, to be precise,

fixing the broken outdoor tap, mysteriously broken off on my return from Los Angeles, and water gushing everywhere.

Frances is here to stay for a few days and she's a boon, washing down paintwork and cleaning cupboards. The 'settling in' process here at the mansion is well under way. Every now and then I think, Gawd, what have I done? But I wander from room to room rubbing my chin and Fanny keeps discovering new bedrooms and is cautious but wide-eyed. It's going to take a while.

Went to Deptford to collect Stephen yesterday, brought him here then took him to Heathrow airport where he's off to see his mother in Belfast. He was very thin and petulant and given to panic attacks. He disappeared in the terminal to find a cash point but was gone half an hour. Came back breathless and manic, snot running down his face, saying, 'I'm having a heart attack.' There was a terrible smell and he said he'd gone to fart and shat himself. We dashed to the check-in and he was whisked through, holding his side with fingers covered in too many silver rings. Again, as I watched him disappear through the tunnel and the check-in woman said gravely, 'He doesn't look well,' I thought: That will be the last time I see him. I've been thinking that for six months or so. He's so frightened of death that he's hanging on every inch of the way. Swigging from a bottle of morphine in the car he said, 'Go on, have some. It won't do you any harm.'

Meanwhile, I've been to Los Angeles to record a Travelog programme. Mikos flew out when I'd finished filming and we went to San Francisco for a week. Stayed at the Inn on Castro in a bedroom full of papier mâché parrots and wandered along the Castro hand in hand.

I have inherited a cleaning lady called Jackie from the previous owners. 'I know the house, you see,' she said, mysteriously. This house is like a big baby and needs lots of attention. Someone called Fred is coming to clean out the guttering. That should do Housey the world of good, I reckon. The dwelling equivalent of a thorough colonic irrigation.

1 October 1993

Stephen died at 9.05 a.m.

I didn't find out till this afternoon. I had been on the phone to the hospital in Belfast this morning and thought it was just Irish officiousness when they said they couldn't give me any information as I wasn't next-of-kin.

So sudden for him, no morphine required.

Last night Penelope and Barb came over and we burnt incense and carried it through the house, wafting at doorways and cleansing every corner. We burnt 'double happiness' candles in every room (including the garage) and Barb incanted under the bay tree in the garden. They left cooing at the full moon and we did a three-handed kind of salute to it as clouds skidded across its face and it hovered over the house. Then I got embarrassed in case any of the neighbours were watching and scuttled indoors to Mikos. 'Oh, you're so lovely,' he exclaims quite often. He melts my heart.

God bless Stephen. What great adventures are you having now, I wonder?

24 October 1993

It's 2.40 a.m. Can't sleep. Just put the lights on and there is Fanny asleep on her chair, and Gloria, my new kitten, asleep by the radiator. She is such a sweet cat. Loves to be in the room we're in and purrs as soon as I touch her. Mikos is asleep beside me. He turned over a while ago and said, 'Don't leave me!' This may refer to the fact that I sometimes retreat upstairs when the snoring gets too much.

4 November 1993

'It's like living with Widow Twankey,' said Mikos. And it must be. I shuffle around the house in my dressing gown, slump in front of the TV and talk endlessly about bedside cabinets.

Had the *My Glittering Passage* video launch at Madame Jojo's last night. So I went dolled up and tucked into the cheap white wine. Then a crowd of us went to the Yard where we drank Champagne, then on to Substation briefly where we moved into beer mode. So today was mainly hangover, although I did nip into Channel 4 where Jo Brand and I recorded some trailers. Planning our links at the bar we invented some cocktails. The Putney Towpath was one: 'It's smooth and dark and creeps up on you from behind.' In the interests of light entertainment we pretended we were two supermodels. I was Claudia Shafter and Jo was Linda Vaginablister.

19 November 1993

Addison rang me from a taxi in Soho and shouted down the phone the details of his Italian restaurant lunch with Seamus Cassidy. 'I told him, my lad don't know what's going on. I told him I've got to get you on the box next year or you're finished. I was straight with him. I worry about your career as much as you do, you know.' Then he was cut off. I was busy feeding the cat so I didn't mind. I have a sense of impending doom.

20 November 1993

Tony Kushner: 'Life is about losing. I don't believe that as human beings we can do anything other than struggle to face the loss with grace.'

21 November 1993

Mikos just arrived from his first day at work – cable TV computer doings. I thought he was coming for his dinner (chicken, rösti and leeks) but I was wrong. 'I want to finish it,' he said, and he wasn't referring to the meat and two veg. I felt immediate relief, like squeezing a spot. Something about an 'Andrew' he met at the Black Cap and went to Heaven with. He asked for a photograph and hugged me. I managed two tear-filled eyes and one tear escaped as he departed.

'Was it a bolt from the blue?' he asked as he left.

'No,' I said, although it sounds like an interesting effect. So there we are. Divorced.

2.30 a.m. Couldn't find Fanny just now. She had gone to sleep in another bedroom. She's never done that before. Double abandonment!

23 November 1993

Recording *Camp Christmas* at London Studios all day. I was the voice of Whitney the Reindeer, thrown out of Santa's pack for wearing nipple clamps that jingled too much for the sleigh bells.

Somehow it was dire, despite a brilliant set and a cast that included Lily Savage, Stephen Fry, Lea deLaria, Colin Bell, Justin Fashanu, Quentin Crisp and Armistead Maupin. Even Derek Jarman was there looking poorly, and made me cry during the finale song when he waved to the camera and mouthed, 'Goodbye!' I was hovered over all day by Amanda, a journalist from the *Independent* and quite agreeable. She's got to write 3,000 words on me. She doesn't know the half of it.

Feeling quite sad today. Missing Mikos, his warmth and affection. Fanny is now completely deaf, so consequently doesn't run to greet me when I get home. I have to go and find her. Tonight she was asleep in a bedroom

I never use on the top floor, and was confused and bewildered when I woke her.

28 November 1993

Mikos has just left after a tearful prolonged hug. His final words were: 'I still care for you. I'm not laughing at you.' Just what you want to hear as a comedian, but he meant well. He seems to think I'll be fine without him. There was lots of 'But I do love you' talk, but the 'I'm doing this *because* I love you and I don't want to betray you' didn't really convince, any more than the 'I'm only doing what I think is right in the long run' tack.

Now I need to reframe myself on this matter. Enough tears, I must relish my solitude. I'm free. I'm single. I'm 34. I'm living in a big house in Holloway. I'm wealthy. Why does it all sound so dismal and depressing?

30 November 1993

Gave Mikos rather a hard time of it tonight on the phone, prolonging the conversation long after he'd tried to terminate as politely as possible. Rang him twice yesterday but they were cheery. Tonight was back a few steps. I think I have to stop now. Agonising, compulsive phone calls is not something I should get addicted to. I have to accept that it's over.

'For your own good. For the sake of your self-esteem,' said Barb. She was sweet. She was my friend and she hadn't left me, she'd always be there, she said. The house is gloomy and ridiculously large for one homosexual, his kitten and his deaf dog. We keep losing each other. Unless they are avoiding me.

2 December 1993

Rohypnol is taking effect so this will be brief. After recording late-night links with Jo Brand all day went to do the *Clive Anderson Show* then came home and took a sleeping pill. Put Mariah Carey on and had major tears, thinking there is so much wrong with my life, Mikos was the only thing that was right. Tears were squeezed out and I overcame my fear of crying. Then, as Mariah screeched out, the phone rang: Mikos, thanking me for my card ('Deep Devotion' by Saudek), which I sent to apologise for my dreary phone marathon of the other day.

It was nice to see Paul Merton and Caroline Quentin. They'd been tipped off over my state and were genuinely concerned for me.

Feel like escaping, running away.

9 December 1993

Again, Rohypnol in attendance. Just want to note the interesting thing I've done today: transferred all the Mikos trauma to Christopher, which is the underlying reason for such disproportionate drama anyway and is somehow easier to cope with. Just the occasional (if I'm strict!) pang.

Went to the doctor yesterday. Valium and Rohypnol. I cried. I've been quite a worry all round.

11 December 1993. Swindon

Arrived at my parents' and burst into tears on the doorstep. My mother looked shocked and pulled me to her then whisked me upstairs. I know I have driven Mikos away with my tears and traumas. Why do I care so much? Why am I tortured with thoughts and memories? I'm dreadfully restless.

Psychic Penelope paid a visit this morning (I think my friends are on a rota system, keeping watch). She said my heart was numb. My brain is, too, but Valium is better than the panicky madness. She quoted a Chinese proverb, along the lines that you have to set someone free then they can come back and you have to set them free again. But I don't think Mikos will be back. 'You're going from bad to worse,' he said the other day.

13 December 1993. Middleton Grove

Extraordinary fuss in the tabloids about my remarks on the British Comedy Awards last night. Front page of the *Mirror*, *Sun* and *Star*.

Mirror: 'GAY CLARY'S SICK TV GAG.'

Star: 'LAMONT GAY JIBE BY CLARY ROCKS TV AWARDS.'

Sun: 'OBSCENE. STORM OVER GAY CLARY'S SEX JIBE AT LAMONT.'

Said I'd just been fisting him in the wings. (The set looked like Hampstead Heath, you see. The punchline was 'Talk about a red box...' but I don't think it registered after the F word.)

Anyway, attempted a writing session for the second series of *Terry and Julian* with Paul Merton and John Henderson, but was too Valiumed to achieve much. Passed Mikos as I drove down Camden Road. He was waiting for a bus, hood pulled up as it was raining and lighting a cigarette.

Then it was the new Comedy Store opening in Oxenden Street. Had a great time in the dressing room with Paul and everyone. Paul was very sweet and concerned about me. He surreptitiously got me to eat something, I noticed. Compèred part two.

Then home and there was a message from Penelope telling me it was a new moon. Feeling stronger.

So there we have it. I thought I should put the infamous Norman Lamont incident in context for you. Taxi drivers reminisce about it still, punters in supermarkets tell me where they were and who they were with as if it was the day Elvis or President Kennedy died. It was just a joke, a daring one perhaps. Nowadays it is widely perceived as the moment my career was derailed; I had crossed the line and gone too far. LWT issued a kind of fatwa banning me from live television for evermore. A retrospective documentary about gay comics I saw on Channel 4 recently made it sound as if I was dead. 'The first soldiers always fall...' said some pompous talking head. He seemed to imply my downfall was necessary to pave the way for Brian Dowling to host kiddies' TV. Well, that makes it all worthwhile. The real wonder is that I was able to come up with such a top-notch joke while in such a dysfunctional state. I have learned to live with it, of course, and cannot regret something that has given so much pleasure to so many. Boy George likened it to his 'Sex? I'd rather have a cup of tea!' remark. We will never escape our infamy, and fully expect it to feature in our obituaries when the time comes. Incidentally, fisting isn't an exclusively 'gay' activity, whatever the press may tell you. It's an activity open to anyone lucky enough to be born with a hand and an arsehole.

But because I was so engulfed with melancholy at the time, so drugged with Valium and alcohol, it does not evoke happy memories for me. I finish the book here at what was for some a deserved public dishonouring in the tabloids, and for others just a jolly good laugh. But it was a pivotal moment, let's face it, and I'm sure the reader appreciates the drama of such a signing off as much as I do. In the context of the times I can now see that fame uncentred me, love distracted me and rejection unbalanced me. You live and learn.

What you do need to know is that my malaise passed eventually and I recovered. But not before I sold the house in Holloway, put everything in storage, had some counselling, went on another five-month tour of Australia and a twelve-month course of Prozac. Apart from the occasional panic attack I was fine. (A chat show with Ruby Wax, Ivana Trump and Dana International, for example. Well, wouldn't you panic?)

When I returned I bought a house back in jolly Camden Town where happiness reigns. I aspired to it as a teenager and as soon as I moved there I knew I had found my spiritual home. Somehow, at the age of 13, I knew I wanted to live in Camden Town and drive a Citroën 2CV. I think Nick and I had been to the market one weekend, and where the 2CV fantasy came from I don't recall, but I think it's more to do with ley lines and ancient pagan goings-on. Such things are not for analysing. Best just to go with the flow. I flirt with Norfolk, Majorca and Brighton, but only in Camden does the never-specified tribal contentment settle over me. I know what's what there. The tweeness of Primrose Hill and the desolate harshness of Kentish Town fill me with horror. As soon as I enter my safe half-square mile, I know the gods are with me. This is also where Christopher and Fanny reside. Whether they could face a move, I'm not sure. But it's them I scurry home to.

The front door bell went yesterday. I picked up the intercom.

'Sorry to bother you,' came the voice of a young Scottish woman, 'but I wonder if you've got any steel cutters I could borrow? Only my car's been clamped outside, and as the clampers are shut the police told me I should just get something to cut it off with.'

'I'm sorry. I've only got a pair of scissors.'

I met a former neighbour from Holloway in the street one day. She'd lived opposite me in Middleton Grove, and I would often see her standing in the street outside her house gazing up at the ornamental turrets on my roof. I asked her what she'd been star-ing at all those months ago. 'I sometimes thought I saw a girl's face peering out through the little window,' she said, spookily, a bit like Fraser from *Dad's Army*. 'We locals refer to your house as "Lover's Leap"...' It seems no one has been happy in that house either before me or since. Indeed, I've seen it for sale in the window of Hotblack Desiato every year or so since I sold it.

Things will never get that bad again, I'm glad to say. The pendulum swings back and forth until it stops. The extremes are no longer as far reaching. I have learned to be suspicious of negative thoughts and to remove myself from suspect environments. I protect myself these days.

EPILOGUE

'Memories are the specific invisible remains
in our lives of what belongs in the past tense.'

JANET FLANNER, *PARIS WAS YESTERDAY*

Maybe, in the course of this book, I've gone too far. Tales of sex, drugs and private anguish are usually kept, if not from the family, then at least from the public. This has obviously not been the case with this particular book. Or, let's face it, with what one might loosely describe as my 'act'. We should none of us feign surprise. I have never aspired to cautiousness. Never mind. There's been a lot of dirty washing down the old Ganges since 1993. Keeping quiet about the years since then is my attempt at discretion. For the moment, anyway.

'He talks a lot about sex in his act, but not a mention of love,' wrote Lynn Barber in an *Observer* article. There was some confusion in my mind those days, as I recall, between love and sex. Of course, a good seeing to, expertly administered, can be a real tonic. A glint in the eye, a spring in the step, an aura of well-being, not unlike visiting Stonehenge, all these can be ours from a stranger. A gift from the Gay God. Not love, of course, but better than watching television or eating food covered in breadcrumbs.

As for drugs, well, I've been there, as you know. You don't work in television for years without being lured into the occasional toilet cubicle for a line of cocaine refreshment, at the very least. If it hasn't happened you know you're doing something wrong.

I've moved on since the days when a puff of a joint caused me to faint, and can acknowledge that drugs, be they paracetamol, alcohol or speed, have their uses. I saw it as self-medication at the time, but found out the hard way that there's a price to pay. If you go up you must come down, and although one dealt with the inevitable depression a gram of coke delivered a day or so later, dismissing the sudden emotional earthquakes for the chemically induced nonsense they were, I must, in my mature years, question whether or not the whole experience was worth it. There's a lot to be said for a clear mind and a fresh face. Drink the water, swallow the green tea, just say no.

As for private anguish, these days I simply repeat to myself as a mantra the words of retired actress Norma Talmadge to an autograph hunter: 'Go away, dear. I don't need you any more.'

The sense of destiny I sought at the beginning of this book has not emerged with any clarity, I'm sorry to report. It was far too lofty and philosophical a question to get a clear answer to anyway. The wisdom of my own creation remains a well-kept secret. I just turned up, I guess.

Which brings me back to my parents.

I was filming a while ago in a dogs' grooming parlour. It was part of another quality light entertainment television show called something like 'Celebrities Behaving like Dogs', that was simply too exciting to go into. Bouncing around the parlour was a young kitten, white legs and underbelly, tortoiseshell back and cheekbones. She bounded towards my dog Valerie and me with all the enthusiasm and charisma of David Bowie. She was bright and attractive. I could see at once she was a special cat. 'Looking for a home,' said Meg, mistress of the parlour, a pleasing 25-year-old. Turns out the kitten was abandoned by the occupiers of a neighbouring squat during the drama of a recent police raid. Who knows what left-wing, communal, free-loving, drug-induced social structure had created this extraordinary creature? Half cat, half socially skilled hippy, she crashed into me, the epitome of life: bold, adventurous, funny.

Gloria wouldn't welcome a sister, so I called my parents and planted the idea of a fun-loving kitten in need of a home.

'I haven't been able to sleep,' said my mother the next day.

'You realise this kitten might well outlive us?' said my father.

A few days later I delivered the kitten to them. Now they're obsessed. They call her 'Puppy' and follow her wherever she goes as if they were Moonies. 'The kitten's on the windowsill... She's looking outside!' they tell me, breathless, over the phone.

The first time she was allowed into the garden they both went with her. Ashen-faced, my father turned to my mother. 'She's gone in the hedge!' They watch her every move.

'She's such a curious cat, we're worried she'll wander off or someone will steal her.'

Last night I had to listen to her purring over the phone. They're born-again parents. Barely able to go to the shops without her, they scurry round the aisles buying any old nonsense, the quicker to return to Puppy and her demands.

'She's become interested in books!' my mother announced. 'It started in the lounge, when she noticed the bookcase. Then last night we heard a noise in the kitchen. Puppy had found the cookery books on the shelf. Suddenly there was a loud crash. She'd dislodged a huge Delia Smith! How clever, she's only small... Oh yes, books is the latest thing with her...'

Their delight in the kitten, together with my mother's admiration of Shane Richie and their newly discovered ability to live in the moment, however mundane, tells me they are getting older. Just as children are born with big eyes and Walt Disney proportions, the better to inspire the protective instinct of all who gaze upon them, so it is with the elderly. I can see them still as young adults, vibrant and as lusty as the 1950s would allow. When they became parents, the sudden responsibility, the sacrifice, the endless round of hair washing, feeding, nappies, baths, homework, the diplomacy required for the difficulties of adolescence, the letting go, the worry that never ends, the need to dole out their unconditional love in equal portions, their satisfaction in a job well done, their eventual return to their own lives. Now they are carefree and happy. They can snooze, guilt-free, in front of the television. Still together, despite or because of all that life has made them deal with. Perhaps part of the recipe is their ability to regard each other with a dispassionate, critical eye.

'Your mother can't walk as fast these days.'

'I sometimes think your father's losing the plot...'

I'm so glad I got the kitten, Puppy, for them. Diverted by her charming personality, they seem young again, and joyful.